# THE
# QUILTING PRIMER

# THE

# QUILTiNG

# PRIMER

## Second Edition

## DOROTHY FRAGER

CHILTON BOOK COMPANY RADNOR, PENNSYLVANIA

*PROJECTS ON THE COVER:*
Front panel, Ulster County Bicentennial Quilt, *left to right from top:* Kingston Point Park, Overlook Mountain, Old Dutch Church, Horse-Drawn Fire Engine, Ashokan Reservoir, Ulster & Delaware Railroad, Sugarbush, Locust Lawn, Ellenville Pottery, Woodland Valley Scene, Ice Harvesting, Stone Ridge Library, Esopus Indians, Henry Hudson's Half Moon, Fur Trading, Peter Stuyvesant and the Stockade, Old Hurley, The Senate House; First Reading of State Constitution, Governor Clinton, Burning of Kingston by British, Hurley Spy House, Huguenot Street in New Paltz, The Senate House Kitchen, Esopus Meadows Lighthouse, Maverick Concert Hall, Greenfield Schoolhouse, Mary Powell—"Queen of the Hudson," Sojourner Truth, N.Y. Steamboat Co. Warehouse, Slabsides, Rosendale Trestle, The Fitch Office, Delaware & Hudson Canal, Bristol Glass Factory at Shady, Kripplebush Cooper, West Camp Lutheran Church, Highland R.F.D., Perrine's Bridge, Woodstock Village Green, Rip Van Winkle, Tuthilltown Grist Mill. The names of the 242 original settlers are embroidered diagonally along the border. Courtesy of Ruth Culver, quilt coordinator. Front panel, accessories: *on the wall,* Indian Bird wall hanging, stamp-appliqued handbag, pin cushions; *middle row,* Beardsley Print quilt, Crazy Quilt, velvet abstract and City Scape pillows; *foreground,* stained glass pillow, 3-pocket ziptop purse, three Medallion applique potholders, strip eyeglass case and makeup case in front of Loonie Bird pillow and Mixed Wrench ruffled pillow. All made by Beverly Panitz, except the handbag by Doris Wickman and Audrey Didriksen and Crazy Quilt pillow by Dot Frager. Back panel, Learning Sampler by Betty Dufficy, left to right, from top: Bride's Block, Star Puzzle, Honey Bee, Harvest Moon, Grandmother's Flower Garden, Bear's Paw, Fancy Dresden Plate, Mohawk Trail, Missouri Star, Clay's Choice, Star & Cresent, Log Cabin. Photo courtesy of *Quilters' Newsletter;* Roy Hale, photographer.

# Contents

# Preface

This text was written to teach the beginner as well as to widen the knowledge of the experienced quilter. There are many ways to put a quilt together, and combining techniques and new ideas makes a quilt a work of art.

To best use the text, it is important to understand how the book is arranged. Chapters 1 through 3 give technical detail of each step in making a quilted item. Each of these chapters outlines both antique and modern variations of patterns and technical methods. The quilter then has the opportunity to put her own craft articles together, drawing on the preferred variations.

Chapters 4 and 5 give detailed instructions regarding quilted articles shown in the book with references to technical points found in Chapters 1 through 3. At the end of each project, there is a list of suggested design variations which change the appeal of the article shown. Throughout the text, there is great attention to identifying the easy versus the more difficult methods, noting small details (for example, needle size and number of stitches to be used), and suggesting coloration and size for various patterns.

Chapter 6 is devoted to today's popular Sampler and Pictorial Quilts. Chapter 7 details a new method of making and quilt stitching each block separately then joining the blocks for a large quilt.

Chapter 8 deals with using scrap fabric. This is something we all want to do but find difficult when we come to a new craft. Here the ever popular Log Cabin and other strip patterns are discussed in the light of producing quilts very quickly. Pyramid patterns are discussed and three quilts detailed. The Crazy Quilt, so popular at the turn of century in its array of silk and velvet fabric, has been updated for use in today's "easy-care" society.

The new, important Chapter 9 presents patterns for the reader's use. The patchwork patterns shown in the book are supported here with a unique set of basic concentric shape patterns. More complicated patterns are detailed specifically. All the applique patterns shown in the book are represented here, as are many patterns seen in the Sampler Quilts.

Current sewing terminology is used and all yardage determination is based on 45-inch wide fabric currently available to the retail customer. When possible, suggestions have been made to use scrap fabric the reader may have on hand.

For the reader's ease in choosing projects, the quilts have been rated: one asterisk for easy or beginner's quilts, two asterisks for quilts of average difficulty, and three asterisks for more difficult or experienced quilter's projects.

Having had the opportunity to teach quilting over the years, I have seen patterns selected and quilts actually finished. It is with this background that I selected the patterns in this book, giving them the names that I know them by. To the selection, I have added some very "mod" designs popular today and suggested some up-to-date colorations for old favorites. Occasionally, I have simplified some of these old favorites to enable the reader to visualize and repeat material offered in this book.

# *Acknowledgments*

To my husband, Victor Frager, who believes all women should have a creative and professional life of their own. My warmest thanks to my mother, Mrs. Inez Lange, who taught me to sew and to appreciate excellence in all craft workmanship.

Special thanks to my sons, James, age 17, and Colin, age 16, who were paragons of patience throughout the work of both editions.

I am grateful to Mrs. Kurt Heinrich for helping as a sounding board for my original ideas and for typing. To Mr. Kurt Heinrich for his professional advice and to Mary Lou Hemmingway for technical assistance in organizing and typing the final manuscript.

A special thanks to the staff of the Westwood, New Jersey, Library: Mrs. June Adams, Former Director; Mrs. Nancy Rotella; and Mrs. Esther Miller for endless securing of materials in the creative crafts area.

Special thanks to Crissie Lossing for her excellent editing assistance of the first edition, to Senior Editor Lydia M. Driscoll for her help in developing the format for the second edition, and to Manuscript Editor Kathryn Conover for her fine work on this second edition. Grateful appreciation is extended to Bonny Leman of *Quilters Newsletter* for permission to reprint photographs used originally for that publication. Although Hal Lindner of Target Photo did most of the superior, complicated merchandising pictures, I also have to thank Roy Hale for the fine work on three of the single quilt photos. Professional photography makes a teaching text realistic.

Particular thanks to all the talented Bicentennial Quilt Coordinators who taught, organized, and publicized the many quilts shown here: Ruth Culver, Kingston, N.Y.; Evelyn Barclay, Newburgh, N.Y.; Mary Helen Foster, Syracuse, N.Y.; Kay Schtichting, Ely, Vt.; Alice Valentine, High Falls, N.Y.; Norma Hubbard, Poughkeepsie, N.Y.; and Stearns and Foster Company of Cincinnati, Ohio, for their many sponsored contests which stimulated interesting pictorial quilts.

To Chris Edmonds and Beverly Panitz, both individual artists in their own right, go sincere thanks; to Chris for the beautiful single topic quilts and to Beverly for the many original accessories. Genuine appreciation is extended to the New Jersey quilt shops that always lend their support and original samples to this text: Helen Squire of Quilt In, Woodcliff Lake, N.J., and Vivian Talbot of Closter Fabric, Closter, N.J. Heart felt thanks to those gals I quilt with each month who have loaned their personally designed quilts to be used for all to copy: Anne Chas, Sally Rowe, Jo Ann Schwamb, Anne Smith, Ginny Ruckert, Mary Gormley, Doris Wickman, Audrey Didricksen, Phyllis Shane, Jo Onaglia, Mary Ann Cowan. Thanks to all my students who generously supported this effort and allowed their work to be shown: Suzanne Murray, Barbara Hillerman, Edith Taylor, Janet Stansfield, Jodie Bouvier, and Florence Chapin. Thanks to Betty Dufficy and June Rykert of Colorado, both quilting teachers, for lending their most original sampler quilts.

# CHAPTER

# *Getting Started*

## Introduction

Quilt making develops a sense of history and helps bridge the gap between yesterday and today. All crafts, not only quilting, foster an interest in other peoples based solely on their various artistic contributions to the craft field. Suddenly, age gaps, economic gaps, and social gaps fade away.

Over the years, quilters have refined and interpreted many sewing techniques to suit their own needs and abilities. They have left a wealth of ingenious methods with which today's quilt crafters may experiment.

The word "quilt" has come to have many meanings. Some people mean any cotton-looking blanket, some an artistically rendered handmade blanket, and others the show-off covering for a bed. A quilt is all this plus a lot more. Technically, a "quilt" is a bed covering that is made of two layers of fabric with a thin interlining between. This is all held together with rows of stitches passing through the three layers. It is the stitching that is accurately called quilting.

There are three basic parts to a quilt: the face or show-off side, the backing, and the batting. The face or "top" layer is designed in an artistic manner and shows the originality and personality of its maker. The face is traditionally made in a series of squares, rectangles, diamonds, or long strips that are designed individually and then set together to form one large design.

There are two basic techniques for making the design squares. The first involves sewing together small pieces of fabric commonly called patches. This started with the frugal setting together of small scraps of fabric of pleasing colors. It developed into complicated geometric patterns that often interact with each other to create additional patterns when the face is completed. This is called "patchwork" and can be hand or machine sewn.

The second method is "applique" which is the layering and stitching of separate pieces of fabric to a background fabric to form a design generally of a pictorial nature. Most often it is accomplished with several pieces of colored fabric creating a picture. This can be hand or machine sewn with a variety of stitches.

Sometimes the two methods are combined, generally by *patching* together the main portions of an *applique* and then sewing the applique to the background. This is then called "pieced applique."

After the designed squares are finished, they are sewn together to form one large face. The face is set aside and the underside of the quilt is prepared. The layer on the bottom or the "backing" is pieced together with large widths and lengths of plain fabric to match the approximate size of the face. Over this backing, the interlining material, called the "batting," is placed. The completed face is placed on top of these two layers. All three layers are basted together and placed on a special frame for hand quilting or are rolled in a special way for machine quilting.

The stitches most often used for quilting are called "running" stitches; they are plain stitches made one after the other. When the stitches are of a fine quality, meaning small and even, and a complex pattern is followed, the intrinsic value of the quilt is increased. The quilts of yesteryear required a great deal of hand quilt stitching which held the interlining in small pockets so that the batting would not lump together after washing. Today, with modern polyester battings, the tedium of having to use a great deal of quilt stitching has been relieved and the design work of the face is now accented.

One point to keep in mind when working a quilt is to *strive for the overall effect.* You can't expect absolute perfection when you are dealing with so many elements: one, two, or three layers of fabric; appliques and patches; needles and thread; the mechanisms and speed of the sewing machine; and most importantly, the human element.

# Planning a Quilt

When planning a quilt, the three basic elements of quilt design should always be kept in mind: *color, design,* and *texture.* Color and design proportion work together but texture is created by the quilt stitching and should be planned in the early stages of a quilt design.

The prize of this heritage craft is the blanket quilt and it is important to carefully plan your project. First consider who will use the blanket and consider the decor of the room in which it will be used. Will the quilt be made in blanket proportions to be used under a bedspread? Will it be used as the decorative covering for the bed, called a coverlet?

Consider the design of the room itself. If you are starting with an empty room, use the quilt as a focal point, since the bed is the largest item in the room. If the room is decorated, then consider the period of the furnishings. With the mixed furnishings that are so popular today, a dramatic quilt can pull the entire room together.

Here is a general rule for a room already decorated: If there are floral patterns in either the draperies or the floor covering, then select a sharp geometric design. If the walls and floors are solid or close to giving a one-color look, then choose an applique type or a bright geometric patchwork. Although the colors of the wall can be echoed in a quilt design, it seems very trite to reproduce the exact pattern of the paper onto a quilt. It rarely comes off as artistic and of heritage quality.

## Color

Color is the factor that will make a quilt sparkle as a showpiece or be just another loving, hands-at-home project. When you first begin, work only with colors you like very much. Remember the color wheel and keep a few basic art rules at hand. Primary colors are good blends: red, blue, yellow. They work well in pairs or all together. Secondary colors—orange, green, purple—offer good blends with each other or with primary colors (Fig. 1 – 1).

To highlight a color, select its complementary color (the color directly across from it on the color wheel) to sit next to it. Any two complementary colors will make each other stronger: blue/orange, yellow/purple.

Select colors that are alike in feeling. There are clear colors such as the six major colors of the color wheel. There are colors with white added to produce pastels. Generally, several pastels are needed to balance the strength of a small amount of one darker color. Then there are tints of primary colors to change the effect of the original color. Red and yellow tints warm up colors; green and blue have a cooling effect. Avoid the grayed colors; they are the dull colors that so often have a clothing fashion revival, but they offer very little to the excitement of the quilt.

When appliqueing onto a tinted ground, place all selected colors on that ground. Don't guess how it will look. Remember the color values, the lightness and darkness of color, give clarity to the shapes of the pattern. Trust your instincts to keep the proportion of colors in good balance and seek to achieve harmony. The strongest harmonizing factor is the background color and one other strong color to complement this ground color. From that point, as a solid or print is added, ask yourself, "Does the addition add strength to the design without overpowering it?"

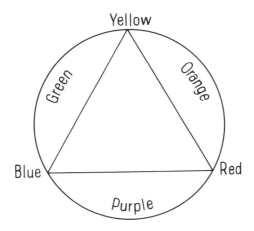

Fig. 1 – 1 Color wheel.

Fig. 1−2 Working pattern uses a 16-inch design block called Floral Wreath. Finished size is 74 by 100 inches. See Chapter 9 for pattern.

## Design Proportions

The first proportion to contemplate is the overall size of the quilt to be made. Start by measuring the size of the top of the mattress. Standard mattress sizes popular today are twin (39 by 75 inches), full (54 by 75 inches), queen (60 by 80 inches), king (76 by 80 inches).

To this, add the drop, which is the portion that hangs over the sides and the foot. It can be just enough to cover the mattress and boxspring or it can go all the way to the floor (Fig. 1−2). If it is to be used as a coverlet for a decorative purpose, then add 8 inches total for the tuck under the pillow plus the measurement over the pillow (Fig. 1 − 3). Tuck is not absolutely necessary; your design may flow over top of the pillow without the tuck.

*Example Measurements For Full Size Mattress*

|  | *Length* |  |  | *Width* |  |
|---|---|---|---|---|---|
| Drop | 10'' | | Drop, right side | 10'' | |
| Length to the tuck | 63'' | | Mattress width | 54'' | |
| Tuck | 8'' | | Drop, left side | 10'' | |
| Over the pillow | 20'' | | | | |
| Total | 101'' | | Total | 74'' | |

Using these measurements as a starting point, you will be able to determine the right size quilt for your bed. Any design can be enlarged to give the proper proportions when you know how.

The prime space for exhibiting the design work will be the top of the mattress. Select a design that will be effective on this focal point. For example, do not have the wings of an appliqued eagle drooping over the edges of the bed. Select your design with these measurements at hand.

Most designs are made individually in squares, rectangles, diamonds, or long strips. These are then multiplied many times before they are sewn together to form the completed "face" side of the quilt. For example, you can have nine squares 24 by 24 inches each for a 72 by 72-inch face or you can have fifty-six squares 10 by 10 inches to make a 70 by 80-inch quilt face. The squares can be further accented with colored bands of fabric intersecting each square. Large borders of colored fabric can be added to the circumference of the quilt to serve as a frame or to enlarge it (see Chapter 5 for suggested patterns).

The next question is always where to get the *original* designs, particularly for appliques. Use the children's section of the library. Pre-school coloring books offer a host of ready-made line drawings. Most children's pictures are simple and drawings are kept to a minimum of lines. Watch all periodical publications for pen and ink line drawings and add them to your collection. In the adult library sections, look for books on sewing and related crafts, such as early American, Indian, Scandinavian, Oriental, tole painting, weaving, and needlepoint.

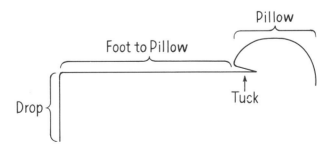

Fig. 1 − 3 Side view of measurement for drop.

## Making a Scale Layout

With the measurements in hand and some idea of your quilt design, plan your quilt on graph paper, purchased or homemade. With a pencil, very lightly draw the mattress position. Start by fitting in the design squares until a suitable number covers the mattress area. The best size squares to begin with are 12 to 16 inches. Add the measurements for the side and foot drops, the pillow tuck, and over the pillow measure for a coverlet. Continue to add the design squares and border measurements to accommodate this additional area.

Suppose you were to plan for a twin bed using 13-inch squares. To get a good size blanket, use five squares across and six squares down to arrive at 65 by 78 inches overall, with thirty squares of pattern. If a 3-inch border is to be used around the circumference, this would make the blanket 71 by 84 inches.

## Making a Working Pattern

Using graph paper with a ¼-inch grid, make one design square its actual size. (Check Chapter 9 for the actual pattern elements that may be required. If they are not given in the exact size, enlarge or reduce them for your needs.) Now try out your colors and fabric prints. Retrace one of each repeating pattern element onto graph paper. The ¼-inch grid on the graph paper gives an immediate seam allowance beyond sewing line. Cut out the paper pattern (¼ inch beyond sewing line) and retrace onto cardboard (bristol board) or thin plastic (flattened side of a bleach bottle). It will look like a picture frame when finished. (See right bottom, Fig. 1 – 4.) Accuracy in patternmaking is one of the important keys to good quiltmaking. When tracing out the pattern on the fabric, use a hard pencil; be sure to indicate both sewing and cutting line (Fig. 1 – 4). On dark colors use a light colored pencil that can be sharpened easily.

Some advanced quilters work with a solid template the exact size of each pattern element, trace it onto the fabric to indicate the sewing line, and then estimate the ¼-inch seam allowance. This is not suggested for the beginner as the ¼-inch seam allowance is very hard to judge, even for the experienced dressmaker who is used to the ⅝-inch seam allowance given on all patterns.

When sewing patchwork together, the novice crafter will invariably place the raw cut seams together thinking the seam lines will match. This is wrong. Place pins through the *seam lines* only and sew on seam lines, checking both back and front to make sure you are accurate.

A word should be said for grain line. When cutting out the pieces, particularly for patchwork, they should be cut on the straight of the grain. The reason for this is that when we sew them back together, the threads will lay naturally as originally woven and when the item is quilted, the upper layer will not buckle and stretch. Study Fig. 1 – 4, where we have a square and rectangle. They present no problem to being cut on the grain. The triangle is thought of as half a square and the two short sides are placed on the cross grains and the long side is placed on the true bias. Keep grain line in mind as you cut and sew. In applique work, as long as the background is on the straight and cross grain, then the pieces applied will not be distorted.

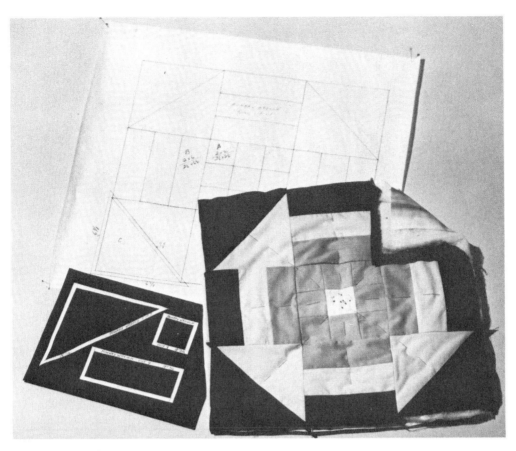

Fig. 1-4 Patchwork. Original pattern for "Monkey Wrench" pillow drawn on 1-inch graph paper with pattern letters and sizes of pieces noted. Bottom left shows actual patterns for the three elements. At right, a Monkey Wrench pillow front basted in sunburst pattern from center and ready for quilting. Note upper right corner of basted unit showing three layers of material.

## Tracing Patterns

When using the patterns for patchwork designs, place the patterns on the *wrong side* of the fabric. With a hard pencil trace both lines. The outer line will be the cutting line and the inside one the seam line. (When making the pattern tracing for applique work, place patterns on the *right side* of the fabric.) Indicate both the cutting line and the inside line very lightly. The seam allowance will be turned and basted to the back in most cases. The exception is the use of the zigzag machine-stitch method of applique.

## Estimating Yardage

Figuring yardage is a nagging problem. The easiest way is to know how many times the design square will repeat itself on the face of the blanket. Square

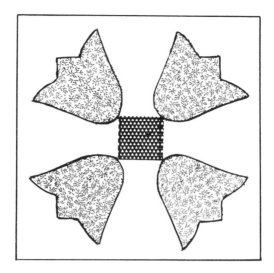

Fig. 1 – 5 Tulip Corner. See Chapter 9 for
pattern.

off each element of the design on graph paper, approximating an irregular shape
into a square. If you are using two triangles, they can be combined into one
square.

Most woven fabrics available in the retail stores are 45-inches wide. It is up
to the quiltmaker, when creating a new pattern, enlarging or reducing a pattern,
to work out these repeats according to the fabric width. Each amount per square
is divided into the width of fabric selected to find the number of design repeats
that will fit across your fabric.

*Yardage Chart*
*Number of squares in 1 yd, 45" wide, including seam*
*allowance*

| Size of square | Number of squares | Size of square | Number of squares |
|---|---|---|---|
| 3'' | 180 | 9'' | 20 |
| 4'' | 99 | 10''-11'' | 12 |
| 5'' | 63 | 12'' | 9 |
| 6'' | 42 | 13''-14'' | 6 |
| 7'' | 30 | 15''-18'' | 4 |
| 8'' | 20 | | |

You may find that there is a waste amount at one side but this cannot be helped. In some cases, the fabric can remain folded and two pattern pieces can be cut at a time, but no more than two or else distortions will occur. For example: If twenty-four 10 by 10-inch squares were required from a width of 45-inch fabric, then cut only four across a 45-inch width and cut six rows of four down the length. This would require 60 inches in length of the 45-inch fabric. There would be a 5-inch waste at one side (Fig. 1−6). This can be saved for another quilt.

In most bordered quilts, the dominating color in the design is used for the large borders. The borders are generally cut in long strips, the longest being the head to foot measurements; and four borders are needed so that length is initially required. The total border requirements should be figured out when cutting first begins.

For example, a quilt that was 70 inches long by 70 inches wide called for four 3 by 70½-inch borders and twenty-eight 7 by 7-inch squares of *one color.* The borders are to be cut from the selvage side first and would take 12 by 70½ inches which would leave 33 by 70½ inches for the remaining pattern pieces (Fig. 1−7).

The next question is, will the remaining pattern pieces required in the same color as the border fit the remaining fabric of 33 by 70½ inches? The pattern called for twenty-eight squares 7 by 7 inches. This would require only 28 by 49 inches of the remainder, giving an additional 21½ inches at the bottom and a 5-inch remainder at the selvage. If the 7 by 7-inch piece was not a square but a flower or a star, you should still figure the layout yardage on a square figure. This can all be worked out very accurately on graph paper and will provide an ample amount of fabric.

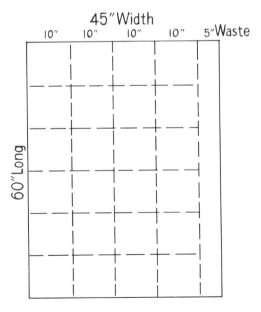

Fig. 1−6 Fabric layout suggestions.

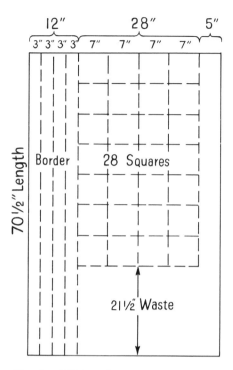

Fig. 1 − 7 Fabric layout suggestions.

## Fabrics for Quilting

One characteristic of a quilted item is its lightweight quality. Select fabrics that are light in weight, opaque, but not sheer. Yesterday's quilters only had cotton to work with and they called their favorite solid color "percale" and their favorite print "calico."

Today we are confronted with many new strange names when purchasing fabrics. Here are some fabric tests to help you select your material.

The "crush" test: As a bolt of fabric stands before you, clasp a warm fist around the loose end of the bolt of fabric and hold it a minute. If you see a handful of wrinkles, this is not a fabric for quilting; it is not resilient.

The "fray" test: Pull a few threads from the raw edge. If they all slip loosely away and leave long frayed-looking edges, it means the fabric is too loosely woven and will be difficult to handle.

The "thread" test: Look at the quality of the threads. If they are thick and rough looking, it will create a heavy appearance and will generally be too hard to work with.

The "grain" test: Check to see the lengthwise threads are at right angles to the crosswise thread. Look at the entire piece that will be purchased before cutting to see that there are no waves in the crosswise threads. This distortion very often happens at the end of the bolt.

The "width" check: Make sure that the width of the fabric corresponds to the width mentioned on the end of the bolt and by the shopkeeper.

Here is a general rule to apply to fabric: *"Select a tightly twisted yarn that creates an opaque, firm, and lightweight fabric."* Wash all yardage before cutting.

Personally, I like to use the Dacron and cotton blend fabrics and thin but firm cottons like the weight that would be used in good blouses and shirts. Buy from a reputable store. Know exactly what the fabric content is and what minimal shrinkage to expect. Test for "shrinkage:" Cut a 4 by 4-inch square and wash it as you would expect to wash your quilt; then measure again. Washing will also be a test for dark color bleeding.

You can use tissue-weight wool. If you want to be able to wash a wool quilt, then all fabric must be washed in cold water before making the face. Wool is used in a patchwork style since it is generally too bulky for applique. The quilt should have a lightweight backing since the wool face will make it very heavy. Do not work with corduroy or any high pile fabric; they make very bulky seams and are too heavy for comfort.

Some stores have remnant tables which always offer good buys for the quilter. Soon you will have a box full of small yardages at advantageous prices. Also watch for fabric sales, having in mind several different quilts that you would enjoy making. Try to have all your fabric needs on hand before you start. I know a gal who is waiting for some cherry red cloth to arrive at her local store to finish a quilt—she has been waiting four years!

The backing fabric should be purchased at the same time as the face fabrics and should be in harmony with the colorations of the face. It is most difficult to match colors after the initial purchase because even the same color from the same manufacturer, but from a different dye lot, may be dissimilar. (See Chapter 2 for lengthy discussion of backings.)

## Fabrics Available in Today's Market

*Batiste*   Plain weave, soft, sheer, originally of cotton, as in handkerchiefs, but generally combined with some synthetic blends.

*Broadcoth*   Plain weave, closely woven, will not admit light when held up to daylight. This is available in the widest range of all cotton and cotton and synthetics. The weight and quality is often determined by the finishes applied. The best fabric for all quilting needs.

*Calico*   Plain weave, closely woven, relatively soft, characterized with very small prints of a geometric or floral nature.

*Chambray*   Plain weave, thin, but closely woven. Characterized by having a colored warp (lengthwise thread) and white filling thread (crosswise thread).

*Duck*   Plain weave, tightly woven of a heavy yarn in cotton or cotton and synthetic blends. This is very good for zigzag machine applique technique.

*Gingham*   Plain weave, medium-weight fabric characterized by woven checks or plaids. True gingham will have the checks appearing on both sides. Occasionally, the checks are printed on one side and are advertised as gingham, but this is not a true gingham.

*Indian Head Cotton*   This is a brand name fabric most often known by its trade name. It is plain weave cotton of heavy yarn, creating an opaque, firm fabric, available in clear solids and prints. Excellent for zigzag machine applique but too difficult to work for hand applique.

*Lawn*    Plain weave, sheer, but crisp cotton or cotton and synthetic blends. Not good for applique; but if it is opaque enough in the prints, it is good for a pieced quilt.

*Muslin*    Plain weave, medium-weight fabric characterized by its light beige color sometimes called "unbleached." Can be purchased in a loose weave at a very low price or a very tight weave with a fine, soft hand of cotton and synthetics at a better price. The better grades can be used for background for applique, in a pieced quilt, or best for backing fabrics.

*Percale*    Plain weave, fine, lightweight cotton or cotton and synthetics characterized by having the same number of threads going crosswise; nice in floral prints.

*Pique*    A double weave, characterized by a novelty surface. This is strong fabric that can often create interest in machine appliqued quilts or a pieced quilt.

*Poplin*    Plain weave, very similar to broadcloth but has a fine rib crosswise. Comes in a wide variety of weights and finishes.

# CHAPTER

# *Making the Face, Batting, and Backing*

## Face

Designing a quilted item is a most satisfying craft experience and it can be as costly or as thrifty as one's time and ingenuity care to make it.

### Selecting a Method

The first step in the simple process of quiltmaking is to examine the many methods of producing the face (the pretty show-off side) of a quilted item. The overall effect of design and color work will coordinate at this point.

The face is usually put together in a series of repeated design squares or rectangles. In this chapter, you will find the most versatile designs currently in fashion today. The total face can be composed of one enlarged design square for a pillow or fifteen to fifty squares combined for a large blanket item. These designs can be formed in three ways: first by joining fabrics together with seams to form a patchwork design; or by appliqueing colored fabrics to a background to form a design: or by combining the two techniques.

There are four ways to assemble the design squares to form an attractive face for the quilted item. The easiest way is by sewing each square to the next. This is traditionally done for most patchwork designs (Fig. 2 – 1). It is especially handsome for applique work of a floral nature.

The work could be planned with solid color framing borders around each square. After all squares are finished, apply the frames first, add the short horizontal pieces to unite the squares into long strips, then add the long vertical pieces. The applique-type designs look particularly good with frames (Fig. 2 – 2).

If there is a shortage of fabric for the long lengths required for top-to-bottom measurement of the vertical strips, then form the vertical frames by piecing with small squares where the horizontal and vertical intersect. This is usually done in a contrasting color and adds to the design of the quilted item. Very novel effects can be worked with patchwork designs and it is an easy technique to add an intricate look to a simple applique.

Fig. 2 – 1 Kaleidoscope quilt, made by Mary Gormly. Pattern given in Chapter 9.

Fig. 2–2 The large quilt in the background is called Sunbonnet Sue. Note each figure holds a different object. The quilt is fresh out of the quilt frame and has not yet been bound. Designed by Jo Ann Schwamb, the design was first seen in *Quilter's Newsletter*. Foreground shows design squares with pieced corner borders. This quilt has a nine-patch set in the intersections. Courtesy of Helen Squire.

The second step is to select a method of piecing or applique that appeals to you. Select the right method for your level of manual dexterity. Not all hands have been created equal; but you can progress to a high performance in this craft if you do not let yourself become overanxious. Sampling the work will help you to find the techniques you feel most comfortable with. *Simplicity* is the first motto. The methods are listed from easy to more elaborate.

## Patchwork

A patchwork design is formed by sewing small pieces of fabric together to form design squares. This design form started with the setting together of simple blocks of color. As piecing became more sophisticated, the use of rectangles, triangles, diamonds, and hexagons all combined to form unique patterns. Each individual unit in the design will have a ¼-inch seam allowance. The patterns are formed into squares anywhere from 8 to 25 inches when finished. These are then sewn together to form the face of the quilted item.

The design squares often interact with each other, forming additional movement in the pattern. Begin with designs requiring few colors and piece elements and then graduate to more complicated designs.

The only prerequisite for the fabric is that it be of common type. Always use a small, regular presser foot on your machine and a throat plate with small holes, never zigzag attachments. Thread will not show so it will not matter what color is used. Set machine for ten stitches to the inch. When handsewing, use a small, running stitch and a short needle to help make many short stitches. Many people enjoy using the "between" needle for quilting. Many hand-stitchers enjoy using the special, strong quilting thread to sew patchwork together although the standard dressmaking thread works well.

*Tricks in Assembling Patchwork Squares*   When forming designs, try to assemble them into partial units or strips that go together easily. Press all seams open or to one side; finish by uniting the larger strips together (Fig. 2 – 3). Sew all number 2s to Number 1, press, add the number 3s to form one long strip, press, and set aside. Then add two number 5s to each number 4, forming the two end strips, press. Add the two end strips to the center; the work goes very quickly if you follow a set method.

When uniting two pieces of patchwork, place the pins at right angles to the marked seamline (Fig. 2 – 3b) and line up other seams with pins. After stitching the first few stitches, check the back to see that the stitches line up on both markings. Sometimes, when assembling two strips of a block that has many small patches, it is wise to begin at the center and work out to either end with two separate threads. This prevents shifting. Seams can be pressed open on the wrong side. Bulk is to be avoided where seams meet. Opening seams will guarantee no bulk where seams meet; however, flipping the seams toward the darker fabric will ensure that if a seam opens, with wear, it will not be so noticeable. In simple patchwork, sew from raw edge to raw edge; but if you have to join a third piece into a corner such as Fig. 2 – 9, sew only on the penciled seam line and not through it to the raw edge. See Figure 2 – 3c—finish off at point* and pin the third piece in and sew from the center point out to the raw

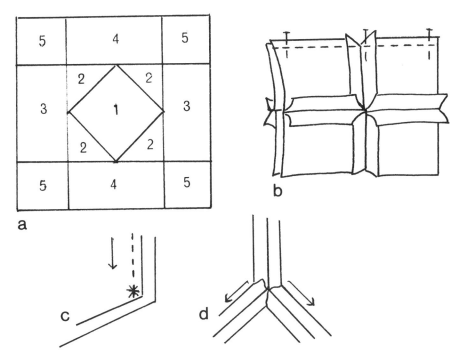

Fig. 2−3 (a) Diamond on end pattern. (b) Sewing patchwork together. (c) and (d) Fitting piece into sharp corner.

edge on both sides. Figure 2−3d—typical examples of this would be found in Fig. 2−9a, b, and c.

*Patchwork Patterns*  Patchwork patterns began with the primitive four-square patches sewn together and evolved to nine patches. The "nine patch" gave the patchwork crafter an opportunity to make use of novel color effects. Figure 2−5a shows the use of large and small squares combined for one patch.

The simple use of rectangle patches to create small squares has always been a favorite. Many times, squares made of three strips each were placed in alternate directions. Another effect is the combining of light, medium, and dark rectangles in long strips, not squares, joining the short ends only. When the next long strip is joined, its vertical seams are centered between the row above, then stitched. Thus a tri-colored "brick wall" pattern emerges. This can be quilted in straight lines. The most artistic use of rectangular patches is in Rail Fence (Fig. 2−5b). The placing of the four-piece squares in alternating directions causes the one dominating rectangle to move diagonally across the quilt in step-like fashion. The quilt stitching outlines the dominating color. (See Rail Fence blanket color insert and directions in Chapter 5.)

The next event in patch design is to cut the simple square in half on the diagonal, creating the triangle. This triangle then can form endless light and dark combinations. It is always cut with two short sides on the lengthwise and crosswise grain. The long diagonal is on the true bias. Always sew a block that is formed of two triangles together first, press seams open, and treat as one square.

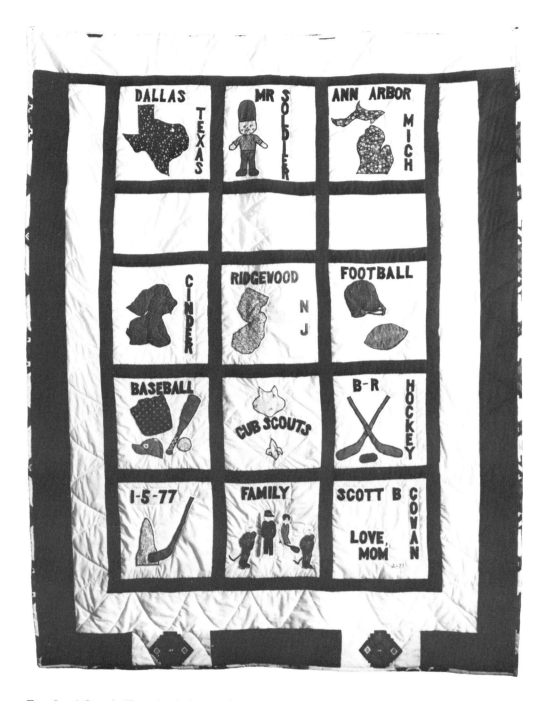

Fig. 2 – 4 Scott's Travels. A first quilt machine quilted by Mary Ann Cowan showing a boy's world and the different cities he has lived in. Note the set of blank blocks planned for tuck under pillow.

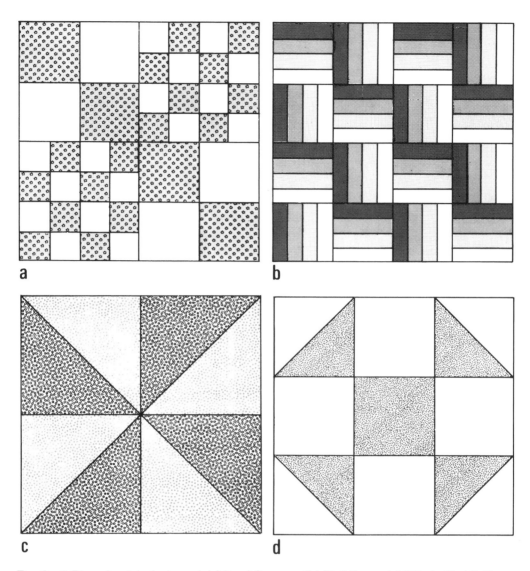

Fig. 2 – 5 Pieced patch designs. (a) Mixed Squares (b) Rail Fence (c) Windmills (d) Shoo Fly. Pattern elements are given in Chapter 9.

| Finished Size of Block | | Size of Element | Cut |
|---|---|---|---|
| (a) | 16″ | 4″ square | 4 light,   4 dark |
| | | 2″ square | 16 light, 16 dark |
| (b) | 8″ | 2″ x 8″ rectangle | 1 each, 4 assorted colors |
| (c) | 10″ | triangle, ½ of 5″ square | 4 light, 4 dark |
| (d) | 12″ | 4″ square | 4 light, 1 dark |
| | | triangle, ½ of 4″ square | 4 light, 4 dark |

The design in Fig. 2-5c is a basic "four-patch" square divided into light and dark triangles. (See Windmills blanket color insert.)

"Shoo Fly," Fig. 2-5d, is a fundamental "nine patch" with its corner squares divided in half diagonally.

The use of some popular diagonally divided blocks in large designs, as shown in Fig. 2-6, suggests many interesting color combinations. Birds in the Air, Fig. 2-6a, is traditionally done with half of its small triangles in assorted colors; the other half of the small triangles are of a background color and the large triangle is generally a strong color.

Figure 2-6b has several names: Flying Geese and Handy Andy. Again, it is a variation on the basic "nine patch." If the same pattern has one large triangle in each corner and a single small one following it, then it is called Duck and Ducklings.

Mixed Diamonds, Fig. 2-6c, offers an opportunity to use assorted colored scraps of fabric for the centered four-patch diamond, narrow borders, and corner pieces.

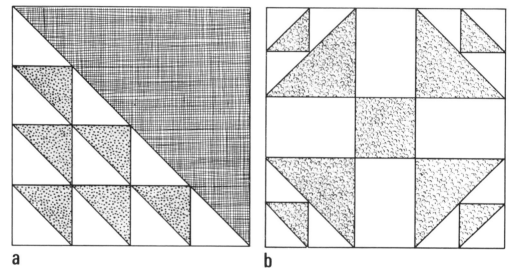

a                                          b

Fig. 2-6 Pieced patch designs: (a) "Birds in the Air" (b) "Handy Andy" (c) "Mixed Diamond" (d) "Yankee Puzzle."

| Finished Size of Block | | Size of Element | Cut |
|---|---|---|---|
| (a) | 12″ | triangle, ½ of 12″ square | |
| | | | 1 dark |
| | | triangle, ½ of 3″ square | |
| | | | 6 assorted colors |
| | | | 10 background |
| (b) | 12″ | 2″ square | 1 dark |
| | | 2″ x 4″ rectangle | 4 light |

Yankee Puzzle, Fig. 2 − 6d, is a complicated piece of geometry. It is actually four small patches each divided into four triangles and put together to form one square whole. Another way to interpret this is to use three colors: two on the inside to form a Windmill in a diamond shape and one other color forming the corner triangles.

A one-patch design capable of increasing variations consists of equilateral triangles (Fig. 2 − 7) placed one next to the other in varying colors to form long strips, rather than square patches. They are easy and fast to work but the design and coloration must first be conceived and understood.

Pyramids (Fig. 2 − 7a) is smart when set together in monochromatic harmonies. Striking patterns can be arranged when placing strips composed of two colors in position to form Diamonds (Fig. 2 − 7c) or Streak of Lightning (Fig. 2 − 7d).

The triangle can take on a wider or elongated shape by making two sides equal and one side longer. The two equal sides will be sewn one to the other to form long strips with the elongated sides as the raw edges. It is this elongated side

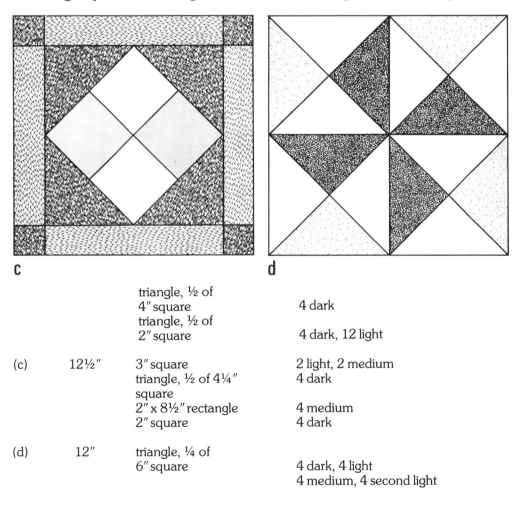

c                                                    d

|     |       | triangle, ½ of 4″ square | 4 dark |
|-----|-------|--------------------------|--------|
|     |       | triangle, ½ of 2″ square | 4 dark, 12 light |
| (c) | 12½″  | 3″ square | 2 light, 2 medium |
|     |       | triangle, ½ of 4¼″ square | 4 dark |
|     |       | 2″ x 8½″ rectangle | 4 medium |
|     |       | 2″ square | 4 dark |
| (d) | 12″   | triangle, ¼ of 6″ square | 4 dark, 4 light |
|     |       |  | 4 medium, 4 second light |

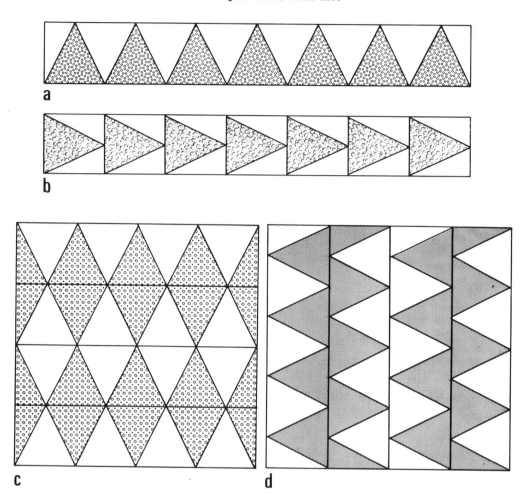

Fig. 2−7 Pieced patch designs: (a) "Pyramids" (b) "Flying Geese" (c) "Diamonds" (d) "Streak of Lightning." See Chapter 9 for patterns.

| Finished Size of Block | | Size of Element | Cut |
|---|---|---|---|
| (a) | 15″ | 5″ square | 4 background, 1 light |
| | | triangle, ¼ of 5″ square | 4 medium light, 8 medium, 4 background |
| (b) | 20″ | 4″ square | 5 light, 4 dark, 8 background |
| | | triangle, ½ of 4″ square | 8 light, 8 background |

that will be sewn to the next strip of triangles so you can have short, squat Diamonds or long, soft Streak of Lightning. The Lightning is probably the easiest to quilt since the stitching can be worked from top to bottom.

Another interesting use of the triangle is to cut the pattern from one square as in Flying Geese (Fig. 2−7b) and Combined Basic blanket (Fig. 5−17).

It is not surprising to find the quilter's ingenuity turn to the star. It is a common historical and political symbol. The innovations follow two forms (Fig. 2 − 8). The first was built on the fundamental "nine patch" design. The easiest is the Variable Star (Fig. 2 − 8a). Only four of the nine squares have interlocking small triangles. Make those first and treat each as a single square. Sister Star (Fig. 2 − 8b) is a larger innovation on the star, evolving from a set of twenty-five blocks. When seen as a line drawing, only eight of the twenty-five blocks are cut in half on the diagonal. The trick to assembly is to stitch all the diagonally cut blocks first, press, and treat as one block. Then the four short vertical seams are stitched to make long strips. Next, the four horizontal seams are made to complete the overall square.

On the way to working out complicated stars, an engaging four-point star was made called World Without End (Fig. 2 − 9a). Its pattern takes its name from early Episcopal prayer book liturgy. It is an outstanding interlocking design generally made of two solid colors or a reverse calico-type print. It is important that color values remain the same. As squares are placed one after the other, suddenly another and larger star begins to appear. It is one of those optical illusions popularly called "op art" today. The movement in this pattern never ceases. If the pattern is to be used to accent the star only, then the center and the points should be much darker than the background. It can also be made with half the squares in the quilt having the center diamond and wide background triangles of one tone and the point of another tone. The other half will have the reverse coloration. The squares will be placed in an alternating pattern for an intriguing effect.

The handsome Friendship (Fig. 2 − 9b) is no more than a variation on the "four patch." To make this design, make a square divided into four parts. Divide each square into fourths again. With a few diagonal lines, this pretty little star shape comes to life. There are only three pieces to the total pattern—one triangle; one square; and one parallelogram which is a plane figure having four

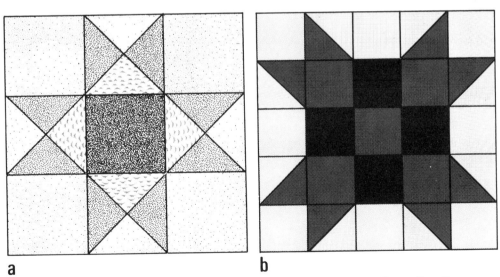

a                                          b

Fig. 2 − 8 Pieced patch designs: (a) "Variable Star" (b) "Sister Star."

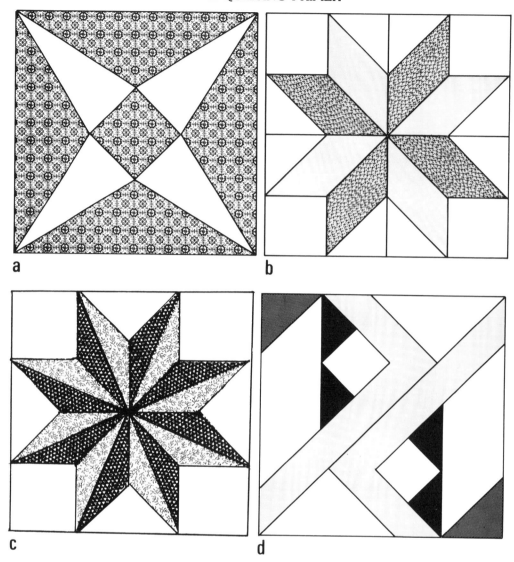

Fig. 2−9 Pieced patch designs. (a) World Without End (b) Friendship Star (c) LeMoyne Star (d) Chinese Puzzle. See Chapter 9 for patterns. Also see Eight-Point Star, Radiating Star, and Whirling Star in Chapter 9.

sides, the opposite sides of which are parallel. The parallelograms form the points of the star. The triangle and the square are of common color. The parallelograms are generally of contrasting colors.

The popular Eight Point Star pattern is made from a basic diamond figure with all sides equal. When the diamond is divided in half lengthwise, it is called LeMoyne Star (Fig. 2−9c). The traditional patchwork technique is to assemble the star then fit the background corner squares and center triangles to complete the star. The star may also be assembled, then the edges turned for applique to a larger background fabric. (Patterns are given in Chapter 9.)

The trick in making the star is to begin by marking with the *greatest accuracy* the cutting and seam line on each star point. If you are making a LeMoyne Star sew the two half diamonds together, press seams open, and treat as one piece, trimming excess seam allowance from top and bottom points. Begin by stitching only on the seam line to join the first two points together with a running stitch. Stop the stiching at the point to be the center on the star, fasten with a strong backstitch, do not press. The third diamond is added to the second seaming only on the pencil line. Continue in this manner until all eight points are attached. To secure the center, use a short thread to sew through each point in a circle. If you have a noticeable hole then you have not stitched or marked correctly. Press all the seams in a clockwise position and the center will fan out and can be pressed with the tip of the iron. (See Fig. 5 – 34.)

The pattern known as Chinese Puzzle (Fig. 2 – 9d) is an interesting bit of geometry. It is important that the long stripes running through this pattern be of one dominating color. Lay the pattern out carefully on graph paper. Each square when finished should be from 12 to 18 inches. Anything smaller would make the small pieces of the design hard to work with. (To see this design as a blanket, see Fig. 5 – 25 and directions for the large blanket in Chapter 5.)

## Applique

This is the technique that offers the most pictorial means of expression. Write this motto on a card where it can be seen, "Applique is the art of *shapes and colors.*" Very minute details are rarely seen and very seldom appreciated; so don't be a "Fanny Fussy," be a "Brenda Bold."

The art of applique involves applying many pieces of fabric in an overlaying technique to a background. In the case of a quilt item, the background fabric will be the face of the quilt. For all appliqueing, select pre-shrunk, colorfast fabric; then *wash and press* it before starting.

The first rule of this method is to think out the *pictorial design* to find which piece will be applied first. If in doubt as to the layering of the design, then cut each piece out of colored construction paper and work the layout. Think of the human figure, as an illustration, and the technique becomes obvious. Look at how the Indian Boy (Fig. 2 – 10) is put together:

1. All number 1s are applied first. They are the body.
2. Then add the pants, covering the top of the legs.
3. Next add shoes, covering the bottom of the leg.
4. Then add the jacket which covers all the upper limb appendages and the top of the pants.
5. Last, but not least, add hair to the figure.
6. Then, add a feather to his head.
7. Last, add a band to cover his hair and the feather end; use a few quick embroidery features for his face.

In other words, first select your design and the applique technique you wish to use. Then make a pattern piece for each element in the designs.

*Placement of Appliqued Patterns*   Since most patterns repeat themselves many times in a quilt design, it is important to place the applique pieces exactly in the same place each time a square is made. The placement technique is as simple as folding and lightly pressing the background squares. The pressed

Fig. 2 – 10 Indian Boy.

fold acts as a guideline; use only enough folds as will be needed for the design, then press out completely after finishing the applique.

Here are two ways of folding your background square to press your guidelines.

First, fold square in half and then in half again, forming quarters. The result is two long intersecting fold lines.

Or, fold on a diagonal, from corner to corner. Then fold on the opposite diagonal; the result is a large folded X on the square.

Either method will give a square with four intersecting lines. Any combination or number of folds can be used—just be consistent.

Placing a design, used for hand and straight stitch machine applique and some satin stitch applique, now becomes an easy task.

The second method is to use tailor tacks to indicate top, bottom, and sides of the main sections to be appliqued. Draw the actual design on a square of heavy paper. Then punch holes in this pattern with a small scissors to indicate points of reference for tailor tacking. Place pattern over face and pin to background. Place a tailor's tack at each hole. Remove paper. Repeat for each square. This method is excellent for marking the zigzag machine's satin stitch applique method.

Applique is basically a pictorial mode of expression. Unlike the geometry of patchwork which finds its expression in size and color, applique allows for free expression of ideas. The designs can be constructed on squares 8 by 8 inches to

Fig. 2 – 11 Pictorial applique of man on a horse. Bottom center shows original tracing on ¼-inch graph paper. The enlargement to 1-inch graph paper is on the right. In the center, each element has a ¼-inch seam allowance basted back. Then each element is basted in place with a second row of stitches, as shown. Next each piece will be slipstitched to the background. At bottom left is a circle with the curved edges notched and basted back. Note fold lines to assure accurate placement.

36 by 36 inches and put aside to be assembled on the background later.

The simple way to construct a pattern is to begin to draw it on homemade one-inch graph paper. Then trace one of each repeating element of the design. Cut each element from construction paper or from scrap fabric in actual size proportions (without seam allowance) and place on the background. Carefully note how the squares will be folded to attain a perfect repeat and note which pieces are to be put on first so that no raw edges are uncovered.

Now figure out where the quilting lines will be placed by drawing them in with pencil and ruler, if necessary. Quilting gives a dimensional effect to the work and it is as much a part of the design work as color and pattern selection. (See Chapter 3 for suggestions on quilt stitching.)

When all proportions are decided upon, then each element can be retraced onto a permanent cardboard pattern with seam allowance added. The total number of design squares should be planned. (Check Chapter 1 for determining yardage.) Trace all applique patterns onto the right side of the fabric.

Many times, the pictorial designs are so vivid that they need blank squares surrounding them to make them more visible. As the eye becomes more accustomed to the various designs, more complicated versions will be sought, such as combining two or more patterns. (See Fig. 5 – 26 showing a very controlled use of several patterns and Fig. 5 – 27 showing harmonious arrangement of eighteen completely individual designs applied to diamond-shaped background squares.)

*Pieced Applique* This is the penny-saving way yesterday's quilters learned to take advantage of the scrap box and to create something artistic. It shows the ingenuity of the quilt designer who pieces together the main portions of a design and then appliques the pieced portion to a background square. Make sure that the background color does not show through any of the pieces of the patched design. The designs selected here are the most popular ones.

The Honey Bee is a piece of patchwork with applique representations of a three piece bee in the corners. The center looks like the beehive (Fig. 2 – 12a). Make the entire background patchwork then applique the bees. The Peony in Fig. 2 – 12b is a floral take off on the Eight Point Star. Set six diamond points together, turn the remaining outer edge to the wrong side and fashion a curved stem and a few leaves and applique to a spacious background. Read information on star making given with Fig. 2 – 9c. Pattern is given for two size stars in Chapter 9.

The most popular of all quilt designs and one of the easiest patterns to make is called Dresden Plate (Fig. 2 – 12c and d). It can have from twelve to sixteen pie-shaped wedges, depending on the size of the circle originally drawn. The center circle should be approximately one-fifth the size of the outer rim. This center circle can be left open to show the background color, may have an additional novel applique placed in the center, or may be overlayed with another circle of contrasting color.

The outer rim offers the most variations. Each wedge can have pointed edges as shown in Fig. 2 – 12c. This is the most popular version. The wedges may have rounded ends added (Fig. 2 – 12d, left) to give the dimensions of a flower-like design. Another striking variation is the combining of larger and longer wedges with smaller and shorter ones. (See variation in Fig. 2 – 12d, right.)

This is traditionally a scrap quilt but works extremely well in highly stylized colors. Each finished square may be successfully placed one after the other, as in Fig. 2 – 1, or may have bands of color set between called bordering frames, as in Fig. 2 – 2. The Dresden Plate is probably one of the easiest and least expensive to begin with whether the quilter is sixteen or sixty-six years old. (See Chapter 4 for tablecloth instruction.)

To make the design, take a square of paper, fold it evenly four times, open it up, and draw a circle on it, using the folds as a guide. (You could trace a dinner plate or any round shape.) Using these four folds as a guide, begin to *divide* the circle into wedges. Trace out one wedge from the main design, with pointed or rounded outer edges, cutting off the center point to form a blunt lower edge. Add ¼-inch seam allowance all the way around. The wedge pattern is complete. Stitch the wedges together on seam line only, starting and stopping the stitches at

---

Fig. 2 – 12 Pieced applique designs. (a) Honey Bee (b) Peony Flower (c) Dresden Plate (d) Dresdan Plate Variations (e) Grandmother's Fan (f) Flower Basket. Patterns are given in Chapter 9 for a, b, c, and e. Design (f) is same as Fig. 2 – 6a with the addition of a handle and flowers and leaves from Chapter 9.

a

b

c

d

e

f

29

the ¼-inch seam allowance of the outer edge. Baste the outer and inner edges back and applique to the background.

Grandmother's Fan (Fig. 2 − 12e) is another interesting way to make a scrap quilt. Very similar to the Dresden Plate, the fans may have four to sixteen individual segments. Each fan is carefully stitched down along its outer rim to a background square. The finished squares are traditionally placed on the diagonal. The fan pieces may be of assorted colored scraps but the background is always a common color. It is generally assembled for a bed quilt as shown in Fig. 2 − 1. For a pillow, stitch one fan into each of the four corners of a large square so the rims face toward the center.

As patterns come and go over the years, certain ones such as Flower Basket (Fig. 2 − 12e) remain constantly refreshing to any age. By dividing the design in half diagonally, we see that the basket portion is a basic pieced pattern seen earlier as Birds in the Air, (Fig. 2 − 6a). To create the illusion of a basket, it is generally worked in two colors. The flowers and basket handle are appliqued to the other half of the background triangle. It is most charming to use assorted color scraps and create different flower shapes for each basket. It makes this look like a designer piece. The trick is to make a few flower and leaf-shaped patterns, about six or seven at least, the size of one of the two-tone squares of the basket portion. Using the patterns, cut a number of flowers and leaves from fabric on hand and arrange the pieces above the basket until you are pleased with the proportions. Then cut out the flowers with seam allowances and stitch down. Three or four flowers above a basket, repeated consistently, is extremely harmonious, too. After the two halves are sewn together, a leaf may be appliqued dangling over the basket for a note of realism.

*Direct Applique*    Here are the most traditional of all applique designs. The elements of the designs should be large enough to make a statement. For small details such as flower pistils and seeds, embroidery floss should be used. Both the motif of flowers in the ring (Fig. 2 − 13c) and the large central flower with small buds or leaves peeping out around it (Fig. 2 − 13a) offer endless variations. The tulips in the four corners of Fig. 2 − 13b offer such a pleasing and easily reproduced balance.

The basic designs in Fig. 2 − 14 can be repeated using assorted colors for heart and floral motifs. Harmony will be achieved by having all the stems and petals the same color. Hearts and rings, in Fig. 2 − 14a, are almost always found in bridal quilts of yesterday. Although hearts are traditionally seen in the red to pink color family, the simple heart applique takes on new dimensions when combined with interesting print backgrounds. Figures 2 − 14b and c are particularly sensational when brilliant colors are used against a dark ground or when made in pastel shades for a crib quilt. The leaves pointing out from behind the large floral pattern in Fig. 2 − 14d need to be of a strong color to make a statement.

Patterns planned on the diagonal are a little hard to visualize but make vibrant arrangements when planned artistically (Fig. 2 − 15). At one time, the pineapple in Fig. 2 − 15a was a traditional sign of welcome. Any small yellow print will do for the pineapple itself when combined with a darker tone leaf. This rather simple to produce design arranges well with a common center. Butterflies

Fig. 2 − 13 Applique designs.
(a) Gardener's Delight (b) Crossed Tulips
(c) Floral Wreath. Assorted floral designs
are in Chapter 9 to mix and use as you like.

in Fig. 2 − 15b are less static when placed on the diagonal and this motif is always a welcome relief to the floral designs. The Love Apple, (Fig. 2 − 15c) originally the American name for the tomato, always has a curved stem. The Turkey Tracks (Fig. 2 − 15d) is a large, crossed diagonal that should be styled in bright, sunny colors, often on a tinted background. Motifs appliqued to a square diagonally can be combined with four squares with one common center, as shown in Fig. 2 − 15e. When a floral is used, curve the stem slightly to give a feeling of movement. By keeping the flowers on the same diagonal, they form diagonal stripes (Fig. 2 − 15f), while the square they are placed on remains easy to assemble into a large quilt.

The use of circular shapes shows great imagination in both Figs. 2 − 16a and b. Sometimes they take on an almost stark modern look but they are true traditional patterns.

a  b  c  d

Fig. 2 – 14 Applique designs. (a) Ring of Hearts (b) Gentle Turn (c) Bird in the Bush (d) Tulip Basket. See Chapter 9 for patterns for (b), (c), and (d).

These designs were made by intersecting circles, using the outline of almost any round object that was on hand at the time (dishes, pails, or one's own embroidery hoop).

Note that each oak leaf of Fig. 2 – 16b is slightly different, though they remain basically the same size. You can substitute any leaf you like.

The stylized tobacco leaf of Fig. 2 – 16c is a simple one with only a two-piece pattern: one center circle and one half of the leaf pattern. This is particularly striking in the earth colors of browns, rusts, golds, and greens.

Fig. 2 – 15 Applique designs. (a) Pineapple (b) Butterfly (c) Love Apple (d) Turkey Tracks (e) common grouping of Wind Blown Daffodils (f) diagonal grouping. See Chapter 9 for patterns for (a) to (e).

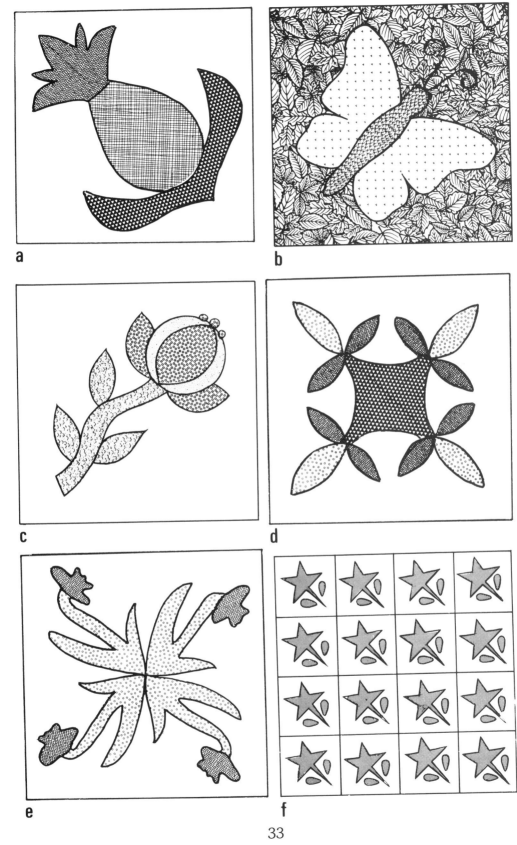

a

b

c

d

e

f

33

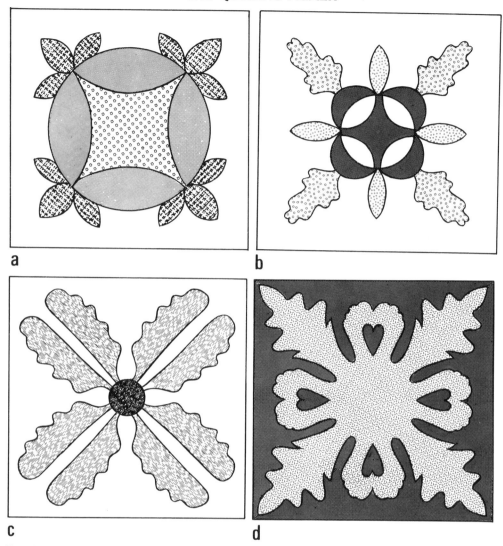

Fig. 2-16 Applique designs. (a) Reel (b) Oak Leaf (c) Tobacco Leaf (d) Hawaiian Star. All patterns are in Chapter 9.

The Hawaiian-type pattern of Fig. 2-16d is cut of one piece of cloth that has been carefully folded four or eight times, cutting a design the same way you made snowflakes as a child. It is elegant in two bright colors, the applique being the most prominent. The women used the shadow cast by nature as an outline for their designs.

The designs in Fig. 2-16 are unique because they can be enlarged up to 36 by 36 inches square. In that case, only four squares, plus a wide outside border, would be necessary for a blanket. In patterns that have definite leaf-like shapes, it would be worth quilting in the pattern that would form the veins of the leaf, as in Figs. 2-16b and c. All the patterns in Fig. 2-16 have noticeable centers. Therefore, it would be an excellent place to have an exceptionally intricate quilting design. It is rare to see any of the enlarged designs with framing borders between the squares. The scope of the patterns, plus the quilting, creates enough interest on the surface. Other patterns that would look well enlarged over 20 inches would be:

Fig. 2 – 8b, up to 25 inches
Figs. 2 – 13a and b, up to 24 inches
Figs. 2 – 14a and d, up to 30 inches
Figs. 2 – 17b and c, up to 36 inches

Some appliques take on a fresh, modern look through bold interpretation as the designs of Fig. 2 – 17 show. The vibrant heart with its modern message is so in step with the times (Fig. 2 – 17a).

a     b

c     d

Fig. 2 – 17 Applique designs. (a) Vibrant Heart (b) Eagle (c) Thunderbird (d) Owl. See Chapter 9 for patterns for (b) and (c).

The imaginative birds have simplified shapes for the appliquer's needle. The precious American eagle, with its many meanings, looks fresh and vigorous worked in large proportions. It sits well on a square, a rectangle, or a diamond. Of course, the bird does not have to be an eagle at all; worked in colors other than red, white, and blue, with a change in the beak shape, the bird takes on a new character.

The takeoff on the thunderbird is just one of the many very beautiful designs of Indian heritage (Fig. 2 – 17c). The impeccable simplicity of this bird is what makes it so adaptable to a pieced applique. It has tremendous appeal to anyone with a sense of history. Little boys are mad about it, especially if it is worked in bold colors and has a pieced border of diamonds or triangles as shown in Fig. 2 – 7. Owls have always fascinated man. This humorous face worked in brilliant colors is sure to compete for the dominant spot in any room. The brighter and more amusing the owl, the less need for other novelty effects in the room. The squares, any size from 14 to 18 inches, should be placed side-by-side in all-over pattern. One owl with a winking eye or an open beak randomly placed will add to the amusement of the overall effect.

*Machine Applique, Using the Zigzag*   Automatic machine is the fastest and strongest applique method. The fabric should be opaque and of the most sturdy type. Pieces of very sheer fabric will cause puckering and will reflect the color under it. Fabrics should have a crisp finish and be closely woven, such as the broadcloth, poplin, percale, and Dacron/cotton blends. You must experiment with your machine. The stitch is called a *satin stitch* and must be closely sewn so as not to show the fabric underneath the stitch line.

On many machines, you can select the width of the satin stitch. The narrow satin stitch is more versatile; it is easier to get into small places. Bobbins should have the same color thread as the top; and if the bobbin thread shows to the face, then consult your machine instructions to make a small adjustment on your tension. Thread should be number 50 mercerized cotton, or you can use cotton covered polyester thread now on the market. Do not use 100 percent polyester thread. It tends to break a great deal when worked on a heavy weight project. Never use silk with washable fabrics because it will shrink when washed. You will get the most consistent satin stitching effect when you create a good tension in your hands, pressing the fingertips down firmly on work and guiding hands and fabric as a single unit. Never pull work from back under the presser foot; this will create uneven stitches.

The first step is to cut the design from a cardboard pattern, forming the outline of each piece. When drawing the pattern onto the piece of fabric to be appliqued, choose a piece that is at least one inch larger than the pattern itself. Place against the background, being careful to line up with tailor tack markings, or use the folded ground techniques described previously. Secure the loose piece to be appliqued to the background with pins (Fig. 2 – 18). Do not place the pins in such a position that the satin stitch will ride over a pin.

An alternate method would be to baste by machine on the drawn design line, using the largest straight stitch of the machine. The satin stitching can be sewn right over the straight basting line. This creates a very firm bond. Follow the

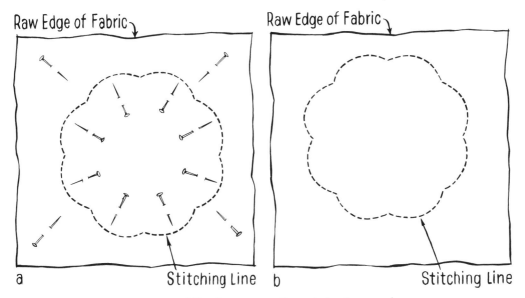

Fig. 2 – 18 Pin-basting applique to background.

design, outlining it completely with a satin stitch. Then trim away excess on the outer edge of the satin stitch very carefully with a small pair of scissors (Fig. 2 – 19).

*Tricks.* When appliqueing more than one piece, stop the satin stitching about six stitches beyond where it will be covered by the next piece. As is the case with a stem, stitch only three sides, not the part tucked under the flower (Fig. 2 – 20). If the stitches did extend to the top of the stem, it would make a ridge under the flower.

Fig. 2 – 19 Trimming excess away from stitching line.

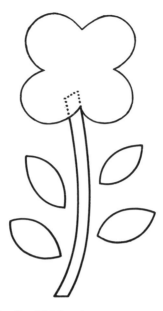

Fig. 2–20 Floral applique.

When coming to the 90 degree angle, zigzag up to the corner, *leaving the needle in the fabric on the outside line of your stitching,* then lift the presser foot and pivot the fabric. Bring presser foot down, overlapping the corner of the original line as you proceed away from the corner in new direction (Fig. 2–21). Stop often when forming circular lines: leave the needle in the down position, lift the presser foot, turn the fabric, lower the presser foot, and begin to sew again. Most of the time, the thread color should match the background color of the material to be appliqued, but sometimes a stronger tone of the thread or a complete contrast will add to the design.

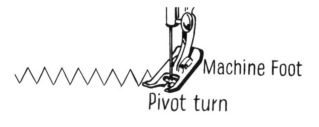

Machine Foot

Pivot turn

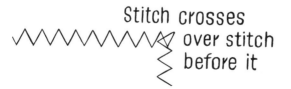

Stitch crosses
over stitch
before it

Fig. 2–21 Zigzag stitching a corner.

*Machine Applique with Straight Stitch*   For home sewers who do not have the satin stitch on their machines, appliqueing with a straight stitch will do. Select and cut out a design, this time leaving a ¼-inch seam allowance beyond the pattern line. Fold the seam allowance to the back of the fabric and baste all around (Fig. 2−22). Now *press* with your iron to prevent the edges from popping up again. On curved edges only, clip notches ⅛-inch deep in seam allowance. Fold background square in such a manner as to have enough fold lines to indicate placement of design. Work the layering as previously described with the Indian Boy. Baste *each* piece by hand to the background (Fig. 2−23). With same color thread for top and bobbin, a fine machine needle, and twelve stitches to the inch, proceed to straight stitch on the top 1/16 to ⅛ inch from the edge.

*Tricks.* Never apply a piece that has *not been pressed.* On any square corner or pointed place, such as a leaf point, miter the excess fabric by first folding the corner point toward the inside (Fig. 2−24). Press. Second, turn in the seam allowances on both sides leading to the miter. There are times when you come to the corner or point and have to turn with a pivot stitch. Try to remain as close to the edge as possible. Sometimes one extra stitch will put the needle over the appliqued piece. In that case, reduce the size of this next stitch from twelve to fifteen stitches to the inch. This will give approximately a half-size stitch and bring the needle within the applique and not over it. After stitch is completed, change back to the original size, lift presser foot, pivot on corner with needle in down position, lower presser foot, and continue stitching.

Fig. 2−22 Fold edge of heart shape
for practice. The deep V is cut to the
sewing line and the points are
mitered. On deep curves, stitch close
to the fold and notch out the excess.

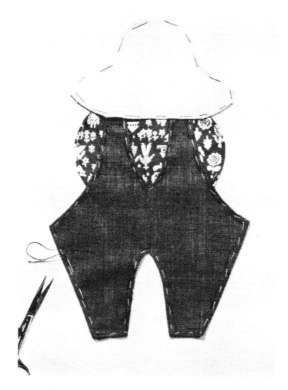

Fig. 2 − 23 Farm Boy. Three-piece applique
showing first row of basting in light-color
thread, second row of basting stitches
attaching applique to background in dark
thread, ready for final applique stitching.
Pattern given in Chapter 9.

*Hand Applique*    This is the form of applique most preferred because the
stitches will not show. It was the only method open to early needlecrafters.
Prepare your pieces as you would for the above-mentioned straight stitch
machine method.

This technique requires a hidden stitch called a slip stitch (Fig. 2 − 25). After
cutting, the edges are basted to back but not pressed (Fig. 2 − 22 and 2 − 23), it is
secured to the background with a hand basting stitch: a "sharp" needle is
threaded with a medium length of matching colored cotton thread and applique
is slip stitched to the background. To start, secure the thread in the backing
material under the piece to be appliqued, then bring it up through the backing
and the folded edge of the applique. The stitch goes particularly fast if you can
pick up the work in your hand, folding the backing material back to form two
folded edges (Fig. 2 − 25). Then you will see yourself slipping in and out of each
folded edge, ⅛ to ¼ inch per stitch, one stitch slipping through the applique, the
other through the fold of the background fabric. The stitch should be small and
tight on the face. There is only one real *trick* to this and it is good stitching.

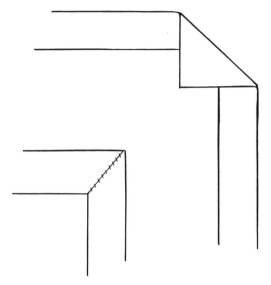

Fig. 2 – 24 Mitering a corner of an applique.

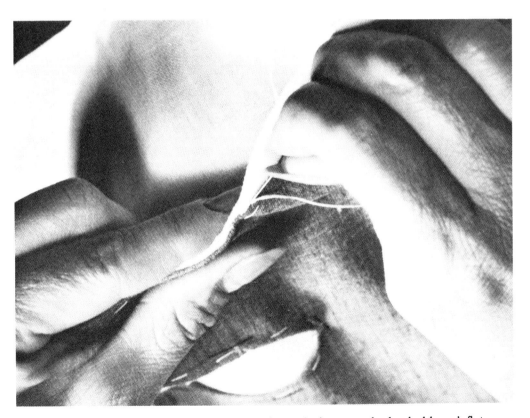

Fig. 2 – 25 Slipstitch technique on straight work; for curved edge hold work flat.

Learning this will take some time. Never stretch the fabric on an embroidery hoop or frame.

After the work is finished, it can easily be quilted by the machine, or by hand. Just pull out basting and *press*. Overcast stitching, much like tiny hemming stitches, are the second most acceptable with running and bottonhole stitches coming next. To secure the points or deep ''V'' cuts, make two or three small overcast whip stitches. Although they will show, they are necessary to prevent fraying. When using the slipstitch, try to make several stitches before pulling the thread through. This will help to speed up the work. Finish by securing thread behind applique.

## Embellishments

If you would like to get a more three-dimensional effect to your work, then try these embellishments. First, use the cotton embroidery floss sold in a myriad of colors. (All libraries have books on embroidery.) Consider only flat, tight stitches, not loop types (Fig. 2−26). My favorites are cross-stitching on checked material and buttonhole stitching on edges to make them more outstanding. Then there are the great number of star types that can be added. On bold designs, or for stems, couching works well.

Couching can be done on your zigzag machine (check your instruction book). Pull a heavy yarn up through the back and place it over the line to be accented or created. Then, with another thread of thinner quality, tack it down, going across the heavy one or use your zigzag machine stitch to hold it. If it is a stem, then sew it into the backing very securely. Hold your work as taut as possible; here an embroidery hoop is good.

When adding yarns to the quilt, make sure that they are washable. Feather stitches fill up cloud space nicely if done with a washable, fuzzy-type yarn. Then there is the cluster of French knots with many services to render.

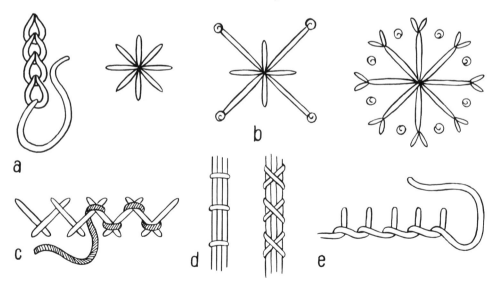

Fig. 2−26 Embroidery stitches. (a) Chain stitch (b) Stars of straight stitches (c) Herringbone interlaced with a contrasting color (d) Couching (e) Buttonhole stitch.

Now is the time to use up all the bits and pieces of braid, rickrack, ribbon, eyelet, lace, and trimmings that you have saved. They really light up some designs, especially children's items. Always tuck under the edges. I use the balls from ball fringe as animal eyes and tails. Do not use buttons on children's quilts. Somehow they get ripped off and the result is a sudden hole that needs a quick applique patch.

Don't forget to personalize your item with your name and the year.

## Bordering

The word "bordering" refers to the wide band of fabric placed around the perimeter of the blanket. It acts as a frame for the work. The word "binding" refers to the actual operation of finishing the raw edges of the quilt item.

The border is an optional feature. It is almost always added to the work when the face is being put together. It will be handled as part of the face. The size of the border depends on the balance needed for framing the main body of the blanket. A vibrant, bold-colored design needs a large, strong border. A small, fragile, delicately colored design may need only a delicate, narrow border.

Sometimes quilts of the same design and size will have different size borders, depending on its colorations: a dark tone will need the statement of a bold, stronger-colored border, while the pale pastels will need only a narrow border of the deepest tone pastel in the design to accent the entire quilt. The simplest method is to place a quilting design in a solid color border. For the first few rounds of quilt making, work on the simplest borders, progressing to the more complicated ones. Borders are actually made of long strips of fabrics. The corners can be handled in two ways: (1) *by forming a block,* that is, a square is fitted in of self or contrasting color and may be decorated with an applique or pieced design; (2) *by mitering,* but if you are unsure of mitering, then baste to form the miter; after permanent stitching, press to make sure the corner will lay flat (Fig. 2–27a and b). (For additional border techniques, see Chapter 7.)

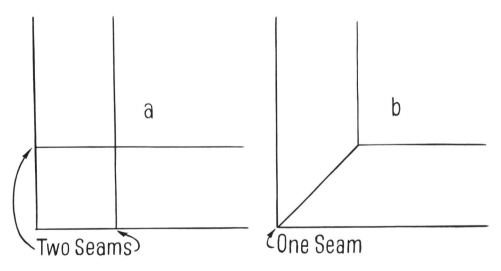

Fig. 2–27 Forming corners of borders.

*Suggested Border Designs*

1. Solid color.
2. Solid color with designs only in the corners (Fig. 2 – 28).
3. Striping together one, two, or three solid colors used in the face design for an easy but dramatic border; always have the darkest tones on the outer edges (Fig. 2 – 29).
4. A pieced design forming the strip of border to coordinate with the main body of the face design. Triangles striped together to form lightning strips; diamonds, chevrons, flying geese, or herring bone (Fig. 2 – 30).
5. The applique of a motif in harmony with the main design of the face. It does not have to repeat the exact motif; but if flowers were used in the main body of the face, then vines and buds would be pleasant around the border (Fig. 2 – 31).

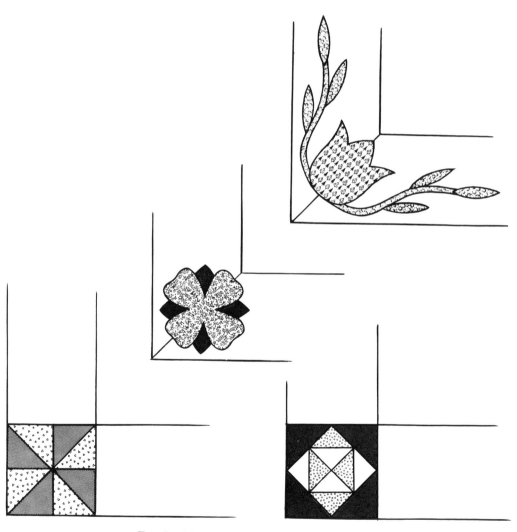

Fig. 2 – 28 Suggested designs for borders.

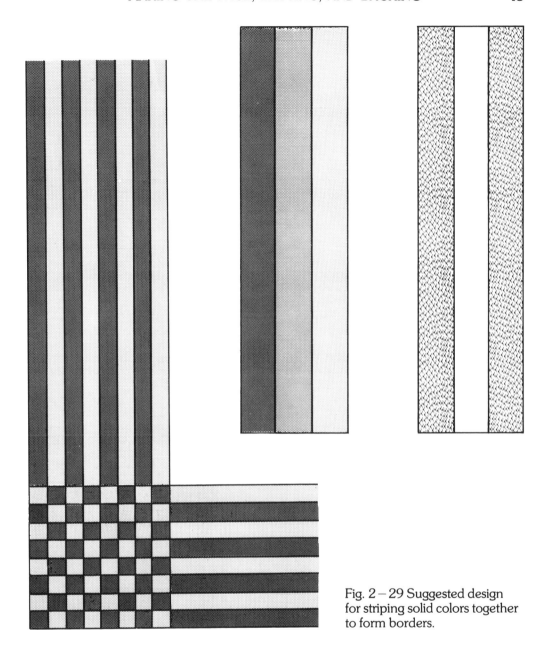

Fig. 2 – 29 Suggested design for striping solid colors together to form borders.

# Batting

"Batting" means the filler that goes between the face and the backing. The traditional reference for this term is "batts." Over the years, quilts have been filled with rags, yarns, feathers, wool, and even corn husks. As cotton battings became more and more accessible, the utilitarian purpose of the craft gave way to more artistic dimensions.

*Polyester* is today's newest material for battings. It comes in large, seamless sheets, is light in weight, and will not ball or lump between quilted surfaces. It

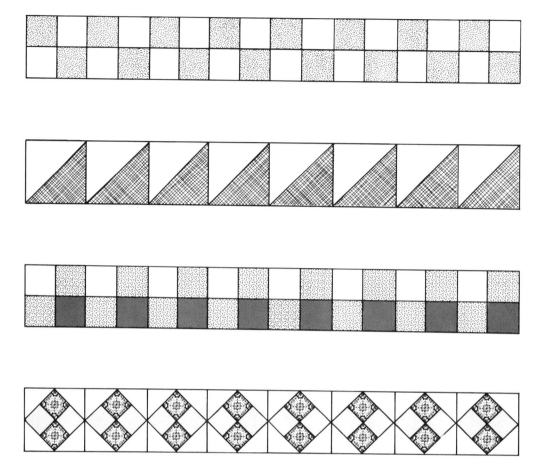

Fig. 2 – 30 Suggestions for pieced design to form borders.

requires less actual quilting since the batting remains soft and resilient in large pockets of quilt stitches. The polyester battings have relieved the quilter from having to work in the old "two-by-two" cross-bar method; pockets of quilting can be as large as 8 by 8 inches.

The most desirable sheets of polyester batting are covered on both sides with a slight sizing. This finish enables the quilter to handle the batting like a piece of fabric. It unfolds without sticking to itself or the quilt crafter. It lays smoothly without forming hills or valleys, is machine washable, dries quickly, never shrinks, is moth and mildew proof, and comes in approximately ¼ to ½-inch thickness. The quilting design puffs up more after machine washing. If you live in a hard water area, a little commercial fabric softener will add to the life of your quilt.

The best battings are sold in approximate blanket sizes (72 by 96 inches, 81 by 96 inches, and 90 by 108 inches) and they will never need pre-shrinking before use.

*Cotton batting* will have smoothly sized surfaces that will be easy to handle and always comes pre-shrunk in blanket size sheets. The shortcoming of cotton is that, over long periods of wear, it tends to lose its initial resiliency and to lump or

Fig. 2 – 31 Suggestions for applique motifs on borders.

flatten out inside the quilted item. For this reason, the actual quilting must be closer than with the synthetic batting. Use no pocketing larger than 3 by 3 inches. In hard water areas a fabric softener will help to increase the life of a cotton filled item.

*Cotton sheet blankets* can be used for a batting. They come in true blanket sizes and are readily accessible in all retail stores. This material will not have the fluffy appearance the other battings have. It will give moderate warmth as is needed in late spring and early fall. The cost will be less and so will the appearance. Pre-shrink this material before using.

*Cotton flannel,* sometimes called "outing," is a cotton fabric that has a napped finish. It will not give the fluffy appearance of the polyester or cotton battings. This material is purchased in the yard goods stores in 36 and 45-inch widths and comes in solid colors. Flannel is particularly good for a lightweight baby quilt since it is a very sturdy material and can be washed often. The selvages are to be placed one on top of the other and sewn down with a straight stitch on the machine or a close running stitch by hand if a seam is needed. This material generally shrinks a little bit, so pre-shrinking is necessary.

# Backing

"Backing" material is the bottom layer of the three parts used in assembling a quilted item.

Yesterday's traditional quilter always used a thin, white muslin, cambric, or lawn-type fabric. Often it was stripped together to form one large backing for hand quilting on frames.

Today's prerequisites for selection are the same as our great grandmother's: a light, but closely woven, opaque fabric. Here, the word "light" can best be defined by popular fabric names available in today's retail market: broadcloth, poplin, calico, gingham, fine muslin, lawn, and batiste. Most of these fabrics are available in either all cotton or cotton and polyester yarn combinations and make excellent backings. Many are available with permanent press and soil-resistant finishes. Solid colors, small, all-over floral or geometric prints are better than pictorial subject prints. Since a large yardage is to be used for a backing, it is most helpful to shop carefully for this fabric. It must be pre-shrunk at home and the center fold should be pressed out very carefully before being used in the quilted item. Backings can be sewn together with a ¼ to ½-inch seam if you need a width wider than those readily available. The most popular width in today's retail market is 45 inches.

Occasionally, you will make a quilted article where the backing is never seen, such as a tablecloth or skirt. Then very low-priced muslins or large lengths from your scrap bags can be used. Keep in mind that an attractive backing fabric on a place mat will allow the user to reverse the mat for additional use.

The question of using a sheet as backing material, particularly for large handmade quilts, often is raised by the novice. It is very hard to set quilt stitches through a top, a batting, and a sheet because of the closeness and stiffness of the threads in a sheet. Sheets may be used for machine-quilted projects, as they have a boardlike quality that helps to keep the backing from wrinkling.

The most popular backings today are the printed calicos—but check these: some have more sizing in them, especially the darker colors. Always take your quilt to the shop, or buy the backing when you purchase the original yardage. If you are purchasing backing after the quilt top is finished, place it over various shades of backing. Tinted backing will sometimes reflect a warming hue through the batting.

# CHAPTER

# Quilting and Binding

## Quilting: The Textural Element

Quilting methods used must take into consideration the design of the face and the way the item will be quilted—by hand or machine. Small items, crib quilts, and hand-quilted blankets will have all the design squares sewn together in a decorative or plain manner and will be handled as one large face. This is the simplest method. All the yardage for the backing will be sewn together in long strips with ¼-inch seams, pressed open, and handled as one large piece of backing.

Large blankets planned for machine quilting will be assembled first in two or three smaller units. The face, batting, and backings will have allowances for the seams that join the triple layered units together after quilting. This is all carefully described under blanket quilts. It is at this point that binding must be considered. The laying together of the face, batting, and backing will depend on how it will be bound and if it will be joined together with another unit. The first time around, use the bias binding, since all outer edges are flush.

### Assembly Instructions

Pre-shrink and press all backing fabric first. Place backing *wrong* side up on a large working surface. Try not to have any part of the work hanging off the table. (Many people prefer to work on the floor.) Smooth out backing so no wrinkles appear. Open batting carefully; place it on top of the backing. Trim to fit where necessary. If batting has to be pieced because it is not long enough, butt edges together, do not overlap. There is no right or wrong side to the batting. Lift the face above the batting and place down carefully, noting where it should be flush with the edges or staggered for later binding finishing.

For all machine quilting, baste the three layers together using stitches 2 to 3 inches long in rows across the narrow width of the quilt. All basting should begin from the center and be worked in lines to the outer edges.

Fig. 3 – 1 This close-up is an excellent example of the textural elements of quilt design.

For small items and hand quilts, the sunburst pattern can be used, starting from the center and running to the outer edges. A light sunburst pattern of basting assures easier handling for placing hand quilting on the frame.

## Placement of Quilt Stitches

Quilting with today's new fiber battings presents very little problem. Batting is to be placed in a pocket of stitched lines, but the pocket holding the batting can be as large as 8 by 8 inches square, in some instances.

Today's quilt crafter should be more concerned about the design of her quilting than the filling. The first rule to apply is never to quilt *on* the seam line with straight machine stitch or hand running stitch. Rather quilt ¼ to ⅓ inch inside or outside the seam. By outlining the main elements of the design, the quilter can make a very dramatic accent while accomplishing her quilting with a minimum of work (Fig. 3 − 2).

For a heavily quilted look, start to outline the design elements with concentric lines, spacing each line an equal distance from the one before it (Fig. 3 − 3). If it is a large area to cover, then proceed like "ripples on a pond," having each line a greater distance from the one before it. For machine quilting, use the presser foot as a guide, noting with your eye the distance the foot is placed from the line before it.

When working on a pieced patchwork design, it is nice if most of the elements can have some definition, but not every patch need be outlined. The quilting itself adds another dimension to the angular forms of the geometric patterns (Figs. 3 − 4 and 3 − 5).

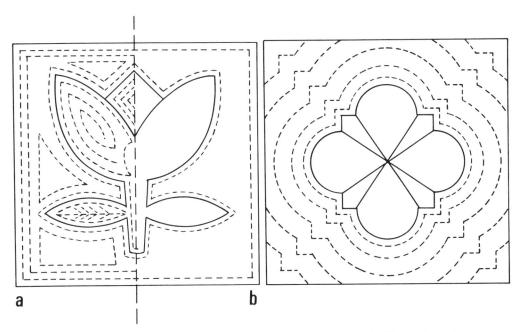

a                                 b

Fig. 3 − 2 (a) Large number of quilting stitches. (b) Small number of quilting stitches.

Fig. 3 − 3 Dutch Tile ripple quilting.

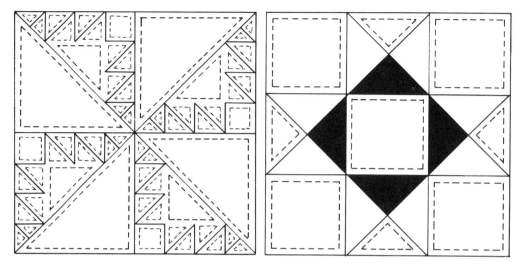

Fig. 3 – 4 Kansas Troubles quilting.            Fig. 3 – 5 Variable Star quilting.

When working with designed squares that are placed in a framing border, all the bordering frames should be quilted in some manner. At the square formed by the intersecting border, it is smart looking to quilt another small design (Figs. 3 – 6 and 3 – 7).

Consider carefully that if the work is done in smaller units to be joined for a machine quilted blanket, the quilting itself will have to match both left and right when the pieces are joined after quilting. This means that you must be consistent in your quilting lines, particularly when working with framing borders. The quilting must not extend into the joining seam allowance. *To protect the seam allowance, mark it with a surface basting line in a contrasting thread ¼ inch from the raw edge.*

Another style of quilting is to produce a box-like design as a background for applique work. This traditional method is called the "cross bar" and has many versions (Fig. 3 – 8). To produce straight line quilting on the machine, sewing shops sell a small gadget called a "quilting foot" that is attached to the machine to serve as a guide. The most popular design is to work on the diagonal so intersecting lines form a diamond pattern. Only the first line must be perfect—all will follow easily after that. For hand quilting, generally all the lines are pre-marked with a hard pencil before top is basted to batting and backing.

You can also quilt in a free-form manner—usually with a random placed applique on a large background, excellent for the crib quilt. This is most successful when started from the center, where the quilting design can be placed in a random fashion around the appliques (Fig. 3 – 9; see crib quilt color insert). Another way to do this is to start in the center with a circular motif and proceed to form a petal-like design from this center (Fig. 3 – 10).

If there is a set of open squares or border areas in your quilt, they can be filled with an assortment of quilt stitching (Fig. 3 – 12). For an odd-shaped space in an applique square that needs some distinction and/or dimension, a simple

Irish Chain by Doris Wickman, on the wall; left, Nine-Patch pillow by Dot Frager; left, Bear's Paw Quilt by Anne Chas; center, Churn Dash quilt by Susann Murray; right from top: Shoo Fly, Mixed Wrench with a Nine-Patch center, and Ragged Star pillows by Dot Frager; bottom right, World Without End quilt by Edith Taylor.

Crazy quilting place mat.

Boutique quilting: Row of Pyramids and Piece and Patch place mats; Lattice Work tablecloth; Geese to the Moon and Variable Star pillows; Vibrant Heart apron.

Hawaiian Sampler quilt designed by Helen Squire of Quilt In. (Courtesy of *Quilter's Newsletter*, photograph by Roy Hale)

George Washington at Valley Forge by Chris Wolf Edmonds. (Photograph by John Bradbury)

Freedom Rider quilt by Chris Wolf Edmonds, inscribed "Proclaiming liberty throughout the land." (Photograph by John Bradbury)

Quilters of the Hudson Highlands Bicentennial Sampler. From left to right, top to bottom: Goose in the Pond; Delectable Mountains; Mariner's Compass; Spools; Palm Leaf; Brown Goose; Shoo Fly; Barrister's Block in center; King's Cross; Nine-Patch; Queen Charlotte's Crown; Blazing Star; Saw Tooth; Turkey Tracks; Monkey Wrench; Jacob's Ladder; Honey Bee; Tea Boxes; Pine Tree; Star Combination; Double T.

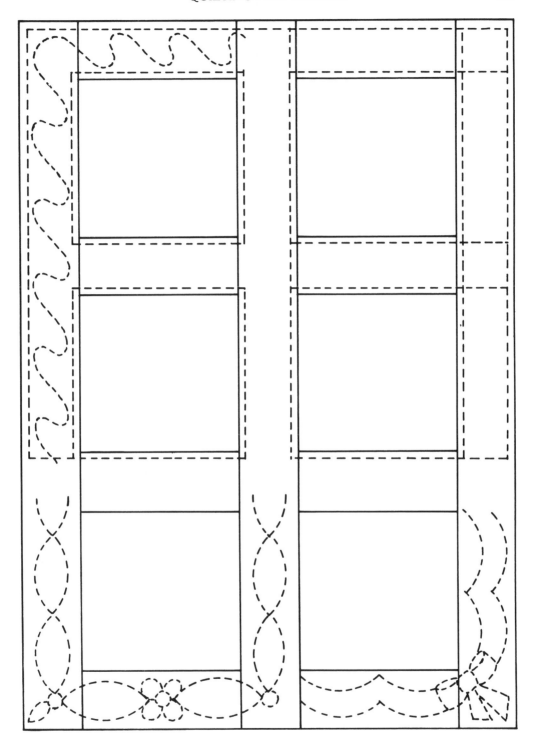

Fig. 3 – 6 Three methods of border quilting.

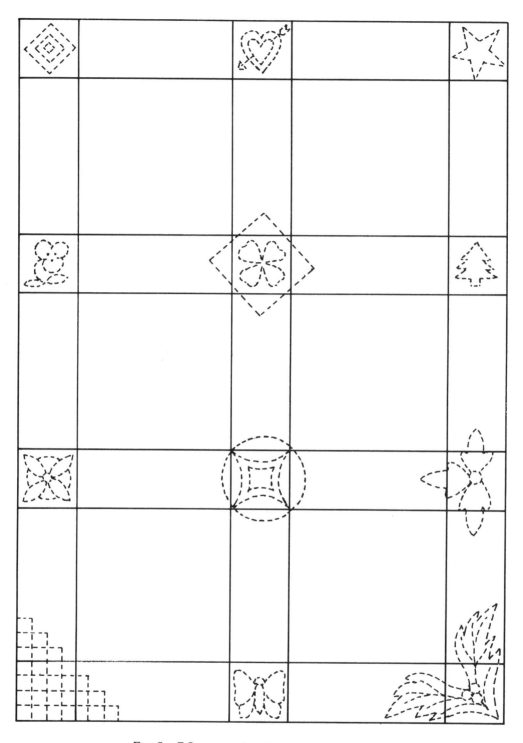

Fig. 3 – 7 Suggested quilt designs for corners.

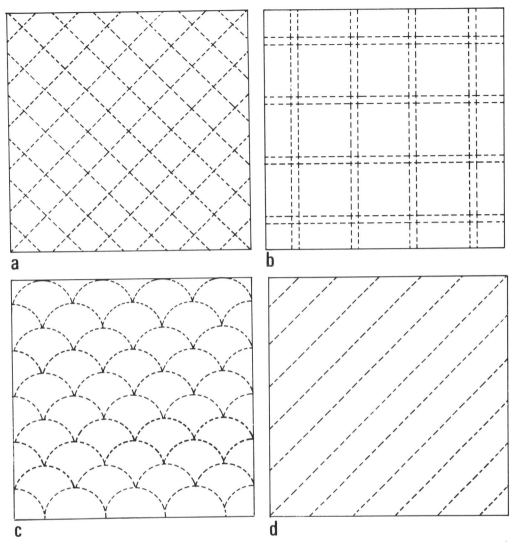

Fig. 3–8 Cross bar quilting. (a) Diamond pattern (b) 2 Bar (c) Clam shell (d) Diagonal pipe line.

design can be made using quilt stitching rather than another applique. Occasionally, a novelty effect can be made by quilting a sun in yellow thread, or stars and waves in blue thread (Fig. 3–14).

## Feather and Novelty Stitches

The only exception to the rule of quilting off the seam line is if your machine can make a feather or other novelty stitch. These fancy stitches should be used only when they do not fight with the design itself. The stitch is centered over the seam line. It is particularly good for crazy quilting, simple pieced patchwork, and outlining applique squares. The lines can intersect each other very successfully. (See color insert Bunnies in a Field of Patches.)

Fig. 3 – 9 Free form quilting.

The feather stitch works very well for free-form quilting or a crib quilt with appliqued birds. (See color insert Birds of a Feather.) When outlining a design, the last stitch should perfectly meet with the first, not overlap it. The trick to perfecting this stitching on the machine is to watch the seam line feed between the opening in the wide hole presser foot. Never watch the stitch being made or pull the work from the back. Create a constant tension by holding the work firmly between index and thumb both in front and behind the presser foot. The stitches are easy and quick when mastered. Practice on a small sample first, using common color thread on both sides.

Fig. 3–10 Petal quilting.

It is possible to employ novelty stitches when quilting by hand, but it takes a great deal of time. It is mostly employed with a crazy quilted skirt or throws made of luxurious fabrics.

## Machine Versus Hand Methods

It will help you a great deal in choosing your method to practice on a sample square of your work. Never judge the work in your lap. Place it at a distance in the position in which it will be used: a blanket on a bed, a tablecloth on a table set with dishes, or, if used as a skirt, view in the mirror at a distance of 5 feet. All quilting will begin at the center of a basted unit (of face, batting, and backing) and

a

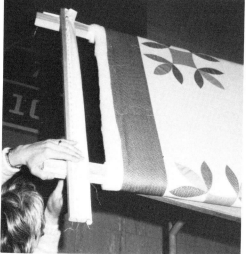

b

c

Fig. 3–11 Turkey Track quilt by Sally Rowe being put into a frame. (a) The backing, batting, and face are basted together in a sunburst pattern, starting from the center. The quilt is basted to fabric attached to long poles the width of the quilt.

(b) After the quilt is rolled to the back, the short stretcher bars are put in position. In this case, the short bars are bolted into the long poles. Also note this stretcher bar has extra fabric attached, as does the long pole. If the stretcher bar is placed close to the edge of the quilt, the quilt may be pinned to the fabric on the stretcher bar.

(c) Note how tightly the quilt is turned to the back, showing the basting which creates cross tension. Sally is beginning to lace the quilt ends to the stretcher by tying 2-inch-wide muslin strips to the crossed end of the

d

frame. This creates tension throughout the length.

(d) Lacing is completed by being pinned to the quilt and laced around the stretcher bar. Start all quilting at the center.

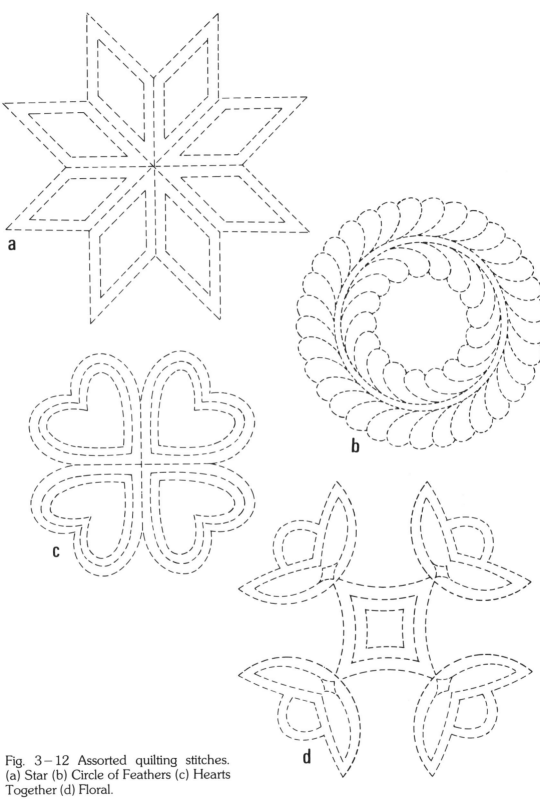

Fig. 3–12 Assorted quilting stitches.
(a) Star (b) Circle of Feathers (c) Hearts
Together (d) Floral.

Fig. 3 – 13 Types of patterns used to mark the design on the quilt. A perforated pattern is shown at center. Top left is a solid template with notched edge. Mark circle from notch to notch, then fit the next circle in below, giving a chainlike pattern. Top right is an open stencil (product of Leman Publication, Wheatridge, Colorado). Bottom right shows another form of outline.

be worked toward one end, then the other. If a complicated quilt design that the eye cannot follow easily is planned, then draw the design on a piece of brown paper and stitch along the line with your sewing machine, using the heaviest needle and no thread. When finished, you will have a perforated pattern. This is then placed on the quilt and marked through the perforation with chalk, or a very hard pencil. A cardboard template of the pattern may be used to mark a simple pattern. The quilt face may be marked with its pattern before or after it is ready for quilt stitching. For hand quilting, it is often marked in the frame and the marking proceeds as the quilt is rolled in the quilting process. The beginner may

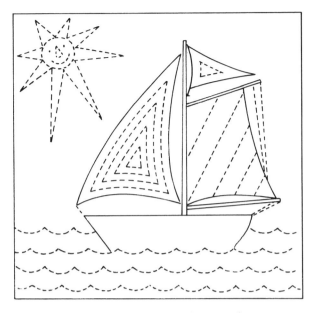

Fig. 3 – 14 Novelty quilting stitches.

start slowly but will pick up speed as the hand and eye develop this simple, coordinated movement. Follow the instructions for machine or hand quilting each time you quilt. For very intricate quilting, make or purchase a stencil type pattern (see Fig. 3 – 13).

## Machine Quilting

Pre-shrink all fabric before using.

Press all fabric before working with it and press all seams open after they have been sewn.

Clean all parts of machine with an absorbent cloth. This will assure that oil will not get on quilt as work progresses.

Set machine at eight to ten stitches to the inch. Count the number of stitches in one inch if you do not have a dial setting that will do it for you.

Release the pressure on the presser foot slightly. If the pressure is too heavy, it will not allow for the thickness of the quilt to pass through easily. If you do not know how to check this adjustment, consult your machine instruction booklet.

Check, on a sample piece of quilting, to see that the machine stitch is locking evenly. A perfectly locked stitch is made when the upper and lower tensions are balanced. For adjustment instructions, consult your machine instruction book.

Use a number 50 mercerized cotton thread, which is traditional. The new cotton covered polyester threads can also be used since they seem to have a greater tensile strength than mercerized cotton—when new.

To start, fill at least two bobbins with the color of the backing fabric or white thread which is traditional.

Use a new, medium-size needle, number 14, since old needles sometimes have burred or blunted ends.

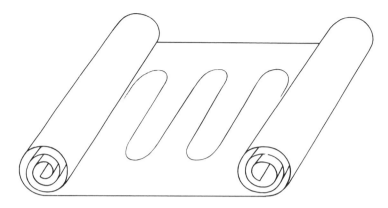

Fig. 3−15 Rolling the quilt.

Use a regular presser foot and a small hole throat plate; do not use zigzag attachments unless using a zigzag stitch.

Make a sample design square and test quilt it on the machine.

If possible, begin to quilt one of the smaller units first. This will give you a better feel for the work.

All quilting will begin at the center of a basted unit (of face, batting, and backing) and will be worked toward one end, then the other.

The machine table should be surrounded by folding card tables or a lowered ironing board to support the work so the weight of it will not cause it to pull under the presser foot of the machine.

The work will be rolled from the ends toward the center and pinned tightly to maintain the roll, leaving about 18 inches of flat surface to work on in the center (Fig. 3−15). As you progress, you can change the position of the roll. Wherever possible, try to keep the bulk of the roll to the left of the presser foot.

When pivoting your work, always place the needle down and release the presser foot; then move the work and replace the presser foot for a new start.

Keep your eye on the edge of the presser foot, using it as a guide through irregular forms. Never look at the needle. Keep concentrating on the work about ½ inch ahead, as it feeds under the presser foot.

Spread the index and middle fingers of the left hand and place them flat on the work, guiding it under the presser foot. The right hand is holding the work behind the foot, creating a constant tension without pulling the fabric (Fig. 3−16).

## Hand Quilting

Most hand quilting is done on a simple wood frame that is composed of four pieces of common pine wood. After the quilt top has been completed, it is placed over batting and a piece of backing material the same size or a little larger. It is basted in a sunburst pattern, all threads starting from the center.

Two long poles the width of the quilt are used. They may be 1 by 2 inches if working alone or 2 by 2 inches if working with a group. These poles, sometimes called the rails, are prepared by stapling or tacking a 2-inch wide strip of sturdy

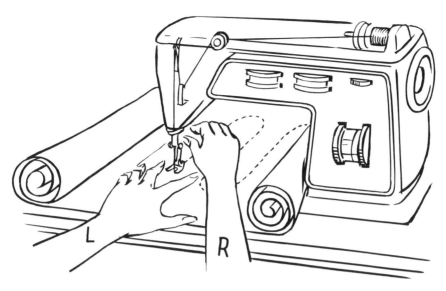

Fig. 3 – 16 Quilting on the machine in sections no wider than 45″.

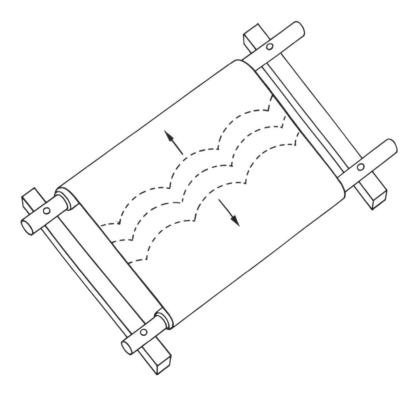

Fig. 3 – 17 Quilting on the frame, working from the center out.

fabric along the length of the poles. At least one inch of the fabric will extend beyond the edges of the pole (see Fig. 3–11). Baste the top of the quilt to the fabric that is extending from the pole; repeat for the bottom. Be careful to mark the center of the pole so it will match up with the center of the quilt. For big quilts, baste from center to outer ends. Each end is then rolled tightly and evenly until about 20 inches of the center appears.

The stretcher bars are then applied to hold the long poles apart. The length of these bars is determined by measuring the distance between the quilt crafter's elbow and hand and doubling the measure. This will allow the quilter to work on one side of the frame and then move to the other side without undue back strain. The two long poles are then bolted to the short end stretcher to hold the surface taut.

The four frame corners can be bolted together with large screws and bolts set through holes at the intersecting corners that are planned before quilt is applied to the frame. Both sets of poles can have several holes so adjustments can be made for various size quilts. Alternate corner assembly could be "C" clamps found in the hardware store or the home workbench. My grandmother had wooden pegs hammered into poles. To support the loose ends of a quilt in a frame, additional strips of fabric are wound around the stretcher bar and pinned to the quilt several times like a lacing to hold the length of the quilt taut (see Fig. 3–11). The stretcher bar may have a strip of fabric attached also and placed next to the end of the quilt. But since the three layers are not always cut exactly even, I find the lacing strips a more convenient method, especially for new quilters.

Legs can be added very easily to the short end bars at just the right height for the seated quilter. The height of the frame from the floor depends on the height of the chair the quilter plans to sit on. The knees are to fit under the frame and the quilter should be seated comfortably. Great grandmother had to put her frame on the backs of four chairs. The frame without attached legs can be stood upright against a wall or layed under a bed when not being worked on.

Today the quilter can purchase very sophisticated frames made of hard woods. The large frames come with many adjustments built in. Most ready-made large frames have long poles which turn on ratchets. It is very easy to roll the quilts on these frames.

Another excellent type of smaller frame is an oval or round frame shaped like a giant embroidery hoop on a pair of legs. It should not be confused with a crewel embroidery frame which generally is mounted on one leg. Starting from the center portion, the quilt is stretched over the lower circle of the frame and the top circle is placed over both quilt and lower frame to hold the quilt taut. To test that the quilt has a good stretch to it on either the large or small frame, a coin (a quarter) should bounce up when tossed onto the center of the frame.

*Where to Start*   Quilt stitching will start from the center of a frame and proceed to the edges. The reason for this is very logical: if at any time a bubble appears due to uneven stretching of face or backing fabric, it can be worked toward the outer edges. On the large frame, the quilter completes one side and then moves to the other side. After the center portion is completely quilted, the long poles are loosened and the quilt is rolled toward one end. After that section of quilting is finished, the quilt is again rolled toward the opposite end and then finished. As each new quilting surface appears, always start the quilting at the center.

*Quilt Stitching* There are two methods to try on a sample piece before deciding on the one you are most comfortable with. Since quilt stitches are actually running stitches, it is quite natural to try to accomplish several stitches at once. Keep it down to two stitches to begin with. Place the left hand under the frame and poke a thumb or index finger up against the line to be quilted. Hold the needle in the right hand at a 45-degree angle and place one or two stitches at a time through the three layers from the top. The finger below can be protected with adhesive tape or a commercial finger tip protector found at stationery stores.

In the second method, place one hand, the right one if you are right-handed, below the frame and the other hand, holding the needle, above the frame. Place the needle at a 90-degree angle to the quilt surface and push the needle and some of its thread through to the underside. The other hand will receive the needle and return it for another stitch. When several small stitches have been made, pull the remaining length of thread all the way through and start anew. It seems awkward at first; but as your dexterity increases, you will pick up speed. Six stitches to the inch is fair, eight good, and sixteen superlative.

Yesterday's quilter used a number 50 mercerized cotton thread because it was strong and drew it through bees' wax to make it stiffer and smoother. This method can still be used, but today's quilt crafter can purchase a spool marked "quilting thread." It is a heavy-weight cotton thread prepared with a smooth finish that will not twist or ravel with wear. This thread is made in white and many colors. The needle used is called a "between". It is short with a small round eye. The most popular sizes are numbers six or seven.

It is best to *start* and end the quilt stitching on the top of the quilt rather than underneath as was done years ago. Always quilt toward you. Pick a point that is furthest from you that you can reach comfortably. Set a pin into the face fabric, allowing part of the head and point to be free. Take a long length of thread, divide it in half, and wind the center in a figure 8 around the pin. Thread the needle on one half of the thread and proceed to quilt until that thread is finished. Take out the pin and continue to quilt in the other direction. This enables you to use a longer thread than usual. (See Fig. 3–19.)

When working on the borders, the quilting will be in rather elongated patterns. Start stitching on top of the quilt by placing a pin into the quilt just beyond the starting point and wind the end of the thread in a figure 8 pattern on the pin. Proceed to quilt the marked patterns until the thread is used up.

To *finish,* make a complete half stitch through the three layers and cover this with a second stitch the size used throughout the quilt. Then reweave the tail back into the last three stitches and take one long stitch under the face, through the batting, coming up again on the top and clipping thread. It will take a long time for this tail to unwind itself. Repeat above for the beginning thread. This puts all the work on top and in sight.

a

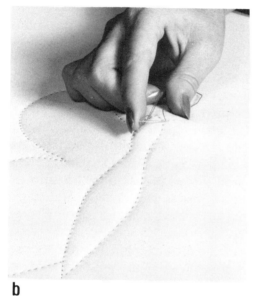

b

c

Fig. 3 – 18 (a) Friends quilting together. Note position of hands of the two quilters seated at the far end of the frame.

(b) The running stitch is worked with the educated hand; the uneducated hand works under the frame.

(c) In the up-and-down method, the less educated hand needs visual guidance and so works on top of the frame. It sends the needle down straight, to be received by the educated hand.

(d) The educated hand is capable of working without the help of eye coordination. It receives and returns the needle to the waiting hand above.

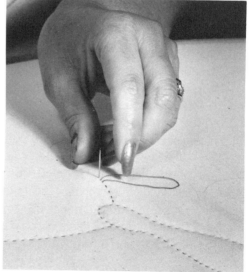

d

66

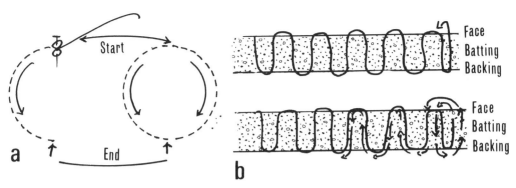

Fig. 3-19 (a) One good way to use an extra long thread is to start quilting by winding half the length of the thread on a pin; then quilt to one side and then the other. (b) The quilt stitch ends with a half stitch, is then covered with a full stitch, and the tail is rewoven into the last few stitches.

An alternate method to start is to make a small knot on the end and begin by pushing up from the back. This is good for pillow tops where the back will not be seen.

# Binding

"Binding" is the way the raw edge of the quilted item is encased or concealed. This step in the project offers another area for artistic expression. Besides adding durability to the outer edges, binding can act as a narrow frame for the quilted work. Binding is not a border and will not add appreciably to the quilt size. The widest a binding should be is 2 inches on each side. Listed below are the many options that a quilter has for binding, beginning with easy methods and advancing to the methods that require more sewing experience. Sample each method before starting and see which one has the most appeal for your project. Binding should be planned as an integral part of the design.

This is the easiest of all the techniques involved in quilt crafting. To prepare the already quilted item for binding, baste around the raw edges of the quilt in a prominent color thread to mark on both sides where the binding should be placed. Bindings are a matter of preference and there are no hard and fast rules to follow.

## Bias Binding

This is a very easy, sturdy method and gives an elegant look. It is easy because the corners are rounded off, which eliminates the need for mitering. It is the method used to form a gentle scalloped edge around a quilted blanket.

*To Make Bias Binding*   Bias binding is formed by cutting many strips of fabric, usually from ¾ to 1¼-inch wide at a 45-degree angle across the grain of a rectangle of fabric. The grain of all fabric is the north and south direction of the threads as they cross the east and west threads. To make bias binding, fold a rectangle of fabric on the diagonal to form a 45-degree angle (Fig. 3-20). Press this fold in gently with your thumb to form a light crease. Cut on the diagonal in strips twice the width needed, plus ¼ inch for each seam allowance. Notice the strips have a great deal of stretch to them that they would not have had if the strip had been cut straight across the width of the fabric.

They will then be sewn together to create one long strip to fit the circumference of the quilted item. To do this, place the short ends with right sides of two strips together so the ¼-inch seam lines match. Sew across on the machine with ten stitches to the inch, or by hand, reinforcing the edges with a back stitch. The seam will appear on the diagonal when finished (Fig. 3–20). Continue in this manner until the desired length is reached. Press seams open.

If time is a great consideration to you, this binding can be purchased in fairly good quality in widths from ½ to 1½ inches wide. It is pre-packaged in attractive colors and can sometimes be found in prints. Check the length in the package against the length that is needed to finish your quilted work. Sometimes, several package lengths will have to be sewn together using the diagonal seam mentioned above.

### *Applying Single Bias Binding Front-over-Back*

1. Trim quilt to a ¼-inch seam allowance. Round off corners of the quilt.
2. Place the face of the binding against the face of the quilt. With raw edges together, baste in place and sew down ¼ inch from raw edge with ten stitches to the inch on the machine, or a fine hand running stitch (Fig. 3–21a).
3. Turn binding over the raw edge to the back of the quilt, turn in the remaining ¼-inch raw edge of binding and stitch by hand with a slipstitch, overcast stitch, or a small running stitch (Fig. 3–21b).

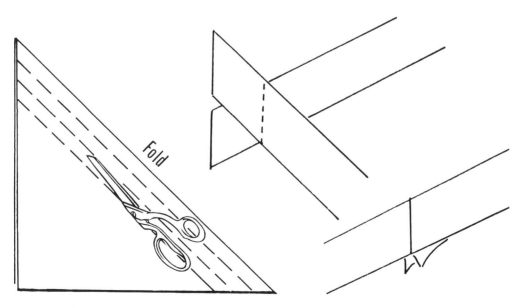

Fig. 3–20 Cutting on the bias and joining two pieces of bias fabric.

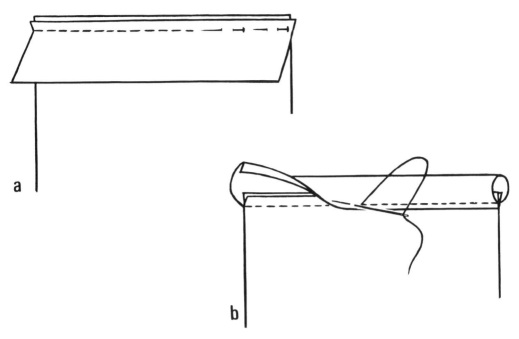

Fig. 3–21 Steps in turning of binding on raw edge.

## Applying Single Bias Binding Back-over-Front

1. The same as step 1 above.
2. Place the face of the binding against the backing of the quilt. With raw edges together, baste in place and sew down with machine, ten stitches to the inch, or a fine hand running stitch.
3. Turn binding over the raw edge to face of the quilt. Turn in the ¼-inch raw edge, baste, and press. Machine stitch down securely with straight stitch, decorative machine stitch, or by hand, using a slipstitch (Fig. 3–21). This method is especially good for the person who is looking for the speed that the sewing machine offers.

## French Binding

This method can be used for strength and durability. Cut the bias strips four times as wide as finished width, plus ¼ inch for each seam allowance. Fold in half lengthwise with wrong sides of fabric together and press. The two raw edges will be together at one side and the folded edge will be at the opposite side. This binding can be applied the same as bias binding described above for front-over-back or back-over-front method. The *two* raw edges will be placed next to the raw edge of the quilt, stitched down securely to the quilt, and the folded edge will be turned to the reverse side of the quilt for final stitching (Fig. 3–22).

## Backing as a Binding (Back-over-Front)

This method is excellent for place mats, blankets, and crib quilts. It has the most appeal in a narrow ½ to 2-inch wide style. This binding must be considered

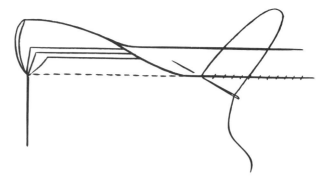

Fig. 3–22 French binding.

and laid out properly before quilting takes place. In this method, all the backing edges of the quilt will be larger than the face and batting. This should be allowed for when buying the backing yardage. When assembling the face, batting, and backing for quilting, allow the backing to be double the width of the binding to appear on the front of the quilted item, plus ½ inch to turn under as a seam allowance. If a 2-inch width is planned on the front, then the backing should be laid 4½ inches larger than the face of the quilt.

The batting will be trimmed just a little less than the width to appear on the front or, for example, 1¾ inches beyond the face of the quilt. It will give a staggered appearance when laying out the work (Fig. 3–23). The large raw edge of the backing should be pinned over the batting to protect it from undue wear during quilting. After the work has been quilted, release all basting so backing lies flat. Press if necessary.

Fold the raw edges of the backing forward ¼ inch all the way round and press gently. Clip off point of each corner ½ inch diagonally (Fig. 3–24a).

Fold each corner of the backing forward over the batting but do not fold the batting. With a pin, secure ¼ inch over the raw edge of the face. It will look like a small triangle. Press, but do not remove the pin (Fig. 3–24b).

Proceed to fold the sides of the backing forward, folding over the batting. Place folded edge of backing ¼ inch over face. The corner will miter itself. Each

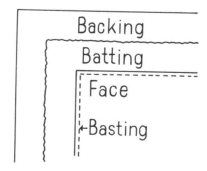

Fig. 3–23 Backing used as binding (back-over-front).

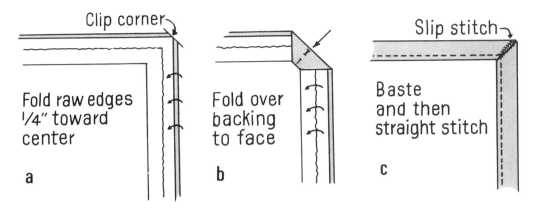

Fig. 3 – 24 Mitering corners on binding.

side will meet to form an angle on the corner of the quilt (Fig. 3 – 24c). Baste this fold to the face all around and press. Set machine for a straight stitch anywhere from eight to twelve stitches to the inch. Sew ⅛ inch from the folded edge all the way round, pivoting at corners. The mitered corner will be caught with this stitching but must be finished with a slipstitch by hand. For those who have new machines with the embroidery stitches built in, here is another place to use them. This type of binding can be finished by hand with a slipstitch, small running stitch, or a novelty embroidery stitch.

## Face as a Binding (Front-over-Back)

In this method, the entire process just described is reversed, having the face larger than batting and backing when laying out the quilted item. The binding is generally kept narrow, ½ to ¾ inch turned to the back. This is usually used when a wide border is wanted as a frame all the way around the quilt. The edge of the border can be planned a little larger so it can be turned to the back as a binding. It is a valuable idea when making a skirt to stop the batting and backing at the *fold* in the hemline and not to quilt the hem allowance (Chapter 4). This relieves the bulk at the hem.

# CHAPTER

# Small Boutique Quilting

The item most often associated with the word "quilting" is the bed covering. Although the blanket is the best known article of this folk craft, there are many boutique projects just as artful which can be carried out on a smaller scale. It is good to start with a simple project and then let your ideas grow with your developing talents. The techniques are very much the same, only reduced in scale.

With the small projects, the crafter has an excellent opportunity to build a design sense, improve dexterity, and gain a comprehensive understanding of the working of the craft. All the designs mentioned in Chapter 2 are well suited for small boutique projects. Some suggested boutique items include: appliance covers; aprons; beach mat; cape; coats, wrap, tied, or A-line; handbags; jackets, fitted or oriental style with frog closing; jumper; laundry bag; lingerie cases; lounge and campaign chair covers; poncho with fringe; rocking chair pad covers; sleeping bag; stocking holder; tea cozy; toys; traveling case; triangular scarf; upholstery; vests, from short to floor length; wall hangings; skirts.

In this section, there is the rare opportunity to use such glamorous fabrics as velvets, satins, and silks. The initial cost and upkeep charges often make these fabrics prohibitive to use in large blanket sizes. The pillow covers, table throws, and skirts are best suited for these glamour fabrics.

For a small item, the hand quilting frame must be reduced in size. A small quilting frame which resembles a giant embroidery hoop with legs can be purchased. If you prefer to work in your lap, use one without legs.

Use the knowledge gained from reading Chapters 1 through 3 as a source of reference for the projects outlined in this section. Once you are inspired with ideas and assurance, there will be no stopping you—for you will be a folk crafter.

# Place Mats and Tablecloths

Place mats are the most fun to make and are a big gift item for shower parties and as hostess gifts. Above all, it is the best way to get rid of those nagging scraps. The only consideration is the color of the dishes. You do not have to keep to the colors of the dishes but can add colors to enhance your entire setting. For the appliqued place mat, remember the design must follow the rim of the plate to be used. It would be a disaster to have the design covered.

After you become skillful at the place mats, enlarge the project and make tablecloths. One of the prettiest is an old design called Dresden Plate which can be worked in a multicolor circle of scraps on a white ground with any color border.

Patchwork design looks really grand and gives an overall geometric effect. Another good scrap quilt tablecloth or place mat can be made of identical size squares. Cut half the squares of assorted colors and half of one common color, alternating the squares between the assorted colors and the dominant color. This is a very attractive casual look for a country table.

An appliqued face can be worked on elongated strips of cloth that can be sewn together before quilting takes place. Try to work an applique design that fills the center of the table and trails off between the place settings. The drop over the table is another important place for applique decoration. The cloths are most often bound on the edges with a narrow bias binding. For a casual look, fringe can be applied over the bound edge.

There are two ways to make place mats and both are easy. The minimum size is approximately 12 by 18 inches. Shape is only a matter of preference. The simplest method is to make the face design and then cut the backing to match. Place the two units face-to-face, sew by machine ¼ inch from the raw edge all the way around, leaving an opening at the bottom. Clip corners, turn right side out, and press flat. Cut batting to match the size exactly, slip batting in the opening at the bottom, baste opening closed, and quilt. Hand slipstitch the opening closed after quilting (Fig. 4 – 3).

Fig. 4 – 1 Rail Fence place mat.

Fig. 4 – 2 Geometric Diamonds place mat.

The second method requires reading Chapter 6 on bias bindings and picking out the method that seems most fitting for your work. For place mats, the use of ready-made bias bindings is acceptable. This method is suitable for place mats with round edges and all tablecloths. Make the face, baste it on top of batting and backing fabric, and quilt. Trim off any irregularities and bias bind overlapping binding at finishing point (Fig. 4 – 4).

Row of Pyramids Place Mat (Fig. 4 – 5, see color insert)

*Materials (for four place mats)*

2 yards assorted color scraps for face
1½ yards backing fabric
1 spool for hand quilting or 2 spools for machine quilting
28'' by 40'' piece of batting

*Cutting (add seam allowance)*

40 assorted color 3'' equilateral triangles for each place mat
batting and backing cut to shape of finished face

Working with the assorted colored triangles, make two rows of nine each and two rows of eleven each. Place the two rows of eleven each in the center, add the two rows of nine each on either end to form the face of the place mats.

Wrong side together

Right side

Fig. 4 – 3 Making place mats.

Fig. 4 – 4 Making a place mat with back-over-front binding.

Press all seams open. Finish the place mat using the first method described (Fig. 4 – 3). Quilt triangles with intersecting lines ¼ inch from seam line.

This is a very effective design when made of scraps as shown in the color insert or if special design effects are used, as suggested in Chapter 2 (Fig. 2 – 7).

### Piece and Patch Place Mat

This Piece and Patch place mat is made of small scraps of fabric, generally of many varied colors and patterns. (See color insert.) Its overall size is 11 by 20 inches and it is made in two steps. Enlarge the drawing in Fig. 4 – 6 to fit on one-inch graph paper 12 by 20 inches. Make a pattern for each of the four elements. For each place mat, cut two number 1s, two number 2s, four number 3s, and two number 4s.

To make the center section, attach a number 1 piece to a number 2 piece

Fig. 4 – 5 Row of Pyramids place mat.

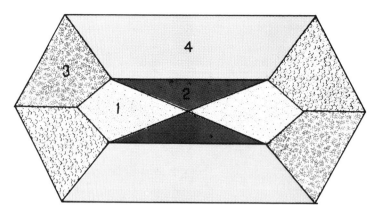

Fig. 4 – 6 Piece and Patch place mat.

and repeat for the other half. Sew diagonally, uniting two center halves. Press all seams open. Turn raw edges back ¼ inch and hand baste, press, set aside.

Sew two number 3s together for the outer rim. Repeat for the other side. Add the two side units to the number 4 pieces. Press seams open.

Place the center unit, (numbers 1 and 2), with its edges basted back, over the raw edges of the outer rim (pieces 3 and 4). Baste, then top stitch in place with a machine or hand running stitch.

To finish the place mat, use the first method described in Fig. 4 – 3. Quilt ¼ inch around each piece.

## Lattice Work Tablecloth

This simple pattern of intersecting borders through printed rectangles can be used for many quilted articles from pillows to blankets. The instructions keep the antique look at the corners but use a front-over-back binding construction to finish the outer edges. It has an optional feature of an appliqued floral motif for the center. Its small size, approximately 52 by 58 inches, makes it attractive for the beginner (Fig. 4 – 8).

### Materials

    2 yards red print for design rectangles
    2 yards solid green for bordering frames
    15'' by 15'' yellow (optional) for floral motif
    52'' by 58'' muslin for backing
    52'' by 58'' batting
    1 spool of common color quilting thread for hand quilting or 3 spools of
        thread for machine quilting to match colors of the quilt

### Cutting

    16 red print rectangles 11'' by 12½''
    3 green strips 54½'' long by 2½'' for middle borders
    2 green strips 63'' long by 4½'' for right and left side borders

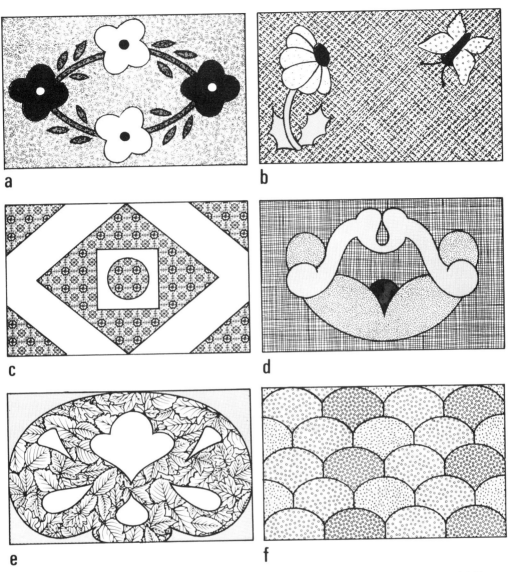

Fig. 4 – 7 Place mats designed by author. (a) Cottage Flower (b) Lazy Daisy (c) Long Road Round (d) Friendship Crown (e) Mod Mix (f) Clam Shell.

     2 green strips 48½'' long by 4½'' for top and bottom borders
     12 green short strips 12½'' by 2½'' for horizontal border
     1 four-petal yellow floral between 12'' and 15''

    Make four vertical rows by stitching four red blocks alternately with three short green strips (12½ by 2½ inches) between each block. Stitch the four vertical rows together using three long strips, 54½ by 2½ inches.

    Add the two strips 48½ by 4½ inches to top and bottom of the squares. Finally add the two 63 by 4½-inch strips to each outer edge, right and left. Note old fashioned look of the corners.

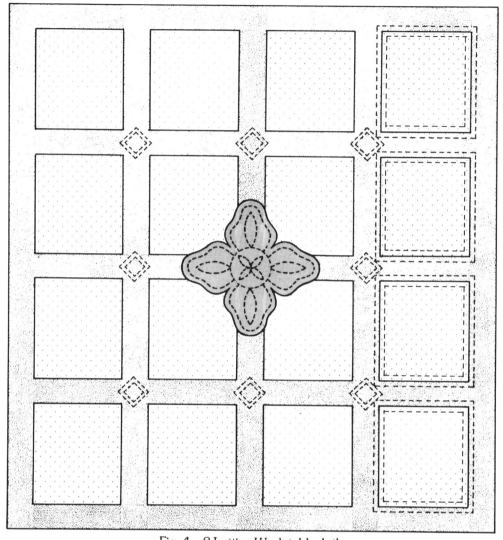

Fig. 4 – 8 Lattice Work tablecloth.

Place entire face over batting and backing (piece backing if necessary). Baste lightly. The face will be slightly larger than the batting and backing which are the same size.

Stitch ¼ inch around each rectangle on borders with green thread and on inside of rectangles with red thread for minimum quilting.

*Optional Floral Motif*   Cut out a four-petal flower approximately 12 to 15 inches wide with the ¼-inch seam allowance included. (See color insert for suggested shape.) Baste back the seam allowance and baste to the center of the tablecloth. Stitch permanently to the three layers with a machine stitch or hand quilting stitch. Use matching color thread if possible. Add as much quilt stitching to the inside of the flower as you please. Add the center circle of red, approximately 2½ inches round, with the edges turned back; and again baste and then quilt to the center of the flower. Quilt in the center of the red circle with a novelty motif as shown in Chapter 3.

In the eight remaining, *intersecting* green bordering frames, place a quilted pattern of two concentric diamonds, using the same colored thread as the frames. If the floral motif is not appliqued to the center, then add the double concentric diamond quilting to the center intersection of the bordering frame.

To finish, turn 2½ inches of the 4¼-inch border to the back, trimming away any excess batting and backing and following instructions given in Chapter 3 for front-over-back construction.

*Variations* Add additional floral motifs at outer corners. Add additional quilting of a novelty nature to the center of the print rectangles or simply make a large X in quilt stitches *across* each square.

## Dresden Plate Tablecloth

This old favorite found in Chapter 2 (Fig. 2−12) shows its versatility as a charming tablecloth. The pieced pattern forms a frame for each dinner plate (Fig. 4−9).

Fig. 4−9 Dresden Plate tablecloth.

*Materials*   This list will vary depending on the size of the table to be covered. Use assorted scraps for the Dresden Plates themselves, or ½ yard each for two colors, or ⅓ yard each for a three-color combination for five plate designs. Cut the pattern at least 2 inches larger than the plate that will sit upon it, so it forms a frame for the plate.

Measure the table. Add a 5-inch minimum drop all around. This generally requires two lengths of fabric seamed in the center. The fabric for the face should be a washable solid or print.

Batting must match the above measurement. Muslin fabric, or a small print if you wish to reverse the cloth, is used for a backing.

Measure the circumference of the outer edge and purchase enough bias binding or fringe to cover it.

One spool of quilting thread for hand quilting or two large spools for machine quilting (one to match face and one to match backing if you wish to reverse) are needed.

Make each Dresden Plate using instructions and suggestions in Chapter 2 and press flat. Also see Chapter 5 for Dresden Plate quilt.

Fold the entire background in half and then in half again, being careful to have all the outer edges matching. Press gently. When open, the folds will serve as a guide for placement of the five-pieced designs. Baste and applique to the face. Press. Place face over batting, backing, and quilt, using suggestions in Chapter 3 and Fig. 4 – 9.

Bind with bias, using suggestions in Chapter 3, and add the fringe or any other novelty trim for a casual effect.

For use on a summer umbrella table, cut out the center portion of the center Dresden Plate and bind with bias.

# Decorative Pillows

The first consideration when planning a pillow is color. Plan the pillow for a specific room, choosing colors that will harmonize with the decorative designs in that room. The second consideration is the design. The most popular pillows have patches of fabric artfully sewn together. Applique methods can be used for carefully chosen designs with a strong central motif or four motifs that reach to the corners of a square.

Prepare the face, lay the face over the batting and a backing such as pre-shrunk muslin, and then quilt. Treat as a single piece of heavy fabric. Pillows need only a ¼-inch seam allowance and can have an unquilted solid color backing.

After the show-off side has been quilted, place the right side of the quilted portion against the right side of the fabric to be used on the back of the pillow. Stitch ¼ inch off the raw edge all around, leaving an 8-inch opening on the bottom. Turn to the outside, press, and fill with a pillow form. Turn the remaining two raw edges to the inside and slipstitch the 8-inch opening closed.

Materials used to stuff pillows are loose style polyester, shredded Styrofoam, or feathers. Make a ticking fabric case filled with one of the above to be put into

Fig. 4–10 Accessories on wall: clockwise from left, Christmas stocking by V. Talbot; three quilted wall hangings by B. Panitz; Christmas wall hanging, nine-patch, by V. Talbot; potholders and mounted Pine Tree wall hanging by author. Pillows: (left to right, top row) Assorted Stripes, Stained Glass, Hearts Delight, Cactus Pot, all by B. Panitz; (bottom row) Dahlia and LeMoyne Star by J. Bouvier, Comedy and Tragedy and Abstract by B. Panitz.

Fig. 4 – 11 Grandmother's Fan pieced applique pillow.

the pillow cover just made. This way, the cover can be easily removed for cleaning. Pre-shaped foam rubber pillows need not be covered.

## Geese to the Moon Pillow

This two-tone pattern pictures the triangular shape of geese flying toward the center square representing the moon. It is generally formed in a dark and light coloration (Fig. 4 – 12).

The following instructions are for a 14 by 14-inch pillow.

*Materials*

½ yard of dark tone
⅓ yard of light tone
14½'' by 14½'' piece of batting
2 small spools of thread to match light and dark tone of fabric
14½'' by 14½'' square of muslin
14'' by 14'' pillow
14½'' by 14½'' fabric for back of pillow

*Cutting (seam allowances included)*

A, cut 16 dark tone triangles having two equal sides at a right angle measuring 2⅞'' and a third side 4''
B, cut 16 light tone triangles 2⅞'' by 2⅞'' by 4''
C, cut 1 dark tone square 2½'' by 2½''
D, cut 4 light tone rectangles 2½'' by 4½''
E, cut 2 dark tone rectangles 2½'' by 10½''
F, cut 2 dark tone rectangles 2½'' by 14½''

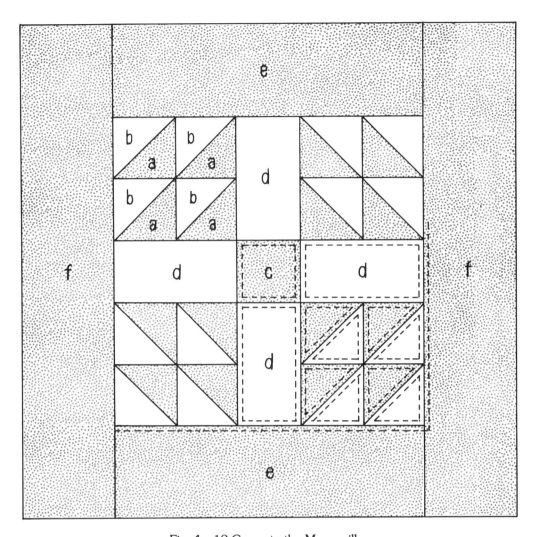

Fig. 4–12 Geese to the Moon pillow.

Sew together all As to Bs to form sixteen two-tone, 2½-inch squares. (Use Fig. 4–12 as a reference.) Press seams open. Sew four of these two-tone squares together to form four 4½-inch squares. You will see that the dark tone represents the geese with the head at the point and the long side of the triangle represents the wings.

Sew one of the 4½-inch squares to the long side of D, keeping the dark tone geese pointing toward the center. Sew another 4½-inch square to the other long side of D. Keep the dark tone geese pointing toward the center. Press and set aside.

Sew the short side of one D to the top of C and another short side of another D to the bottom of the same C to form the center of the design. Join this newly assembled unit to the long unit formed in step two. Make sure the geese point toward the center. Press.

Repeat the instructions in the second paragraph to form the third and last section of the design and attach to the other side of center unit. Press.

Sew one E to the top of the design and one E to the bottom of the design. Press. Sew one F to the left side of the design and one F to the right side of the design.

Place the design square over a 14½ by 14½-inch piece of batting and muslin backing. Baste in a sunburst pattern from the center. Quilt by outlining each element of the design ¼ inch from the seam. Finish as described earlier.

### Variable Star Pillow

This patchwork is worked in three colors (Fig. 2 – 8a).

*Materials*

¼ yard each of three colors
15½'' by 15½'' piece of muslin
15½'' by 15½'' piece of fabric for back of pillow
15½'' by 15½'' piece of batting
15'' by 15'' pillow
1 spool of thread for either hand or machine quilting

*Cutting (add seam allowances)*

4 red 15'' squares
1 white 15'' square
12 blue triangles
4 red triangles

To make pattern for triangles, divide one 5-inch square in half on the diagonal and in half again (see Fig. 2 – 8a). Be sure to add ¼-inch seam allowance to both the square and the triangular pattern pieces.

Begin by putting the four 4-piece triangles together, using three blue triangles and one red. Press seams open and treat as one block. Seam three blocks together horizontally to form three long strips. Press. Seam the long verticals together. Press. Face is finished.

Place muslin on work surface, place batting on top, and then place face. Baste in sunburst pattern. Quilt ¼ to ⅓ inch off seam line of each element in design.

Remove basting and assemble to selected pillow backing as previously described.

# Vibrant Heart Apron

This cute, mod design is very timely for today and fits so well onto an apron. The quilted apron is not only a beautiful object but needs no ironing and allows no dirt to penetrate to clothing. This apron is designed for a medium-sized woman. (See Fig. 2 – 17a and color insert.)

*Materials*

30'' by 24'' square of sturdy fabric for the face
30'' by 24'' backing

Rail Fence patchwork of small strips of fabric quilted in a step-like design by Helen Doyle.

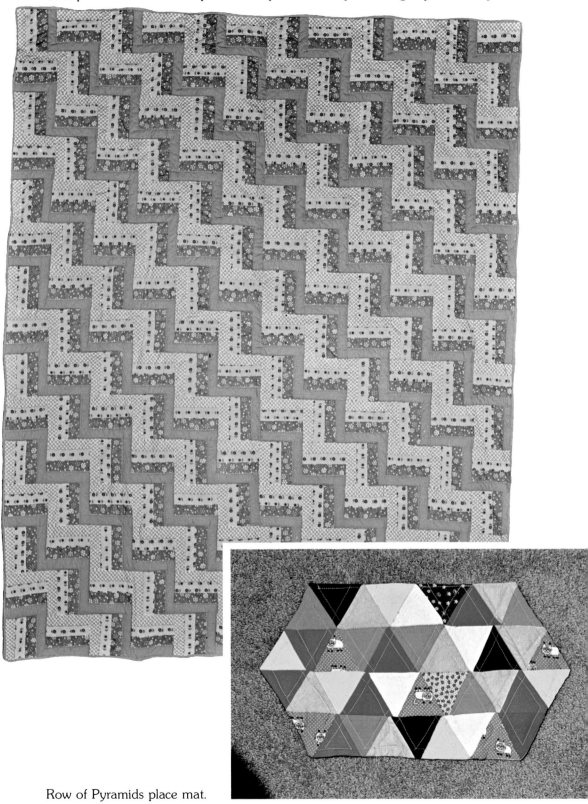

Row of Pyramids place mat.

Around the World quilt by Dot Frager, on the wall; left, Country Blossom by Sally Rowe; center, Ladies Lace-Trimmed Full Fan pillow by Vivian Talbot; foreground, Log Cabin set in the Court House Step design, courtesy of Sally Rowe; right, Flower Vase pillow by Beverly Panitz and Ohio Rose quilt by Dot Frager.

Dresden Plate pieced and appliqued quilt, designed and made by the Young Womens Christian Association of Ridgewood Quilt Club. Contributors to this quilt were Ila Alexander, Helen Bowler, Jessie Cummins, Edith Hayes, Ann Hovan, Betty Jenkins, Florence Kantor, Tina Klee, Matilda Mikoff, Beverly Panitz, Jean Schmid, Fu Jiko Shinozuka, Betty Taylor, Marcia Winick.

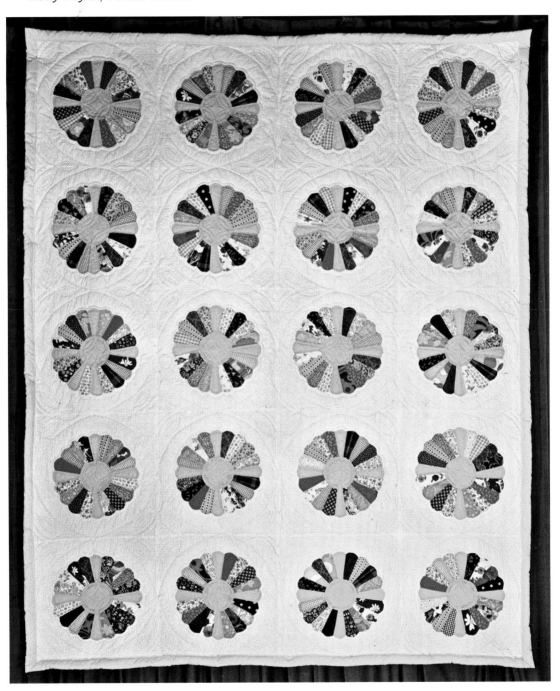

Crib quilts: Bunnies in a Field of Patches and Birds of a Feather.

30'' by 24'' batting

½ yard yellow for applique

¼ yard green for applique

½ yard red for heart applique

6 yards purchased binding, ¾'' wide

1 spool of thread for hand quilting or 1 spool each green and red thread for machine quilting

*Cutting (seam allowances included)*

Cut a pear-shaped apron pattern approximately 30 by 24 inches wide (at hip area). Cut face, batting, and backing from this pattern.

1 red heart, 10'' wide by 13'' high

1 yellow set of letters, 3½'' tall, L-O-V-E (or personal name)

4 yellow flowers about 4'' by 4''

6 or 7 green leaves about 3½'' by 1½''

Apply the letters to the heart before cutting heart from red fabric. Fold face of apron in half to find center. Press fold lightly. Cut out heart and applique to upper center of apron, placing center of heart over center of apron. Applique two yellow flowers and green leaves to heart.

Place the remaining yellow flowers together, face-to-face. Sew ¼ inch from edge, leaving a small opening at the bottom. Turn to right side (Fig. 4–3). Top stitch to lower right hand side of apron on three sides only, leaving top open to form pocket.

Applique the remaining leaves in place to cover opening at bottom. Place face over batting and backing and baste in a sunburst pattern. Quilt with two or three concentric lines of quilting around the heart and flower applique, one line around the letters. In a free form manner, quilt the veins into each leaf.

Fold 54 inches of the purchased bias binding in half so raw edges are covered and stitch along the edge. Cut in three 18-inch lengths. Place two at approximate waist to be used for back tie and one at top to form neck band. Place remaining binding around raw edge of apron on the back, catching all three layers in the binding seam allowance. Turn to the front and stitch by hand or machine ⅛ inch from folded edge to finish.

# Pot Holders and Bun Warmers

Pot holders, a necessary item in any kitchen, can be made from scrap fabrics. Both methods described for making place mats are attractive, keeping this size to at least 8 by 8 inches. Place small plastic rings, purchased in any variety store, in the corner so pot holders can be hung. A good batting material, for pot holders *only*, is the unworn portion of an old mattress pad.

Bun warmers are another gift item that are very useful. A quilted bun warmer need not be set in a basket since it will stand by itself after quilting. Choose a design that will fit into a 14 to 18-inch circle. Prepare the face design.

Cut a backing to match and four 9-inch long by ½-inch wide grosgrain ribbons, color matched to the design. Baste one each of the four ribbons at north, south, east, and west position on the right side of the round face, with one raw edge of the ribbon touching the raw edge of the face. Pin loose ends of the four ribbons at the center. Place the right side of the backing to the right side of the face. Pin and sew ¼ inch from the edge all the way round, leaving an 8-inch opening at one side. Turn to right side out, release ribbons from center. Press.

Cut batting to fit the circle. Place batting inside through 8-inch opening. Baste opening closed and quilt. By hand, slipstitch the opening closed after quilting.

To form bun warmer, place on table, backing side up, and draw four ribbons toward center forming two intersecting bows. The pockets formed by the bows drawn to the center are where the buns are placed to keep warm. The face forms the decorative outside.

# Skirts

Quilted skirts have had continuous fashion appeal since the first Dutch settlers in New York brought the idea to this country. These ladies even quilted together layers of wool for warm petticoats. The simplest skirt is a gathered style and right now the most popular length seems to be the floor length (Fig. 4 – 13). The daytime length seems to be quite serviceable for the younger set.

Here is another opportunity to use the glamour fabrics of silks, satins, and velvets. The crazy quilt designs are charming for this style and so easy to make from the "old scrap box."

Most patchwork designs of a casual nature are easy and appropriate for skirts (Figs. 2 – 3 to 2 – 10). Squares, triangles, and diamonds of any size are the easiest of all. Don't forget the lightning stripes shown in Fig. 2 – 7d; it would be both easy and dramatic. Look at any of the circular pieced and appliqued designs shown in Chapter 3 (Figs. 2 – 12 to 2 – 14). Circles could be placed at the bottom of any skirt. The design motif could be repeated toward the top, getting smaller for each successive repeat. Creating garlands of flowers around the hem of the skirt, topped by small appliqued flowers, makes a stunning design. Remember to leave room to quilt around the appliques.

Measure waist to hem length, add 3 inches for hem at the bottom and 2½ inches for tunneling elastic at waistband. Measure widest part of lower torso and add 10 to 16 inches. This gives the width needed. Prepare face according to this measurement.

Cut the backing fabric the same size as the designed face. Place the backing face down on work surface. Place the batting on top, leaving the 3 inches for the hemline free of the batting. This reduces the bulk at the hemline when finishing the garment.

Place face on top, trim the batting to fit the face and backing, baste carefully, placing small basting stitches across the hem just above the fold. Quilt, checking Chapter 3 for suggestions.

Close the skirt by placing a ¼ inch seam in the back. To tunnel waist, fold the edge of the waist ¼ inch toward the inside and press. Then turn down

Fig. 4 – 13 Patchwork skirt.

Fig. 4–14 Clothing decorated with applique. At left is an applique and lace trimmed ready-made chambray shirt and a child's shirt trimmed with a print cutout, both made by V. Talbot. In the center are three shirts appliqued and embroidered by hand and machine and a unique velvet evening bag decorated with satin, trims, and quilting, all by B. Panitz. At right is a baby's bib with picture cutout and stitching by B. Panitz and a wool vest trimmed with linen applique, made by the author.

another inch toward the back, sew ⅛ inch off edge at bottom fold of the newly formed tunnel. Stop stitching one inch short of place you began. This allows for entrance of elastic. Place a second row of stitching at top of tunnel ⅛ inch off edge. Now place a ¾-inch elastic band into newly formed tunnel, pulling gently to fit waist. Lap the two ends of the elastic over each other and sew securely. Slip elastic into tunneled band and close band with a slip stitch.

Turn up the 3-inch hem at the bottom, covering the raw edge with hem tape and finishing with hand hem stitch.

# CHAPTER

# Crib Quilts and Blankets

## Crib Quilts

One of the most charming items to quilt by hand or machine is the *crib cover*. This item can be handled quite successfully on the machine as one unit. For hand quilting, a small frame must be used. The most important consideration is the size of the quilt. For those of you who have forgotten, or who have not had the opportunity to find out, the standard crib mattress is 52 by 27 by 5 inches.

The length of 52 inches should be adhered to as closely as possible since the

Fig. 5–1 Three Bears crib quilt, made by the author for Shannon Powell.

top and bottom of the mattress lays flush with the two solid wood ends of the crib. The crib cover cannot be easily tucked under at the top and bottom. It can and should be tucked under at the sides. This tucking meets two needs: It covers the mattress when baby is not in the crib and also provides a stable tuck when baby is snuggled under the blanket.

The mattress is 27 inches wide and 5 inches high, which adds another 10 inches to the width, plus a 3-inch tuck under each side of the mattress for a total minimum width of 43 inches.

Another item for baby is the 24-inch square carriage blanket and matching pillow sham, approximately 12 by 16 inches. As a gift for little girls, a small 18 by 18-inch doll blanket is most appreciated and easy to make from scraps.

The standard pink, blue, yellow, turquoise, and green should be strong enough in *their* color values to make the designs dramatic. The baby item is attractive with a two-color face that uses a third color quilt stitching, such as yellow and white fabric with turquoise stitching or pink and blue fabric with yellow stitching.

Original designs for appliques are easy to find in pre-school coloring books and juvenile picture books. The quilt can be designed just as successfully with assorted animal figures, flowers, toys, or vehicles in random fashion in place of the birds. The fabric should be soft and lightweight. The crib blanket may be a showpiece to its maker but baby does not know that and mother will be happy with easy-care fabrics, colors, and designs.

Do not attach any buttons; novelty embroidery trims and rickrack offer endless opportunities for original effects in baby quilts.

## Birds of a Feather

*Materials*

> 45'' by 53'' piece for backing
> 44'' by 52'' solid color for face
> ¼ yard each of 7 different colors
> ½ yard of white ball fringe for birds' eyes
> 44'' by 52'' piece of batting
> 1 large spool of hand quilting thread or 2 spools of thread for machine quilting.
> Assorted novelty trims (optional)

*Cutting*   The quilt shown in the color insert has fourteen appliqued birds. Make seven cardboard designs and use each twice. Draw each bird to fit on an 8 by 8-inch paper to keep them all the same relative size.

Applique birds in a random fashion on the face, being careful not to place any of them closer than 1½ inches to the outer edge. Press.

Assemble face, batting, and backing; and baste in a sunburst pattern. Quilt in a free form fashion, starting from the center and working out to the edges. (See Fig. 3−9.)

Trim batting to match face and fold remaining backing over the front to form a very narrow binding. See detailed instructions, Chapter 3, for back-over-front binding, or use a bias binding. Use one ball from the white ball fringe for each bird's eye.

Suggested colors on white ground: bright yellow, turquoise, navy or skipper blue, bright pink, rose, red, coco, purple or lavender, pastel blue, mustard gold, creamy orange, any strong shade of green.

*Optional Feature*   There is a toy bird in a nest in the upper right hand corner of the picture in the color insert. Make the toy following the pillow instructions in Chapter 4; make the nest a double fold of fabric, applique as a pocket (see apron instructions, Chapter 4).

## Bunnies in a Field of Patches

*Materials*

> 1 yard each of 3 colors (a, b, c) for face
> 1¾ yards 45'' wide for backing
> 6 yards for binding, any color used on the face of quilt
> ⅔ yard white for bunnies
> 45'' by 56'' piece of batting
> 2 spools of thread for machine quilting or 1 large spool of hand quilting thread.
> 1 hank of washable yarn for tails

*Cutting (seam allowances included)*

> 52 squares of each of 3 colors for face, 4½'' squares
> 2 white bunnies 25'' tall and 11'' wide at the foot

There are eleven squares in each row. There are fourteen rows in the quilt. Begin first row, colors a, b, c. Continue second row, colors b, c, a. Continue third row, colors c, a, b. Repeat making above three rows until there are fourteen rows. Press all seams open.

To work the bunny figures, turn and baste the ¼-inch raw edge of figures to back. Center and baste to the quilt with a straight stitch on the machine or hand applique securely to the quilt. Press.

Assemble the face, batting, and backing, having all three layers even at the raw edges. Baste and quilt. The quilt shown in the color insert was machine feather-stitched on all the seam lines, but outlining each square with machine or hand quilt stitching would be just as effective.

Bias bind the edges. (See Chapter 3 for binding details.) Applique the eyes of a strong color fabric and embroider a nose and mouth at this time.

To make the tail, divide the hank of yarn in half. Wind half the yarn snugly on 6 by 2-inch piece of cardboard. Slip it off the cardboard carefully. With a double length of yarn, 6 inches long, slip it around the middle and knot securely. Cut each end of the yarn and it will fuzz out into a little pompon-like ball. Repeat for the other tail.

*Variations*

> Use assorted color pastel scraps in a random fashion for squares.
> Use assorted colors in crazy quilt fashion.
> Use one large applique elephant, sail boat, teddy bear, puppy, or bird.
> Enlarge the design for adult size bed, using sophisticated colorings and either no applique or a more appropriate design.

# Blanket Quilting

Blanket quilting is the prize of this heritage craft. It combines taste, skill, and creative vigor. Because there are so many choices in putting a blanket together, it becomes a highly valued design item. A plan should be formulated before starting, depending on the quilter's craft skills and the amount of time the quilter wishes to spend on each blanket. The basic blanket has five major parts: face, batting, backing, quilting, and binding. Each time a new blanket item is planned, the following decisions have to be made.

Fig. 5–2 School Days, an appliqued 1976 contest quilt. Photo courtesy of Stearns & Foster "Mountain Mist" quilt collection.

*Size of the Quilted Blanket*

|  | *Mattress Size* | *Standard Blanket Size* |
|---|---|---|
| Twin | 39'' by 75'' | 66'' by 86'' to 100'' |
| Full | 54'' by 75'' | 76'' by 86'' to 100'' |
| Queen | 60'' by 80'' | 86'' by 106'' |
| King | 76'' by 80'' | 100'' by 106'' to 109'' |
| Crib | 27'' by 52'' | 43'' by 52'' |
| Carriage cover |  | 24'' by 24'' |

*Determining Materials Needed and*
*Techniques to be Used*

|  | *Yardage* |
|---|---|
| *Face* |  |
| Patchwork | ............... |
| Crazy Quilt | ............... |
| Pieced Applique | ............... |
| Applique | ............... |
| *Batting* | ............... |
| *Backing* | ............... |
| *Binding* | ............... |

## Hand versus Machine Quilting

The hand-quilted blanket is the most easily assembled item. The entire face is designed and fashioned into one complete sheet and assembled to batting and backing, discussed in Chapter 2. Next, it is placed on a frame, quilted, and bound as described in Chapter 3.

The advantages of the hand-quilted blanket are numerous: more intricate quilt stitching patterns can be used; the intrinsic value of a totally handcrafted item is higher; and a more exacting reproduction of an antique item can be made. Its disadvantage is time. The hand-quilted project can take from 5 months for a small quilt to 5 years for a large, complicated quilt.

On the other hand, the machine-quilted blanket has the distinct advantage of being completed in a few days for a small quilt to less than a month for a large quilt. In quilting on a home sewing machine, the large blanket is broken into smaller units for the quilt sewing and assembled into a whole with a simple seaming process. The variety of stitches from simple outline to free form to special effects, like the feather stitch, is a prime consideration. The disadvantage is the difficulty of the machine to follow very intricate quilting patterns.

Special note should be taken that the methods can be combined. An all machine face can be hand quilted. A handmade applique face can be very successfully machine quilted. Big bold designs are as popular as antique copies. Each is a work of folk art interpreted for today's needs—each an heirloom.

Fig. 5–3  13 Colony Bicentennial Friendship Quilt, a 1974 contest quilt. It includes thirty historical applique renderings of thirteen original states. Photo courtesy of Stearns & Foster "Mountain Mist" Quilt Collection.

## Machine-Quilted Blanket

The first thing to consider is just how you are going to put an appliqued or pieced face together with the backing. This requires a little forethought for machine quilting; it is as important a consideration as the design itself. You are working with assembling a face, then a batting, and then a backing fabric. The trick to making light work of quilting is to divide the total blanket into small units. By quilting in small units on the machine and then joining the units together securely, the work is very easy to handle. The newer you are to machine quilting, the smaller you want the actual units for the machine work.

Fig. 5 – 4 Autograph Quilt is an unusual patchwork quilt signed and dated by its makers. The center of the applique star tells us the quilt was made for "Lynn M. Prettyman." It is signed below, "Made by the Females of the Methodist Mariners Church, 1840." The small boat drawing above the signature has the name "Mary Prettyman" inscribed on its stern flag. In the four corners surrounding the center star are Biblical texts. Each patchwork block is signed, and some have pictures drawn in. Courtesy of Florence Treuer.

There are many sizes of blanket quilts; this necessitates the diagramming of several plans for breaking the large blanket into small units that can be easily quilted. Choose the one that suits your blanket best. Then lay up the face, batting, and backing and quilt the two or three separate units. Unite all the units with the simple joining seam detailed in this chapter. The next step is to choose the outer binding method from Chapter 3 that best suits the blanket. Complete the blanket quilt by finishing the outer edges.

*Dividing the Blanket into Units for Quilting*   Consider the following assorted ideas for breaking the quilting work into smaller units. Do not consider trying to machine quilt on anything wider than a 44-inch width. When executed properly, the seam to join the units together becomes *invisible* on the outside of the blanket.

*Two-part unit.* Plan to divide the work into two 44-inch (or less) wide pieces by the length from head to foot. Two 44-inch wide units give a completed width of 88 inches and two 35-inch wide units give a completed width of 70 inches. Quilt each width and join your work together with one "joining seam" at the center. Remember that the quilting forms a design, too, and must match left and right. This two-part construction would require two lengths of backing fabric (Fig. 5—5).

*Three-part unit.* The three-piece section method generally uses a large single piece for the center section and two smaller pieces for the sides. Then there will be a center unit with joining seams at either side. The side panels can be adjusted to any width. For example, a 44-inch center with two 30-inch side panels gives a completed width of 104 inches and would use three lengths of backing fabric. (See Fig. 5—6.)

*Unit Assembly of the Joining Seam Area*   Now that the decisions have been made regarding the designs of the face and the breaking of the work into

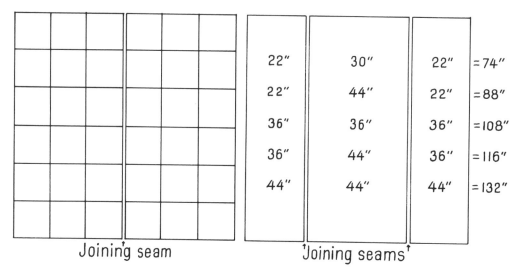

Joining seam                Joining seams

Fig. 5—5 Dividing the work into two units for machine quilting.

Fig. 5—6 Dividing the work into three units for machine quilting.

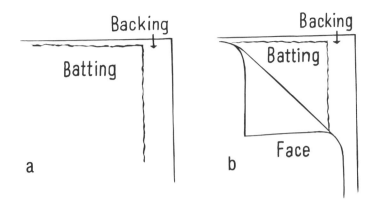

Fig. 5 − 7 Detail of layout for joining seams.

units for quilting, it is time to assemble the face, batting, and backing. There are three different outer binding methods to be considered when assembling a blanket, as discussed in Chapter 3. It makes no difference which method is chosen for the outer edges of the blanket. The "joining seam" process is the same for all assembly. Only the widths and lengths will change, depending on the actual size of the blanket. First, place backing on work surface, rightside down.

Assemble face, batting, and backing (see Chapter 2). Place the smooth cut edge of the batting ½ inch inside the raw edge of the backing fabric where the "joining seam" is to be placed (Fig. 5 − 7a).

The face is now lifted above the batting and placed ¼-inch off the raw edge of the *backing,* covering by ¼ inch the edge of the batting (Fig. 5 − 7b). The outer edges are adjusted according to the plan chosen for the binding of the edge (Figs. 5 − 8 to 5 − 10). Repeat for each unit.

As each unit is laid out, baste at once before removing from the work surface. Work the basting from the center toward ends. Use large stitches, 2 to 3 inches, in lines 12 inches apart. Treat each unit in this manner, then roll carefully for storing. After all units are basted, then quilt using Chapter 3 as a guide. Do not quilt in the joining seam allowance.

*Unit Assembly of the Outer Edges*  For each of the three binding methods discussed in Chapter 3, there is a unit diagram showing how to lay together the face, batting, and backing for a three-unit blanket, indicating the joining seams and how to lay out the outer edges. If a two-part blanket is planned, then cover the center section with a blank card and use only the illustration for right and left sides.

*Bias Bound Outer Edges*  The first and easiest method is to have all the outer edges of the face, batting, and backing even and to apply a purchased or homemade bias bound edge (Fig. 5 − 8). This is very sturdy and can be applied from back to front or front to back, finishing the front with a machine top stitch. This is very effective for patch quilting, antique copies, or when the color of the binding is not violently different from the colors in the blanket. The best sizes are ½ to 1½ inches wide.

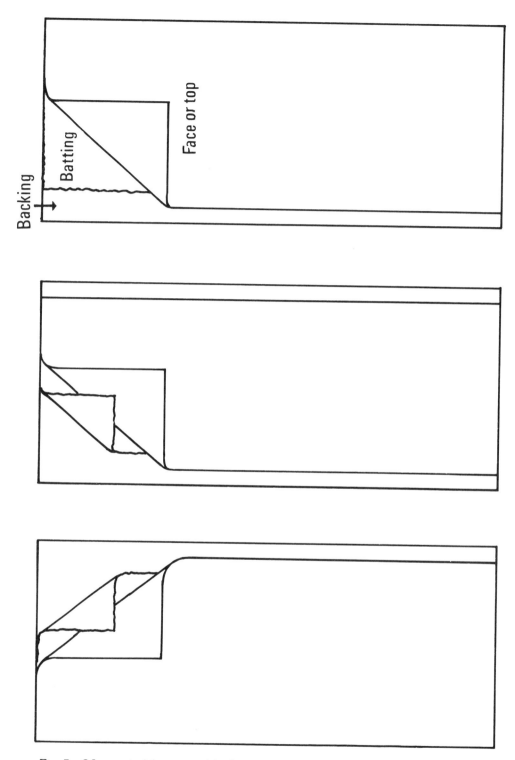

Fig. 5–8 Layout of three-part blanket quilt: even edges with two joining seams.

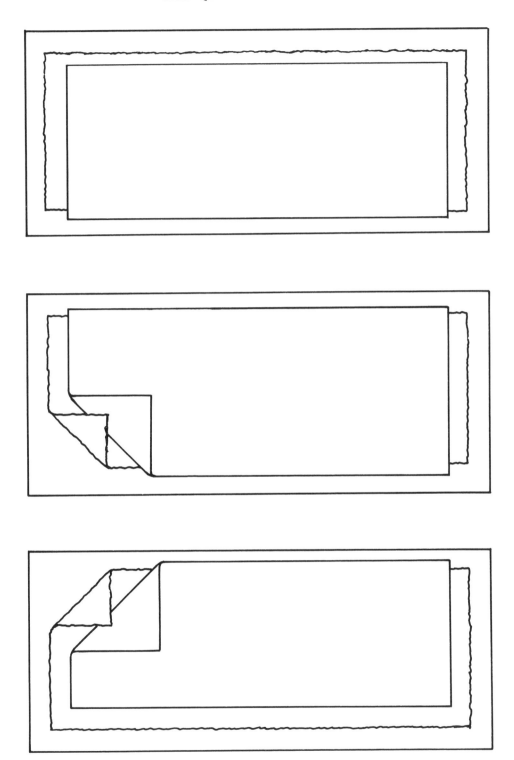

Fig. 5 – 9 Layout of three-part blanket quilt: back-over-front with two joining seams.

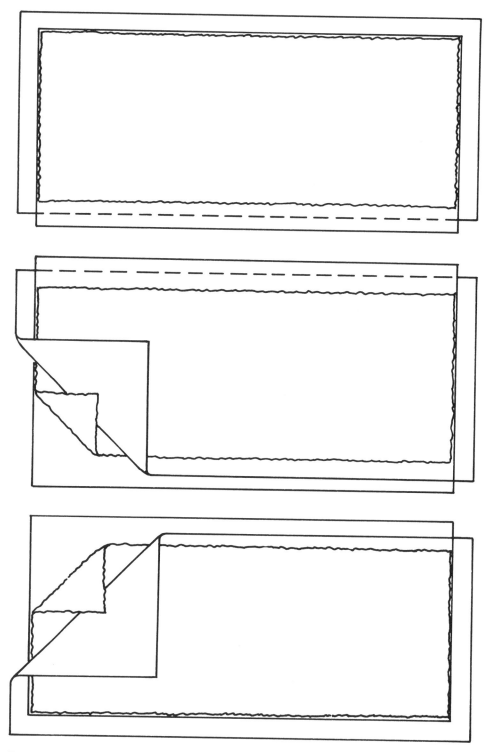

Fig. 5 – 10 Layout of three-part blanket quilt: front-over-back with two joining seams.

*Back-over-Front Unit Assembly* The second method is to use the backing as a binding (Fig. 5 – 9). This is laid out so the backing is larger than the batting and face at all outer edges. After assembling the quilted units, the backing is folded over toward the front. This is very effective when the backing is a color that will coordinate with the face. It saves time, since the backing can be machine sewn very quickly with a straight or novelty stitch. A suggested size would be ½ to 2 inches showing on the front.

*Front-over-Back Unit Assembly* The third method is the reverse of the above (Fig. 5 – 10). The outer edge of the face is larger than the batting and backing. After assembling the quilted units, the enlarged face is folded toward the back and handsewn over the batting and backing. This is particularly good when a solid color border is used and is generally a very narrow piece, ½ to 1 inch.

*The Joining Seam* The seam called a "joining seam" will securely fasten the quilted units. In an appliqued design, consider this ¼-inch seam allowance and plan it into the cutting of the *face*. In a pieced design, the seam allowance is considered part of the *face* design because each pattern piece of the *face* must have a seam allowance on all sides as it forms a pattern. When working with the *backing* fabric, make a special note to add the ½ inch for a joining seam allowance.

Where the "joining seams" are planned, be sure the batting is trimmed to the depth of ½ inch from the raw edge of the backing. If the batting is not cut away, there is too much bulk at the seam after it is sewn.

Use a zipper foot on the machine and place the needle in the left position as the machine faces you. Place the two quilted faces together, sewing only the length of the *face fabric* ¼ inch from the raw edge on the wrong side with a straight stitch, about ten stitches to the inch. The zipper foot will be next to the batting. The backing fabric for this operation is turned back against itself and caught with a few pins.

After stitching, open the seam and lay it flat. The batting now butts together since the seam is flat and is pressed lightly on the face side. Check to make sure all pattern pieces match. Corrections can easily be made at this point (Fig. 5 – 11).

If there is an excess of face fabric in the seam, trim away to ¼ inch and press open lightly. Unpin the backing fabric.

Now there is a loose backing to be seamed. Fold the quilt in half so the face halves lay against each other. On the wrong side, the two raw edges of the backing fabric will be placed under the zipper foot of the machine. The needle will be at the left of the zipper foot as it faces you, raw edges will be hanging out to the right, the bulk of the quilt to the left. Sew with ten stitches to the inch, straight stitch all the way down, closing the two raw edges together. This seam secures the work against hard wear (Fig. 5 – 12). Do not press open. Turn both of the raw edges ¼ inch in toward each other and press down. Now stitch with a regular presser foot on the two folded edges, ten stitches to the inch (Fig. 5 – 13). Turn the finished seam to the right side as the quilt lays open, press down, and hemstitch securely by hand (Fig. 5 – 14).

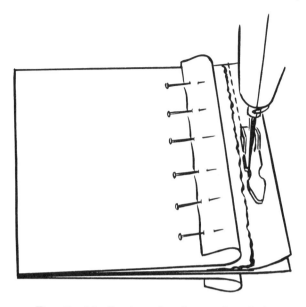

Fig. 5−11 Sewing the face side of the joining seam.

# Five Easy Quilts

These blanket size quilts were selected with great care. Each shows versatility in technique and design. To help the quilt crafter get started, I have outlined in great detail five *easy* quilts. The designs employ different skills, but each allows for a wide variety of interpretation. To reduce the cost of the initial investment, a great portion of the fabric can come from your scrap bag.

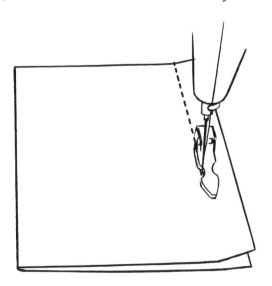

Fig. 5−12 Sewing the backing side of the joining seam.

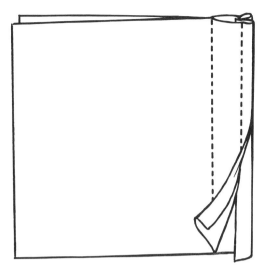

Fig. 5–13 Finishing the joining seam on the backing side.

The designs are detailed for machine techniques so that the reader can use previous chapters as points of reference. However, for anyone desirous of making a totally handsewn blanket, both face and backing are planned as one large single sheet, then placed on the frame for quilting. (Also see Chapter 3 for specific details and quilting ideas.) At the end of the directions, note each quilt has suggested variations. Try to visualize how effective these variations will look.

## Old-Fashioned Patches

The setting together of small squares of color was a mark of thrift and thoughtfulness for our grandmothers. This modern example is the easiest of all

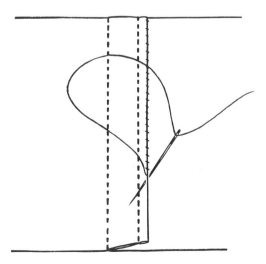

Fig. 5–14 Hand stitching the backing seam.

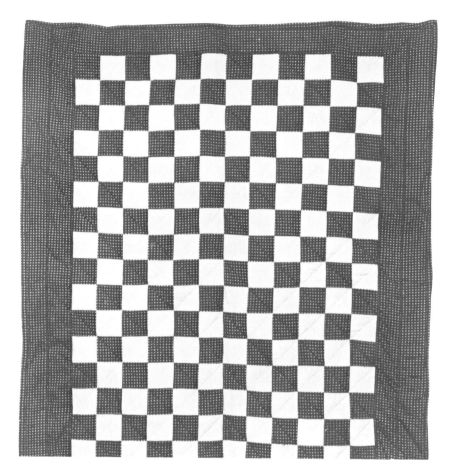

Fig. 5–15 Old Fashioned Patches. Designed and made by Virginia Ruckert.

designs (Fig. 5–15). Its simple pattern of small squares offers an opportunity for the beginning quilter to try her hand at quilt stitching by outlining the blocks or placing a simple diagonal pattern through the blocks by hand or machine.

For an advanced hand quilter, each block could have a pattern quilt stitched into it, such as a star, a flower, or a novelty design. The blanket as shown was made of two colors with a matching color backing. Approximate size is 66 by 82 inches, using a back-over-front binding construction.

*Materials*

2 yards each of 2 colors (red and white) for face
5 yards red for backing
66'' by 82'' piece of batting

*Cutting (seam allowances included)*

96 red 4½'' squares
96 white 4½'' squares
4 red borders 9½'' by 24½'' for top and bottom

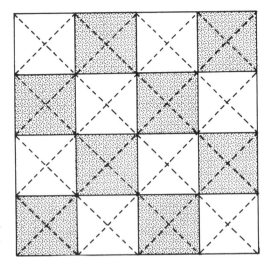

Fig. 5 – 16 Diamond pattern quilting.
Assorted square patterns available in
Chapter 9.

2 red borders 9½'' by 82½'' for sides
2 pieces of backing 34½'' by 84''

Instructions are given for a machine quilted blanket divided into two units for quilting with the backing used for binding (layout design, Figs. 5 – 5 and 5 – 9).

Stitch together alternate red and white squares until you have six horizontal by sixteen vertical. Add two short borders to top and bottom of squares and add one long border to outer edge. Repeat for second unit. Press. Assemble and baste each half of the quilt, using Fig. 5 – 7a and b for joining seam and Fig. 5 – 9 for back-over-front construction of outer edges (use only two outer halves of illustration, disregard center section). Baste together.

To copy quilt as shown, stitch a diagonal line across the squares, starting from the approximate center. This will form a cross in each square when quilting is completedly finished (see Fig. 5 – 16). Join the two units together (see Figs. 5 – 11 to 5 – 14). See Chapter 3 for fine details for finishing outer edges.

*Variations* This would make a wonderful scrap quilt, using assorted colors. The only purchase necessary would be common color borders and backing.

This makes a fine background for an applique. (See color insert of crib quilt Bunnies in a Field of Patches.) This could be assembled combining large and small squares (see Fig. 2 – 5a).

The finishing of the edges could be bias bound or front-over-back. Any binding will look good.

This can be quilted with a feather or novelty stitch as described in Chapter 3.

## Tulip Garden

This easy-to-applique quilt was hand sewn but would be just as effective worked by machine. It can be made with scraps or can combine special color plans. The quilt stitching suggested is the simple outline of a plain running stitch that is easy to follow, using the applique as a guide. It has the added dimension of being quilted between each design square with a novelty stitch on the machine. This offers an opportunity to use rickrack in place of the novelty stitch or, rather than intersecting lines, an all-over quilting as suggested in Fig. 3−8. Approximate size is 60 by 72 inches (Fig. 5−17).

*Materials*

5 yards of light pink for face
½ yard dark pink for applique
⅓ yard pink check
½ yard green for stems and leaves
5 yards for backing
8 yards binding, purchased ½″ wide
64″ by 80″ (minimum) piece of batting

Fig. 5−17 Tulip Garden. Designed and made by the author.

2 spools thread for hand quilting
2 large spools of a common color for machine quilting as shown

*Cutting (seam allowances included)*

16 light pink squares, 15'' × 18''
16 tulips 7'' × 7''
16 inset pieces 4'' × 7''
16 stems 1¼'' × 7''
32 leaves 2¼'' × 4½''

Fig. 5 – 18 Tulip Garden quilt detail. Tulip and other floral designs available in Chapter 9.

For hand applique, turn all ¼-inch seam allowances to back, baste, and press. Baste applique to face square, centering the flowers. (See Chapter 2 for fine details of applique.) Stitch down using thread to *match color of applique*, press, and set each appliqued square aside. This quilt, as shown, is machine quilted in two units (Fig. 5−5) with a center joining seam. Set eight completed squares together to form one unit to be basted to batting and backing. Repeat for other side. (Two across and four down.) Quilt around tulips with a running stitch, then quilt the long vertical with novelty "ball" stitch, then quilt the three horizontal lines of each unit (Fig. 5−18).

Stop the stitching at the seam line of the center joining seam. Do not close seam allowance with quilt stitching. Then assemble both halves together, using as a guide Figs. 5−7 and 5−8. After seam is finished, complete center row of quilting. It will not be difficult because most of the batting has been trimmed out of the seam allowance.

Trim all outer edges of the blanket even with the face and apply bias binding to front ¼ inch from edge. Turn binding to the back and *baste* through the four layers along outer fold of bias binding. To baste, use the same color thread as for quilt stitching. The basting that appears on the face can now be used as a guideline. Use novelty quilt stitching to rim the circumference of the blanket, at the same time permanently attaching the binding to the backing. On this quilt, the backing is pale green, the binding pink, the stitching rose.

*Variations*   Use suggested instructions for size and details but change applique flower.

Add another set of eight more blocks to form a third section to make an approximately 108-inch wide quilt for large bed. Use Figs. 5−6 to 5−8 for assembling design.

Instead of using novelty quilt stitching, place rickrack between squares and use one row of stitching as quilting. Finish as above with rickrack on edges.

Do not section off the design squares, instead use background quilting as suggested in Chapter 3 (Fig. 3−8).

## Windmills

This old favorite two-color design can take on a very modern look by making the design very large or can be made into a complicated geometric quilt by making the design diminutive. The quilt, as shown in Fig. 5−19, is made of a reverse print calico with a wide solid color border. It is machine quilted with contrasting thread, using a two-unit assembly with one joining seam in the center and front-over-back bound edges. Approximate size is 70 by 70 inches. Individual design square is shown in Fig. 2−5c.

### Materials

    1⅔ yards red for face
    1⅔ yards blue for face
    2¼ yards yellow for border
    5½ yards for backing

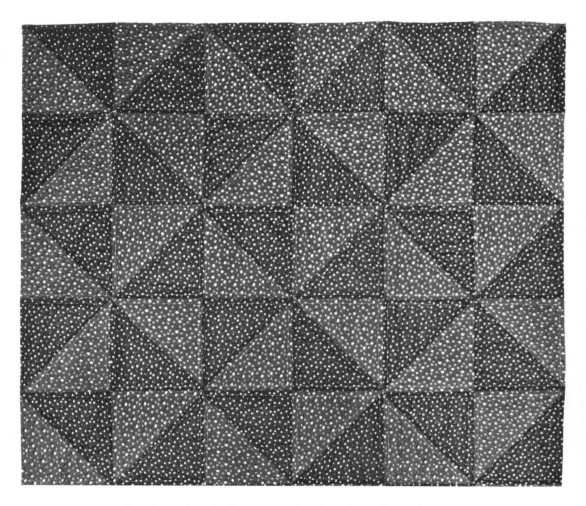

Fig. 5 – 19 Windmills. Designed and made by the author.

70'' by 70'' (minimum) piece of batting
2 spools thread for hand quilting or machine quilting

*Cutting (seam allowances included)*

pattern for triangle 10⅞'' on two short sides and 15⁷/₁₆'' on diagonal
32 red triangles
32 blue triangles
2 yellow borders, 7'' × 74''
4 yellow borders, 7'' × 37''

Stitch together a red to a blue along the diagonal with a ¼ inch seam, to form thirty-two red and blue squares 10½ by 10½ inches. Press seam open. Set three squares by six squares together, forming half of the face. Repeat for other side (Fig. 5 – 5). Make sure that squares form a windmill design. Add each of the long borders 7 by 74 inches to the 60-inch finished outside of each face half. Add the top and bottom strips, 7 by 37½ inches, mitering the corners. After mitering corners, cut off excess and press all seams open.

Assemble the two-unit face to the backing, using as a guide Figs. 5 – 7 and 5 – 10. Baste each half securely for quilting. With yellow thread, machine quilt ⅓ inch off the seam line inside each triangle and stitch plain or novelty design on borders. Assemble quilt halves together with joining seam (Figs. 5 – 11 to 5 – 14). Turn the raw edge of the face ½ inch toward the back and press. Fold the remaining border over toward the back, covering batting and backing. It will be approximately 1½ inches wide. (See Chapter 3 for fine detail of border finishing.) When completely finished, reinforce the outer edge with another row of quilt stitching, pivoting at the corners.

*Variations*   Make another panel and use a three-unit assembly.

Use a novelty solid color border with novelty quilting stitched throughout the length of the border. (See Chapter 2, Fig. 2 – 27.)

Fig. 5 – 20 Combined Basic quilt layout.

Use a variety of borders as shown in Chapter 2 (Figs. 2 − 28 to 2 − 31).

The windmill quilt needs no border and can be bias bound. See Chapter 3 (Fig. 3 − 20). This is a very easy quilt to hand stitch for the beginner.

## Combined Basic

This easy-to-make design combines three very old patterns into one handsome blanket. In the center is a basic nine patch; flying geese sit on both sides with lightning stripes at the outer edges (Fig. 5 − 20). This quilt is considered easy because it is formed from nine long face pieces: five are pieced designs and four are solid colors. It is quilted from top to bottom only and uses its own backing as a binding. It is machine quilted in a three-unit assembly (Figs. 5 − 6 and 5 − 9). Approximate size is 78 by 90 inches.

### Materials

        ¾ yard orange for nine patch
        1 yard gold for flying geese
        1½ yards green for lightning stripes
        5½ yards blue for background for the face
        8 yards green for backing fabric
        81'' by 96'' piece of batting
        1 large spool each of blue and green; small spool of orange

### Cutting (seam allowances included)

        16 orange 6½'' squares
        29 blue 6½'' squares
        4 blue strips 6'' × 90'' for background
        30 gold geese (see Fig. 5 − 21)
        60 blue pieces for background of geese (see Fig. 5 − 21)
        32 blue triangles (see Fig. 5 − 22)
        32 green triangles (see Fig. 5 − 22)
        3 even lengths of backing 93'' long

Form the basic nine patch by first assembling three horizontal squares, starting from the top. Keep adding a row of three horizontal squares to form a vertical center. Note the four basic nine patch squares will each be separated by a horizontal row of solid color blue squares. Press all seams open and set aside. Follow center section of Fig. 5 − 20.

The flying geese units are formed from a two-part pattern as shown in Fig. 5 − 21, ¼-inch seam allowance included. (Cut the blue background pieces for the geese from remains after long panels for background of face have been cut.)

Assemble one blue piece on each of the two long sides of the gold piece. This will form a 6½-inch square when complete. Press seams open.

Sew together fifteen assembled flying geese squares to form one 90-inch strip. Repeat with remaining fifteen squares to make a second strip and press all seams open. (See Fig. 5 − 20 for placement on quilt.)

Stitch one long blue 6 by 90-inch panel to each side of a row of flying geese with ¼-inch seams. Repeat for the other side, press all seams open, and set aside.

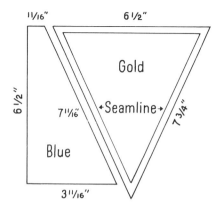

Fig. 5 – 21 Flying Geese detail.

Form lightning stripes in four separate strips (two strips for each side). Alternately stitch together eight blue and eight green triangles, joining them on the 9¼-inch side to form one long strip; press all seams open.

Place two completed strips together so all the *greens touch* (Fig. 5 – 22), forming the zigzag stripe of lightning. Sew together with ¼-inch seams, press seams open. Cut off excess at the ends; it should measure 90 inches long. Add a completed lightning stripe to each outer edge of the flying geese panel, using a ¼-inch seam. Press open. There are now three separate panels: one center panel with patch squares and two side panels with flying geese and lightning stripes combined.

Cut 8 yards of backing fabric into three 93-inch lengths (Fig. 5 – 7 for joining seam detail and Fig. 5 – 9 for three-unit assembly).

From one length of backing, cut a strip 19 inches wide. Place right side down on work surface. Center an 18 by 92-inch long piece of batting on top. Place completed nine patch center unit over batting, right side up, centering so the long right and left seams will extend ¼ inch over batting. Batting and backing will show at top and bottom. Baste and quilt ½ inch off the seam line as indicated at bottom of Fig. 5 – 20.

From a second length of backing, cut a 33-inch wide width; place right side down on work surface.

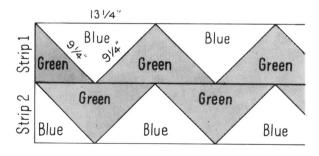

Fig. 5 – 22 Lightning Stripes detail.

Place a piece of batting 31 inches wide by 92 inches long ½ inch inside the raw edge which will be joined to the center panel (Fig. 5−7a). On the three outside edges, there will be 1½ inches of the backing fabric beyond the batting.

Place the flying geese and lightning stripe face on top so that it extends ¼ inch over the batting at the joining seam (Fig. 5−7b) and falls 1 inch from the edge of the batting, on the three outer edges, giving the three layers a staggered look (Fig. 5−9). Baste across every 12 inches. Quilt ½ inch off the seam line as indicated at bottom of Fig. 5−20.

Unite the joining seam as previously explained (Figs. 5−11 to 5−14).

Trim all outer edges of the batting to be one inch larger than quilted face and trim backing 1½ inches beyond batting. Turn the raw edge of backing forward ¼ inch on all four edges of backing; press or baste and fold the remaining 1¼ inches forward over batting to cover raw edge of face.

Miter corners and sew with a straight stitch (eight stitches to the inch) to secure backing over front or hand stitch with blind stitch. See Chapter 3 on binding (Figs. 3−21 and 3−22) for detail instruction.

*Variations*   Use only the two side units of flying geese and lightning stripes, with one joining seam in the center, for a quilt approximately 60 by 90 inches.

Use only the lightning stripe or only the flying geese stripe. Repeat many times across the width of the quilt. (See Fig. 2−7d.)

## Rail Fence

The stitching together of rectangular pieces of fabric has always sparked the interest of the American quilter. The popular Rail Fence design is one of the basic variations of a four stripe patch. The design combines prints and solids. It is dominated by one strong color stripe in each block. The blocks are set so the one dominating color forms a step-like design (Chapter 2, Fig. 2−5b and color insert).

The four chosen colors are numbered so that the dominant color will always be placed first, the other colors should be repeated in exactly the same order for each square. The squares are then set together so the dominating stripe forms the step-like design.

It is machine quilted in two halves and joined at the center with one "joining seam." The quilting follows the lines of the rail fence design formed by the dominant solid color (Fig. 5−23). It is backed and bias bound in its dominant color and is approximately 72 by 90 inches.

### Materials

2½ yards dominant color for face
2½ yards each of 3 other colors
6 yards of backing
1½ yards binding, 1½ inches wide (or 10 yards of purchased binding)
72″ by 90″ piece of batting

### Cutting (seam allowances included)

180 rectangles of dominant color, 2″ × 6½″
180 rectangles of each of 3 secondary colors, 2″ × 6½″

Stitch together one of each of the four color stripes, always starting with the dominant color. Press seams open. Place squares in rows across the quilt, alternating the direction of the dominant stripe (Fig. 5−20): first row, first square, dominant color top; second square; dominant color to the left; repeat. For the second row, first square, the dominant color is to the left; second square, dominant color top; repeat.

The rail fence will quickly form. Assembling instructions are given for machine quilting by dividing into two units for the quilting (Fig. 5−5). Form the first unit by placing six squares across and fifteen squares down. Repeat for the second unit. Do not join the units together, but note the pattern that continues moving diagonally across the quilt at the "joining seam." Press all seams open.

Assemble and baste each half of the face as shown in Figs. 5−7 and 5−8 (noting on Fig. 5−8 that the quilter is using two outer halves only; disregard center section of illustration). Baste together. Starting from the center, quilt stitch only the continuous lines formed by the dominant color. These lines will be on the diagonal across the quilt.

Join the two units together as in Figs. 5−11 to 5−14. (See Chapter 3 for fine details of bias bound edges.) The binding for this quilt was cut 1½ inches wide from 1½ yards of fabric.

# Original Heirloom Quilts

While the designs for quilts are unlimited, there will always remain a few that can be called heirlooms. These quilts are conceived and executed with a true spark of originality. This originality knows no limits. The quilts take on the spirit and vitality of their makers.

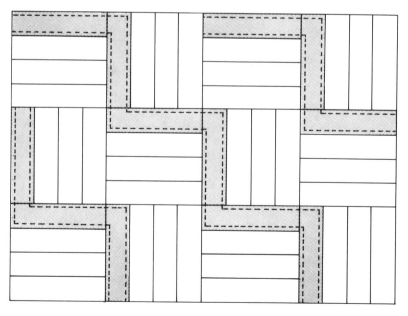

Fig. 5−23 Rail Fence quilt detail.

This section will describe briefly the details necessary for you to style the other photographed quilts into heirlooms of your own. The various techniques of quilt making have been described in Chapters 1 through 3. It is time to choose how to put the elements together to make an original heirloom of your own—by hand or machine.

The quilts in this section are identified for ease or difficulty of working: one star, very easy; two stars, intermediate; three stars, for more experienced quilter.

## Chinese Puzzle ★ ★ ★

This interesting, pieced design, originally worked in blues and greens, begins to form when four squares are placed together (Figs. 5–24 and 5–25). The dominating lines should be of one strong color. The corner colors must all be common. It is worked in a highly stylized solid and print colors, which add dimension to the original designs shown in Chapter 2 (Fig. 2–9d). Working this quilt in solid colors only will make it a lot easier for the less experienced quilter.

The heavily quilted look was achieved on the machine by dividing the work into three units for quilting and has a front-over-back bound edge. The backing is fine muslin and the batting is Dacron. The approximate size is 106 by 106 inches. The finished size of each square measures 12 by 12 inches. There are eight squares down and eight squares across with a 5-inch border all around.

### Materials (for 64, 12'' squares)

4 yards blue for dominating stripe (pattern A, Fig. 5–24)
1 yard white for squares (pattern B)
1¼ yards navy for triangles (pattern C)
2 yards print for parallelogram (pattern D)
2 yards different print for large triangles (pattern E)
¾ yard light green for corner triangles (pattern F)
3½ yards blue for 11'' border
9½ yards for backing
108'' × 108'' piece of batting

### Cutting

128 blue stripes (pattern A, Fig. 5–24)
128 white squares (pattern B)
256 navy triangles (pattern C)
128 print parallelograms (pattern D)
128 print large triangles (pattern E)
128 light green corner triangles (pattern F)

To form each design block, first join two C pieces to piece B to form the inner triangle (see Fig. 5–24 and Chapter 9 for patterns). Attach D to F. Attach inner triangle (BC) to one side of pieces D and E, and attach this piece to A, pivoting at corners. Then attach F. You now have a large triangle which makes up one-half of the design block. Repeat for adjacent half and join to complete the design block.

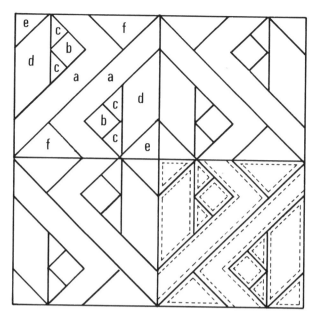

Fig. 5 – 24 Chinese Puzzle quilt detail.

Design blocks are joined into three units for machine quilting. Units are of uneven widths. Two are 36 inches and one is 24 inches. (See Figs. 5 – 7 and 5 – 10.)

Each element is "outline" quilted ¼ inch from each seam and corners are quilted with concentric squares. (See Chapter 3 for front-over-back binding.)

## Pennsylvania Dutch Delight ★ ★ ★

Five old hex designs caught this quilter's fancy. Each has a special meaning to this fine craftswoman (Fig. 5 – 26). The novel way of combining the designs for machine applique shows the clear, fresh spirit that pervades the total design. The true colors of red, blue, green, and yellow are appropriate for the hex designs, considering the Pennsylvania Dutch who created them.

### Materials

    8 yards white for background squares
    ¾ yard each of 4 different colors for appliques (red, navy, green, and yellow)
    2½ yards red for bordering frames
    6 yards for backing
    89'' by 106'' piece of batting

### Cutting

    30 background squares, 16½'' by 16½''
    12 large hex designs approximately 13''

Fig. 5 – 25 Chinese Puzzle quilt, made by Beverly Panitz.

18 hearts approximately 5''
2'' wide borders

The quilt shown in Fig. 5 – 26 is approximately 89 by 106 inches. The work is broken into three uneven units for machine quilting (Fig. 5 – 6). Use "joining seams" as shown in Fig. 5 – 7.

To use the outer framing borders as a binding, plan to make them a little larger than 2 inches.

Each element in the main design is "outline" quilted both inside and outside (Fig. 3 – 2b). The eighteen hearts are quilted with concentric lines (Fig. 3 – 3). (See Chapter 3 for details of the front-over-back binding.)

*Variations* Substitute your favorite hex design or any circular type applique design found in Chapter 2, or clovers, pineapples, or bows in place of the heart appliques on the border.

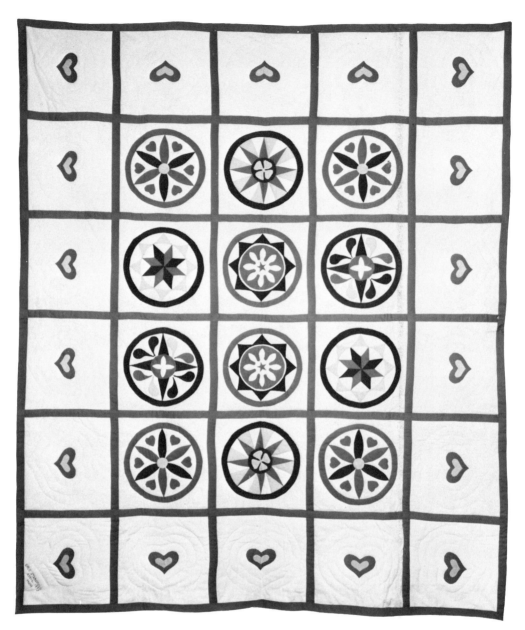

Fig. 5 – 26 Pennsylvania Dutch Delight quilt, designed and made by Jeanette Stansfield.

## Ships Ahoy ★ ★

This creative use of fabric scraps to form eighteen different appliqued boats is particularly well adapted to the diamond-shaped background patch (Fig. 5 – 27). Red framing borders highlight the red and blues predominating in the appliques. Both the zigzag satin stitch and straight stitch were used to applique the fabrics to the background. They were further enhanced with embroidery stitches and novelty trimming. The designs are easily found in children's picture books.

Fig. 5 – 27 Ships Ahoy quilt, designed and made by the author.

The eighteen diamonds are approximately 13 by 13 inches when finished; the appliques are 12 by 11 inches. The framing borders are 2 inches wide when finished. There are ten triangles for the outer edges, which are quilted, and four smaller corner triangles. The approximate size of the quilt is 63½ by 85 inches.

## Materials

Assorted scraps for appliques
4 yards white for background squares
4 yards red for bordering frames and bindings
8 yards for backing
63½″ × 85″ piece of batting.

## Cutting

18 squares 13½″ × 13½″
5 additional 13½″ squares to be cut in half on the diagonal to make 10 triangles for outer edges.
4 triangles 8″ × 8″ × 12″ for corners

The quilt is assembled in two units with the "joining seam" on the diagonal across the quilt rather than from top to bottom (Figs. 5–5, 5–7, and 5–8). Each of the appliques were outline quilted and each of the ten triangles on the outer edges were quilted with a 5 by 4-inch anchor in red quilt stitching.

The bias binding for the outer edges is cut 4½ inches wide to be 2 inches when finished and is stuffed with strips of left-over batting for a puffy look. (See Chapter 3 for fine finishing of bias binding.)

*Variations*  Any applique looks good in the diamonds but Figs. 2–12e and f can be placed so they stand upright and this gives a very intricate look to the quilt.

## Joseph's Choice ★ ★

This unique quilt was originally a crib quilt. As the quilt crafter grew in skill, so did her desire to make a larger quilt—hence, this particularly beautiful, three-dimensional effect quilt (Fig. 5–28). The original twelve white squares were 10 by 10 inches. Each scrap applique was approximately 8 by 8 inches.

To further enhance the appliques, each was hand buttonhole stitched with three-strand embroidery thread. The white squares were then sewn to a 14-inch square of light blue. These were combined with 4-inch dark blue framing borders and hand quilted. The backing of dark blue was turned to the front to be used as a 4-inch border and binding.

It was hand quilted with a four-heart novelty design at the intersections of each framing border. There is a ½ inch of quilt stitching around the appliques, the white edge, the light blue square, and the blue frames. The finished size is 58 by 76 inches.

## Materials

1 yard white for squares
2 yards light blue for squares

Fig. 5 – 28 Joseph's Choice quilt, designed and made by Tina Klee.

2 yards dark blue for frames
5 yards dark blue for backing
58'' × 76'' piece of batting
assorted scraps for appliques
assorted color embroidery thread
1 spool quilting thread for hand quilting

*Cutting*

>12 white 10½'' squares
>12 light blue 14½'' squares
>2 dark blue frames 4½'' × 70''
>9 dark blue frames 4½'' × 15''

## Dresden Plate ★ ★

A superb rendering of an old favorite pieced applique was made by the quilting club of the Young Women's Christian Association of Ridgewood, New Jersey (see color insert). This club was started by the author with members of her first quilting class. Every year, this club makes a quilt for their patron organization to be used to attract contributions. This represents the combined efforts of fourteen women working once a week for a year.

Although the design is not new, the symmetry of a common yellow center and four cross-like wedges in each plate gives a harmony to the assorted colored wedges used in the rest of the design.

The 12-inch plate rims were assembled first; the 5½-inch circular center with its turned back edges were added next. The outer rim of the plate was basted back, then basted to the 19½ by 19½-inch background square of white. There are twenty background squares, four across and five down. The batting is Dacron and the backing is made of two lengths of 44 by 104-inch yellow fabric. It uses its backing as a binding by folding 2 inches of the backing forward around all outer edges.

Each wedge is hand quilted; the center circle is quilted with two concentric convex diamonds; each plate is outlined following its scalloped design and again with a large round ring. Between the plates, an original quilting design by Beverly Panitz was stitched.

*Materials*

>3 yards assorted scraps for plate rims
>1 yard dominant color (yellow)
>6 yards white for background
>96'' by 108'' piece of batting
>6 yards yellow for backing

This pattern is as old and good as vegetable soup. If the ingredients are of good quality with interesting color and it is made with tender loving care, the end result will win the maker praises every time. The simplicity and symmetry of the pattern fascinates the newcomer and the old hand at quilting.

If you own a dinner plate, you can make this pattern in a jiffy. Trace the outline of the plate onto paper, cut the circle out, fold in quarters and cut out a center circle, but do not open. Fold one, two or three more times and open pattern up. You have a kind of doughnut shape with folds forming wedges. One wedge can be cut out and used as the basic pattern element. Shape the outer edge into a point or semicircle (see Fig. 2 – 12d). Add the ¼-inch seam allowance and cut the color to suit. The wedges are sewn into a ring. Stitch on the seam line only, not to the raw edges. The inner edges of the center circle and the outside edges of the ring are turned to the wrong side and basted. The circle of wedges is then centered and basted to a piece of background fabric (see the Dresden Plate quilt in Fig. 5 – 33). As an alternate design, the open center can be covered with a solid circle of fabric with its edges turned under (see Dresden Plate quilt in color section). In that case, do not turn under the seam allowance of the center of the ring. When stitching the additional center circle on, sew through the inside edge of the circle ring and background fabric to hold the center down firmly.

The quilting can be simple or complex. For a simple pattern, stitch ¼ inch off the seam line and the outer edge of the plate too. For a complex look, add intricate bands of patterns between the applique. There are two patterns given in Chapter 9: one large pattern for a 16-inch, twenty-piece plate and one for a 14-inch, twelve-piece plate. These may be placed on any size background that the quilter feels will balance the plates; the size of quilt is determined from there.

## World Without End ★ ★

The quilt as shown in the color section is a double bed size with a bold interpretation of the pattern in a mod geometric effect. The star-like pattern emanates from a white center to rich gold points to a white background. (See Fig. 2 – 9a and pattern in Fig. 9 – 5.)

Each finished block is 15 inches square and the quilt is made of six design blocks across and seven down, a total of 98 by 113 inches. It has a 4-inch border finished in the back-over-front method (see Fig. 3 – 27).

### Materials

5 yards light color for face
2 yards print for face
6 yards for backing
98″ × 113″ piece of batting

### Cutting

42 center squares
168 points
168 side pieces

When attaching the star points to the center square, sew only on the sewing line; do not sew to the raw edge. Fasten the thread securely at the end of the sewing line. This makes a ready-made opening to set in the elongated triangle. Pin the triangle in place with pins in the matching corners. Stitch from the center to the outer edge on one side and then from the center out again (Fig. 2 – 3). This is an easy and accurate way to work; if you are worried that the center point will pull, reinforce with one or two stitches. This rarely happens if the stitches are small and neat. It should be noted that to achieve the effect shown in this rendition of the design the long side triangle should be of a solid color. This quilt is made of the early American-type cotton and linen combination fabrics.

## Double Irish Chain ★ ★

This is a very old quilt pattern that is often passed over as a starter quilt because it looks complicated. It is a very easy quilt if you follow the color pattern as shown in Fig. 5–29 and the color section. It is made up of two large alternating blocks. One is composed of twenty-five (five across and five down) smaller squares of the same size, thus one pattern element.

### Materials

> 3 yards dominating color
> 3 yards medium color
> 3 yards background color
> 6 yards backing (including back-over-front binding)
> 66″ × 106″ piece of batting

### Cutting (add seam allowances)

> 390 dominating color 2″ squares
> 2 borders of dominating color, 2″ × 64″
> 2 borders of dominating color, 2″ × 100″
> 480 medium color 2″ squares
> 120 background color 2″ squares
> 30 background color 10″ squares

In sewing each row of five pieces, the quilter must be mindful of the pattern to be achieved. This finished block of twenty-five squares will measure 10 by 10 inches if a 2-inch square is used and 15 by 15 inches if a 3-inch square is used (this does not account for the seam allowance). It is this author's opinion that the best-looking Double Irish Chain quilts appear with a dominating bright color in the middle, crisscrossing each design block. The secondary color to the left and right of the middle would be complimentary or supportive; because there is actually more of the secondary color, it too becomes strong. The background should be either very dark or, traditionally, off-white. The color pattern as shown in Fig. 5–26 would be, from the top left:

> Row 1. Dark / medium / background / medium / dark
> Row 2. Medium / dark / medium / dark / medium
> Row 3. Background/medium/dark/medium/background
> Row 4. Medium / dark / medium / dark / medium
> Row 5. Dark/medium/background/medium/dark

The second, large block is cut out of the background material. The block will be 10½ by 10½ inches if a finished 2-inch square is used and 15½ by 15½ inches if a finished 3-inch square is used (this includes the seam allowance). A small square of the medium color is appliqued into each of the corners of the large square. Place the two outer raw edges exactly over the raw edges of the background corner and baste in place. Turn the seam allowances of the other two sides to the wrong side. Then baste to the corner of background square and applique only the folded edges.

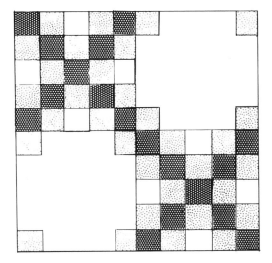

Fig. 5 – 29 Irish Chain. Note use of alternate blocks.

When the multi-pieced square and the plain square with its colored corners are alternated throughout the quilt, an optical illusion is created. The crisscrossing effect of the chain will take place and the background will recede.

Since any 2 or 3-inch square is used for a pattern, it is an easy quilt to estimate yardage. Each multi-pieced square has nine of the dark color, twelve of the medium color, and four background color small squares. For every multi-pieced square planned, cut one large background square and four small medium squares for the corners. The quilt as shown is 72 by 112 inches (6 squares across and 10 down). It uses its backing as a 4-inch binding

## Around the World ★ ★

One basic square is set together to form a concentric diamond effect of varying colors. Whatever size square is chosen from 2 to 5 inches, the colors should be worked out on graph paper first. It is easy to multiply the number of colored squares needed by using the yardage chart given in Figure 1 – 5. The quilt shown in the color section has finished squares of 4 by 4 inches. It has a 10-inch border trimmed with six small 8-point stars (see Chapter 9 for small star). The quilt measures 100 by 104 inches for a king-size bed. It is important to note that there are several shades of one color together. This shadowing effect is to help carry the eye around the concentric diamonds and accentuate the colors. It is sometimes referred to as Sunshine and Shadows.

*Materials*

1 yard dark red
⅞ yard medium pink
1 yard light pink
1¼ yard dark green

¾ yard medium green
1¼ yard light green
¾ yard gold
3 yards dark green for border
100″ × 104″ piece of batting
6 yards of 60″ wide fabric for backing or 9 yards of 45″ wide fabric

## Cutting (add seam allowances)

59 dark red 4″ squares
48 medium pink 4″ squares
62 light pink 4″ squares
68 dark green 4″ squares
38 medium green 4″ squares
68 light green 4″ squares
43 gold 4″ squares
4 border strips approximately 11″ × 108″

The quilting accents the concentric diamond pattern of the colors by running on diagonal lines to form concentric diamond line quilt stitching. The border re-echoes the pattern with overlapping elongated diamonds of white stitching on the dark green.

There are several ways to work this quilt: (1) sew rows across, using pre-colored diagram; (2) sew small sets of squares together such as five across and five down, using pre-colored diagram; (3) start in the center with one square cut and add around that square, according to personal preference (this is the best method if using scraps).

## Churn Dash ★

This very simple nine-patch pattern is designed in the earth colors for a queen size bed, finished it measures 90 by 120 inches.

## Materials

3 yards medium light color for face
3 yards medium dark color for face
½ yard very dark color for face
½ yard very light color for face
6 yards backing
90″ × 108″ piece of batting
12 yards bias binding

What makes this pattern so interesting is that the quilter made fifty-four 10-inch squares in a predominantly dark color combination and fifty-four in a predominating lighter color combination using the same colors. Although the geometric effect is the same, altering the colors creates an interesting effect. The quilting crisscrosses each block, stopping at each center square to outline the square ¼ inch in from the seam line (see Fig. 5–30). It is finished with a biased bound edge. See color insert and Mixed Wrench in Chapter 8 for another version of this type.

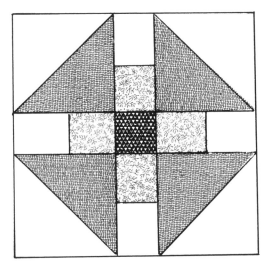

Fig. 5–30 Churn Dash. This is a small,
tight version of a traditional pattern. See
Mixed Wrench Scrap Quilt in Chapter 8 for
another version.

## Drunkard's Path ★ ★ ★

This two-color quilt is an old favorite of most hand quilters; it is sometimes
called Rocky Road to Kansas. It is easy to make and is best made with two
contrasting colors with very little or no print on the surface. It is usually put
together as shown in Fig. 5–31, combining sixteen small blocks into one larger
design square. This block is generally found in old quilts to be 3 or 4 inches,
however, it may be made up to 6 inches for king-size beds of today.

Fig. 5–31 Drunkard's Path. For one
design block, cut sixteen of each element
(eight print and eight solid).

The block is made up of two pattern elements: a small square missing a concave corner and one quarter of a circle, or quadrant (Fig. 5–31). Half the blocks for the quilt are made with dark quadrants set into the light colored, larger squared portion; the other half is made with light colored quadrants set into the darker squared portions. It is best to handstitch the quadrants into the squared portion. When sixteen blocks are assembled together to form a working design square for the quilt, you will note there are eight of each coloration. When the design squares are set together, the pattern then forms crisscrossing lacing throughout the quilt (see Fig. 5–32).

## Materials

4 yards dark fabric
4 yards light fabric
5 yards backing
90″ × 86″ piece of batting

## Cutting (add seam allowance if using pattern in Fig. 9–3)

286 light squares with concave corner cut out
286 dark squares with concave corner cut out
286 light quadrants
286 dark quadrants

One good trick when cutting out the working pattern is to place a small notch or pencil point at the center of both the circular edge and the concave edge. When setting the quadrant into the squared figure, pin centers first, then two side points, easing the rest in between. You may find it necessary to clip into the seam allowance of the larger piece before beginning to pin. The first three pins will be easy to set because you can match up the centers and sides with the pins. Do not allow excess fabric to cause bulk in seam allowance; clip bulk and press seam to one side. Do not open curved seam.

The quilt as shown in Fig. 5–32 is approximately 78 by 66 inches, having twenty-six small blocks down and twenty-two across. There are a total of 572 individual squares, using the 3-inch pattern. (Two sized patterns are given in Chapter 9.)

## Eight-Point Star ★ ★ ★ and Le Moyne Star ★ ★ ★

These two designs have to be considered together as the Le Moyne pattern is just a slightly more complicated version of the basic eight-point star pattern. The pattern can be pieced together or the star can be made and then appliqued to a background. In Fig. 5–33, the eight-point star quilt is called American Stars Forever; see Chapter 7 for materials and cutting information. The star is appliqued to the background and quilted in the block-by-block method. The two tone blue Le Moyne Star, also shown in Fig. 5–33, has a pieced background and was quilted on a large frame.

To begin, we must master the pattern. Our great grandmothers made this pattern by the age old oriental technique of paper folding. You can turn to Chapter 9 for patterns or make your own.

Fig. 5 – 32 Drunkard's Path quilt (on wall) shows the charming crisscross pattern of this design. In the foreground, Floral Wreath (Fig. 2 – 13) quilt and Mixed Diamond pillow (Fig. 2 – 8c). Courtesy of Sally Rowe.

A compass allows us to draw this in a jiffy. Draw the circle as big as you would like the star and mark its center point. Divide the outer ring in eight equal parts by knowing that the full circle has 360 degrees (every 45 degrees). Draw a second, concentric circle half way between the outer one and its center point. Divide that into eight equal parts but place the dots between the outer points. By joining the center point and dots on the two circles, mark the diamonds. Use one

Fig. 5 — 33 Crazy Quilt (on wall), designed and finished by Sally Rowe; worked by Sally Rowe, Vivian Talbot, Mary Lou Bella, Anne Smith, Anne Chas, Jo Ann Schwamb, Vivian Egeland, Lorna Blauvelt, Virginia Ruckert, and the author. Pillows, left to right: Free Form Heart (Beverly Panitz), 9-Patch and Stripe (Dot Frager), School House (Anne Smith). Quilts, left to right: American Stars Forever (author), Dresden Plate (Anne Smith), and LeMoyne Star (Jodie Bouvier).

diamond for a pattern. This can be set onto graph paper and into a square the same size so that a piece of patchwork can be formed or the star can be set together and appliqued onto a larger background. You never again have to be limited to the size of the star you want to make.

The most important part of putting this block together is to get all the pieces to lay flat. Cut this pattern like a picture frame so that both the cutting line and the sewing line can be marked on the wrong side of the fabric. Mark no more than one piece at a time as that sewing line must be accurately marked for the success of a flat star. Place the pattern on the length of the grain. The diamonds will fit close together so as not to waste fabric.

Begin by placing two diamonds together, right sides touching. Align two sides by placing pins at the top and bottom points and one in the middle (see Fig. 5 – 34). Sew the diamonds together on the sewing line only; do not sew from raw edge to raw edge. The seam allowance must not be stitched; it must be free to be manipulated. Use a backstitch at the beginning and end of each seam as it makes it stronger. Place a third diamond on to the second diamond, right sides touching. Pin again along the seam line only. Working from the center, place your first stitch next to the stitch in the just finished seam; backstitch and proceed along the seam line until marking stops. Continue adding diamonds in this fashion until the star is closed to form a complete ring. Knot a small thread and insert the needle through the center of each first stitch in each star in the center, making a little circle of thread and pulling close to secure the center more firmly. If the star is cut and sewn accurately, there will be no hole in the middle. *Press all seams to one direction.* With the tip of the iron gently press all the center points into a little open fan or pinwheel (see Fig. 5 – 34, top).

A special short cut for making a Le Moyne Star is to cut two lengths of different colored fabric that you wish to use in each star point. Sew the lengths together with the ¼-inch seam in the middle; press the seam open. On the wrong side place the pattern for the solid diamond, centering the diamond on the seam line, and cut out the entire unit together. I think it is faster and more accurate and I do it all the time.

*Setting the Star into a Patchwork Square*    On graph paper work out the star pattern set into a square (see Fig. 5 – 34). Cut out the corner squares and the center triangle. The best way to set these into the star is to work from the inner corner out, using two threads. This method secures the corner in the exact place it should be. I teach beginners this method and use it myself. In fact, 95 percent of the quilters I know regularly do it this way.

*Setting the Star onto an Applique Background*    After the star has been pressed, turn under the remaining raw edges. The points should be mitered and the inside "Vs" will open nicely because they have not been sewn completely to the raw edge. Fold the background square in four and use fold lines as a guide for placement of the star. This applique method is particularly effective if it is used in a sampler quilt or in the American Stars Forever quilt worked in the block by block method. The materials list for the red, white, and blue American Stars Forever is given in Chapter 7.

Fig. 5—34 Star making. Top: Sew each diamond to the next, open, and center for patchwork. Center right and bottom: Fit the pieces of background and bordering bands. Stars and border made by Phyllis Shane.

*Materials*

    2 yards light blue
    2 yards dark blue
    3 yards background white
    6 yards backing
    84″ × 96″ batting

The Le Moyne Star in two shades of blue was the first quilt made by Jodie Bouvier. The size of each block is 12 by 12 inches. There are seven blocks across and eight down, 84 by 96 inches overall.

## Country Blossom ★ ★ ★

Country Blossom is a stunning rendition of a floral motif. The block is used to advantage by placing the motif of the upright flower on the bias grain, forming a diamond (see color insert and Fig. 5–35). The sixteen appliqued blocks are alternated for a pleasing special effect with the solid blocks. There are four applique blocks across and four down the length of the quilt with nine alternating solid blocks between in rows of three across. There is a 4½-inch band of color around the main design and a 6-inch additional scalloped border of background color on the edge. The scallops are 5 inches at the shortest point and 6 inches at their longest depth. They are 5¾ inches wide. Although this flower as shown is a

Fig. 5–35 Country Blossom set on diamond figure.
Any floral shape from Chapter 9 can be used.

very pretty one, the solid ground and green leaves can hold any flower shape given in the pattern section. This would look good in calicos too. Approximate overall size is 82 by 82 inches.

### Materials

    7 yards background
    2 yards for border and applique flowers
    1 yard for applique leaves
    5 yards backing
    82'' × 82'' piece of batting
    10 yards bias binding

### Cutting (add seam allowance)

    25 background blocks 11'' square
    16 background triangles ½ of 12'' square
    48 flowers
    16 long stems 6¾'' × ½''
    32 short stems 2½'' × ½''
    32 large leaves
    32 small leaves
    16 triangles for base of flowers ½ of 2'' square
    2 side borders 4½'' × 61''
    2 top and bottom borders 4½'' × 70''
    2 solid side borders 6'' × 70''
    2 solid top and bottom borders 6'' ×  82''

After setting the entire face of the quilt together, but before basting it to batting and backing, pencil or baste in the scalloped edges. Quilt only to the edges of the scallop and after withdrawing the quilt from the frame, then trim off the excess and bind. This scalloped edge is optional. Bind edge with bias binding. (Pattern, Fig. 9 – 33).

## Ohio Rose ★ ★

The Ohio Rose is a traditional heart petal flower combined with buds to fill out the corners (see color section). The pattern makes use of two size hearts with the smaller top one placed over the larger one. The top heart has been padded with batting to give a more dimensional look to the flower. The points meet in the center and are covered with a center circle of the darker color.

The buds extend beyond the bud stems and are placed above the center of each heart.

The border has a set of small tulip buds and a few scattered "wind-blown" tulips. The leaves have been padded here too. The white quilting traces the patterns and the squares with curving lines. The bud stems have been quilted in green thread to give more dimension to the light green color. The backing is a complimentary small rose print. This is made for a twin bed and is approximately 60'' by 87''.

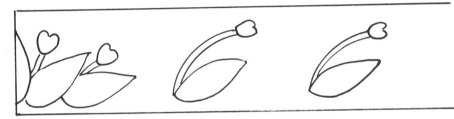

Fig. 5–36 Ohio Rose quilt with double heart can have a dark-on-light or light-on-dark color scheme. Although hearts are usually done in pink and red, this looks good in blues, too, and is very country-looking when worked in calicoes. The quilting pattern is simple outline; the border pattern shows movement.

### Materials

5 yards white background
1¼ yard dark pink
1½ yard light pink
1½ yard green
5 yards backing
60″ × 87″ batting

### Cutting

8 squares 19½″
2 side borders 11″ × 76″
2 top and bottom borders 11″ × 60″
32 dark pink hearts
32 dark pink buds
24 tulip buds for border
32 light pink hearts
8 light pink circles 2″ diameter
32 green bud stems

12 green short stems
10 green long stems
27 green leaves

Patterns can be found in Chapter 9 for both the design block and the borders.

## Bear's Paw ★ ★

This old pattern is perfectly named as you will see if you look at the quilt shown in the color section and Fig. 5−37. You will see four dark paw prints on a light ground—this is *Bear's Paw*. If the reverse coloration is used, four light footprints on a dark ground, the pattern is called *Ducks Foot in the Mud*. It is a pattern derivative of the traditional nine patch.

### *Materials*

3½ yards dark fabric
4½ yards background fabric
5 yards backing (includes back-over-front binding)
66″ × 82″ batting

### *Cutting (add seam allowance)*

80 background 2″ squares
20 dark 2″ squares
320 dark 2″ squares cut on diagonal
320 background 2″ squares cut on diagonal
80 dark 4″ squares
80 background 2″ × 6″ rectangles
16 dark borders 2″ × 14″ for horizontal bands
5 dark borders 78″ × 2″ for vertical bands
2 dark borders for top and bottom 66″ × 2″

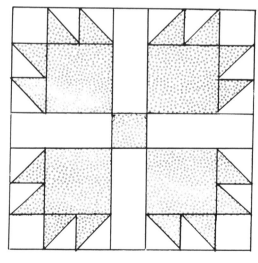

Fig. 5−37 Bear's Paw is tailored looking and is often used in items for men.

When beginning to set the pattern together, always start by sewing 2 two-tone squares together. Add this to large center dark one. Then sew two more two-tone squares together and add the small light solid color corner square. Sew this strip to above to complete one paw. Repeat for the other paws. When the paws are finished and the seams are pressed, add to remaining background rectangles and single dark squares. It is the author's opinion that the pattern blocks are best separated with intersecting bands as shown in the color photograph.

This quilt is twin bed size, 66 by 82 inches. There are four blocks across and five down. Each block is 14 by 14 inches and bands are 2 inches wide. There are 20 Bear's Paw blocks. Pattern pieces can be found in Chapter 9, using basic squares and rectangles.

# CHAPTER

# Sampler and Pictorial Quilts

A traditional explanation of a sampler quilt would be a quilt made up of many different design blocks that a quilt crafter has tried over the years. All needle-crafters have samples of various patterns or stitches, and when the projects are finished, they have just another small sample project. The quilter can put these samples into a quilt. Sometimes these samples look unrelated, but the quilter may have a special feeling for the various patterns which may hold memories of stitchery problems solved just for the fun of it. Today's quilt crafters are designing sampler quilts of related ideas, patterns, and colors. Each beautiful pattern the quilter chooses can now be worked out and integrated into one quilt. Another point to consider is that one pattern does not have to be repeated, thus making each block a new challenge.

The first step to designing a sampler quilt is to decide on the overall size needed, whether for a bed covering or a wallhanging. It would be best to keep the patterns on the top of the bed and have a solid or repeating border of a simple nature on the drops.

Study Chapters 1 through 3 and pick out and draft patterns that you like. There can be a very successful blend of patchwork and applique into one quilt. Samplers are often used for teaching; you can learn a new technique in each block. You too can use this as a teaching tool, trying the different types of patterns suggested and ultimately finding what pleases you most. It would be good to choose one pale background color, one bright color, and a third color to compliment the bright.

## Hudson Highlands Bicentennial Sampler

The Hudson Highlands Bicentennial Sampler Quilt as shown in the color section is a unique response by a group of women who felt the need to record their place in history. These women were very familiar with the quilt patch. This looks like a true sampler of yesterday. The first thing that strikes you when looking at this quilt is that there are both expert and novice design blocks sitting happily side by side. The especially large design in the center is called a medallion; the pattern is Barrister's Block. The quilt is owned by the Quilters of the Hudson Highland's; the quilt coordinator is Evelyn Barclay, a well-known quilt teacher. It is displayed at various shows and benefits and, when not on view, it is gracing the walls of one of the member's homes.

The overall size is 80 by 114 inches with earth colors predominating. The quilters kept a step-by-step photographic record of the progress of the quilt. Originally they decided to have the blocks in various sizes but that proved too difficult in trying to lay out a harmonious quilt. This resulted in having to frame some squares and add additional separating designs. This is a good example of how a quilter will square off and enlarge an accumulation of various size blocks. There are people who are collectors of design blocks. There are traders of design blocks who, for instance, make a really fine pine tree and will trade it for some other finely made block. So a sampler quilt can hold many memories.

This quilt group published a booklet of patterns and, for the purpose of harmony, decided to adjust all the patterns to 15 inches. For a copy of the booklet, write Box 27 – 11, Newburgh, New York 12550.

The quilt was mounted in the traditional way and beautifully hand quilted on a frame. Each design block was to be quilted by its maker, but as in any communal effort there are always a few who do more than the rest. The intersecting bordering bands are 3 inches wide and the Saw-Tooth edge is a brown and white tiny polka dot that is contrasted with unbleached muslin. The border blocks are 4 inches square. See Chapter 9 for Barrister's Block, Nine Patch, Turkey Tracks, Monkey Wrench, Honey Bee, Pine Tree, and Shoe Fly patterns.

# The Super Sampler

This was finished for the Bicentennial in 1976 and is appropriately worked in red, white, and blue. The patterns are the best in the show collection of June Ryker, a quilter and quilt teacher at Quilts and Other Comforts in Denver. June's pattern search lasted over many years. Some were from tiny pictures in old scrap books. Each of the thirty-eight patterns was drafted on graph paper to a 12-inch square. The overall quilt size is 93 by 108 inches (see Fig. 6 – 1). It has 3-inch wide blue framing bands intersecting the quilt with small red squares at each corner. The trick to doing this is to attach a top and left hand band with the corner set in before you call it a finished piece (see Fig. 5 – 30). When the quilt is to be assembled, all that has to be done is to set the squares together and add the outer right hand and bottom bands.

This was hand quilted in a large hoop. It won a fourth prize at the Quilt Show and Exhibition sponsored by the Educational Opportunities School in Aurors, Colorado, and first appeared in the *Quilters Newsletter* where it was showered with praises from coast to coast. A number of star patterns are given in varying sizes in Chapter 9. What makes this quilt so superior as a sampler is that each pattern is drafted with a white background. Each of the patterns is a star variation. This carries the eye in and out and around each square. The white

Fig. 6 – 1 Super sampler of star patterns by June Ryker. The photograph was taken by R. L. Hale and appeared first in *Quilter's Newsletter*. Top row: Royal, Shadow, French, Liberty, Rhododendron, Hexagon. Second row: Hex, Morning, Diamond, Brunswick, 8-Point, Flying Saucer. Third row: Star of Mystery, Union, Star of Many Points, Virginia, Pieced, Double Diamond. Fourth row: Tel Star, Hope of Hartford, All American, Star & Planets, Compass, Ohio. Fifth row: Whirling, Bethlehem, Star & Crescent, Aunt Eliza's, and Bicentennial Stars.

background provides a rest area for the viewer. It also gives a crisp and clean look, helping to lift up the stars. The quilting is different in each block, helping to accent the pattern. The bands have two rows of quilting and the red squares at the intersecting corners have little stars quilted into them.

# Learning Sampler

The Learning Sampler of Betty Dufficy (see back cover) is an example of the work done by quilters out in the Rocky Mountains at a shop called Quilts and Other Comforts in Wheat Ridge, Colorado. Here the different design blocks, mostly patchwork, teach the various techniques of curves, deep "Vs", small diagonal pieces, applique, and strip-type patches. Betty chose twelve patterns that were especially attractive to her for this quilt.

The two components that make this quilt so handsome are the uniform size of the blocks and the smart use of varying sized blue prints. The gold bands that are 4 inches wide serve as a perfect foil for highlighting the many shades of blue. The strength of the triple borders makes a good frame that draws the viewers attention into the patterns of the quilt. Note the interlocking quilt stitch pattern in the bands and borders where quilting will show up best. The blocks are quilted with simple outline stitching to accent the patterns' intricacies. The overall size of the quilt is 84 by 104 inches; the design blocks are 16 inches square; the framing bands are 4 inches wide; and the outer borders are 4, 2, and 4 inches respectively. This will help you get a good perspective on a well planned quilt. Some of the patterns are given in Chapter 9 in various sizes but a set of patterns for this sampler may be purchased by writing to Bernice Fair, Quilts and Other Comforts, 5315 West 38 Ave., Wheat Ridge, Colorado 80033.

# Hawaiian Quilt Sampler

When the missionaries first came to the Hawaiian Islands in the early 1880s, they brought with them cotton woven fabric and their quilting skill. There emerged a special type of pattern. Large pieces of cloth were placed on the ground and folded in half, north and south; then folded again east to west, forming a four fold. It was then folded on the diagonal. It is said that in the early years of Hawaiian quilting the shadow of the trees and fruit plant forms were cut out on the folded piece of fabric. The art of paper folding is not new; the Orientals and the Europeans have done it for centuries. Since early colonial days, American children have been taught to fold and cut out paper snowflakes.

Hawaiian quilts are generally found in two colors with the darker color on the top. When the design is cut out, it is then opened and centered on a pale or white background. This is a departure from the most traditional applique taught throughout this country, and this text. The edges are not turned to the back in traditional Hawaiian applique, but the entire piece is basted to the background about ½ inch in from the raw edge. As the work progresses, the edges are then turned under ¼ inch with the applique needle. Points are mitered, wherever possible, to reduce the bulk.

The quilting follows the contours of the design, generally a fingers width from the edges of the applique. The quilting appears both on the applique design and on the background. It continues in evenly spaced concentric contourings until no more lines fit.

Since this is a rather large undertaking for one single quilt, Helen Squire designed the Hawaiian Sampler shown in the color section with nine existing, traditional designs. Each block is 22 by 22 inches with a 15½-inch border; the overall size of the quilt is 99 by 99 inches. It is on permanent display at Quilt In, Woodcliff Lake, New Jersey. This first appeared in the *Quilters Newsletter*, February 1978. As a monthly series, one pattern would appear each month. The patterns can be purchased in their entirety from the Quilt In, Box 603, Woodcliff Lake, New Jersey 07675.

Anyone can make their own designs by duplicating the traditional methods. If you decide to copy the sampler idea then make sure that you have at least 1½ inches of background material extending around the perimeter of the cut out design. This helps to give the eye space to rest between each busy motif. Hawaiian designs make fine wallhangings, lovely small throws, and baby blankets.

To make your own patterns, cut strong brown bag type paper the size of your finished design. Fold in half, then in half the opposite way, then half on the diagonal, bringing fold to fold (see Fig. 6−2). Draw a design on the triangle, cut. unfold fully. The finished design will be approximately ¼ inch smaller since seam allowance is figured in this cutting. If you like your design, you're ready to cut fabric; if not, try to improve what you have or start again. A word for beginners—try not to have too many deep sharp cuts. Study Fig. 6−2 as it will show steps to follow and see Fig. 2−16 for the finished drawing. Cut out only ⅛ of the pattern and retrace it on strong paper. Then fold a square of fabric as the paper was folded and press each fold as it's made; pin securely. Match pattern on top, lining the points and folds. Pin pattern and draw the cutting line in pencil. Be careful not to cut on folds. Open and press flat. Cut a square of background material 1½ inches larger. Fold and press lightly same as for applique. Place the

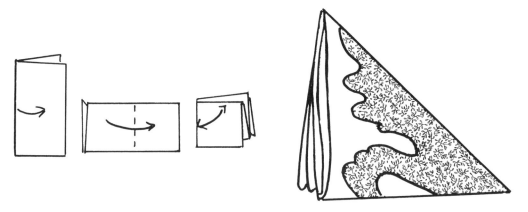

Fig. 6−2 Folding the Hawaiian design.

applique on the top, lining it up with the folds on the background. Proceed as described above. (See Chapter 9 for an exact pattern; use as given or enlarge.)

To make a full-size Hawaiian quilt which is traditionally square, choose two large pieces of fabric for applique, from 60 up to 90 inches square. Fold in eighths as for smaller work to cut center design. After cutting the center design, you will be left with the perimeter fabric to be cut for the border design. Create a free form design along the inner edge of the border piece. The design cut for the border should complement not parallel the center design. The outer uncut edge of the border should line up with the outer edge of the background fabric. It is suggested you try this with two pieces of colored paper first.

# Jenny's World Crib Sampler

The sampler type design need not be relegated to trying out established quilt patterns, but may be brought out to the nursery for the fun of making a child's quilt. Patterns can be found in coloring books and children's storybooks. Appliques of a simple nature are the best. The objects should be easy to recognize by the child, such as an apple, a heart, a flower. Bright colors are best and no loose trim such as buttons should be used.

There are several patterns given in Chapter 9 that would be suitable: the sun bonnet girl, a butterfly, the small star, the schoolhouse, small flowers and hearts, a small fan made from the twenty-piece Dresden Plate, peony, and Bird in the Bush reduced. Some other simple figures are pears, umbrella, hen, small house, ice cream cone, boat, cup, pitcher, calico cat, drum, pine tree, snowflakes, elephant, car, train, fish, balloons, kite, birthday cake, turtle, zeppelin, tree with embroidered flowers, bell, anchor, or an outline of your home state with a star for the capital and the home town name embroidered on.

The sampler as shown is 32 by 56 inches and is tied with embroidery floss. (See Chapter 8, Crazy Quilting, for directions for tying method of quilting.) It has a cotton flannel filler rather than the batting of polyester. This is a good idea because it washes so well and can be tied so easily. This was made by a group of women as a shower gift, but before it could be finished, baby Jennifer came along a month early, so eight friends of mother and grandmother had to work fast.

*Materials*

    ⅞ yard for background of face
    assorted scraps for appliques
    2 yards (print suggested) for backing
    32″ × 56″ cotton flannel filler

*Cutting*

    6 squares for appliques, 14½″ × 14½″
    32″ × 56″ flannel
    41½″ × 65½″ backing

Fig. 6–3 Crib sampler, called Jenny's World. This quilt is appliqued and tied over a flannel filler. Courtesy of Jennifer Rooney. Each quilter designed and worked her own block. Made by Doris Wickman, Phyllis Shane, Jo Onaglia, Sally Jo Gindel, Mary Ann Cowan, Marge Carlson, Audrey Didricksen, and the author.

Make the appliques and sew two blocks across and four down. The finished face will be 24½ by 48½ inches. Place the backing right side down on the work surface, center the flannel over it, and then place the face over that, right side up. The three pieces will have a staggered look. Bring the backing over the flannel to cover the raw edge of the face. This edge can be covered with rickrack, lace, eyelet, beading, or fancy embroidery stitches. Feather stitch the edges to give it more stability (see Fig. 8 – 10).

# Pictorial Applique Quilts

This quilt is composed of a series of blocks that depict different pictures, scenes, or symbols. This is a very personal form of decorative art. Due to the nature of working with fabric, this picture applique takes on the look of folk art. It needs embroidery to help with small details. The bicentennial really helped to stimulate local artists and quilters to design and depict history of regional areas more often as wallhangings than bed covers. They were often sponsored by historical societies, libraries, and community-minded social groups and county extension services. They were made to be kept by the community as an example of folk craft of the era, a teaching tool, a history of our times, and as a fund raiser in a few instances. Most often the quilt is designed, appliqued, and quilted by the same group of crafters; thus it would be called an "historical pictorial."

When quilts are made by one person, they usually picture the events or symbols that have significance to one family. They are called "album quilts."

Start by deciding just what you want to picture in your quilt. If you are working with a community group, be prepared for a bit of polite discussion as feelings can run strong on what each one considers important. This calls for the good old democratic vote, with the majority making final decisions. Try to get this settled in one session and get on with the quilt. A good trick to help the situation come to a speedy end would be to make lists under topic headings: historical houses, historical events, historical people, natural resources, and industries. Decide on the number of blocks to be planned for the quilt—that helps to narrow down the above list—and give each category a certain number of blocks. You can diplomatically remind everyone that categories which were voted out this year can always be included in another quilt. That helps to smooth out the ruffled feathers and gets you on to the matter of work.

Match the number of blocks to the number of needlecrafters you can count on. If you have more volunteers than needed, suggest that duplicates of certain blocks could be made and then one will be picked for the quilt and any alternates will be used as a pillow for sale or raffle. By now you should be ready to start.

Other topics for quilts would include American Indians in special dress and habitat, the Space Age, Scout merit badges and ranks earned, Zodiac Quilts filled with all the beautiful star signs, or a tribute to an author or artist, such as Beatrix Potter or Norman Rockwell.

The next part of the process is to select the size of the individual design square and the overall size of the quilt. This type of quilt looks best with bands running through it, as the bands act as picture frames for each representation. If it is to be a wallhanging, then it could be square; but if it's to be a bed covering, then it should be rectangular. The size of the design square should be, in this author's opinion, anywhere from 14 to 18 inches square. The block size should be drawn onto graph paper and, with a second colored pencil, a one-inch measurement marked inward. All drawings of the objects are done inside this line. This margin allows room for quilting and helps to carry the view inward toward the object represented. Using a third colored pencil, add a ½-inch seam allowance on the outside. Draw the pictures to fill the space up to the margin line. Sometimes a tree, a path, a brook, or mountain has to slip out of the margin and this can't be helped.

There are many good sources for help with drawing. Local historical societies, libraries, and newspapers have photographs and line drawings of historic spots. Libraries have dozens of specialized books and magazines that relate to what you may think is an odd subject. For example, cricket and skiing can be found in outdoor magazines; Victorian dress, in costume books; an old stone springhouse, in books on Pennsylvania Dutch folk art. Then there are greeting and Christmas cards; this industry employs top notch artists and you can use their work for reference to help you get started. Children's books utilize super artwork, using a very simple representation. Among my favorites are song books, nursery rhyme books, and poetry books. Last on the list, but by no means least, are the better coloring books in which appear marvelous line drawings.

Embroidery thread can be used for small detail such as trees on a faraway hill, personal features, decoration of clothing, and almost all flowers.

Facial features seem always to worry the nonartist, but this is easy, with the help of newspaper advertisements. Find a head the same size and view as your fabric drawing. Pencil in the newspaper on the reverse side of the face; then place it over the fabric and, with a sharp pencil, trace off the features. Embroider with one or two strands of cotton embroidery floss. I do this after the face has been appliqued.

Overall, this type of quilt should be kept to conservative colors and shapes—not too extreme. The quilting will supply enough texture. Details such as clap boards or stones on the side of a house, roof tiles, or brick walks can all be worked in with the quilting or embroidery stitches for texture. Many times it is the quilting texture that gives a block its personality. A friend of mine wanted to make a block to commemorate ice fishing. No matter how she tried the drawing, it all looked a little lonely and bleak with the blue sky, the pale blue lake ringed with green, and the three little ice shacks. It was the quilt stitching that saved the day. Quilting on the ice to represent skating marks and the addition of a few birds stitched into the sky gave the dimension needed to compete with the rest of the patches in the quilt. By the way, if you want to represent snow, remember the embroiderers' French knot; or for the look of window glass, an overlay of sheer dotted swiss fabric.

Highly textured or novelty fabrics should not be used for this art. When adding corduroy to indicate a furrowed field or fake fur to cover an animal, you are saying you do not have the skill to embroider these fine details. Unless every block has this added texture dimension, the quilt looks unfinished. Sometimes these quilts are done all over in highly textured fabrics and, while they look okay as beginner work, they lose their intrinsic value as a highly skilled piece of craft work. So aim for the best you can produce.

The selection of the fabric is rather easy; it should all be a basic broadcloth type with perhaps a few exceptions. Since most of these designs feature outdoor pictures, include at least three greens that please you, maybe even a small green print, and brown for tree bark, paths, and small dogs. One color should be chosen for the daytime sky and all sky pictures should have the same background. A dark blue would be used to offset a building at night. Don't limit yourself to all daytime presentations—one house in our area had a special history of being on the underground railroad and only operated at night. Besides, Paul Revere did not ride at noon. Two or three more blues may be added for water colors. When choosing black and gray, try to find those shades that have a bit of blue in them as they will appear warmer. After this, it is best to make individual color selections based on what is needed for each presentation.

Hard colors to find include barn red, so settle for maroon, and sandstone, so settle for a reddish brown. The only yardage that must be in adequate supply is the daytime sky, as dye lots are hard to match at later dates. The rest may be small pieces with many contributions from the scrap basket. Keep in mind that you want as much harmony as possible. The bands can be selected after the picture blocks have been completed. Reds and browns seem to be most popular with darker blues next. Remember, the use of the band is to serve as a picture frame and should be a minimum of 1½ inches.

# Pattern Making and Use

Place the basic drawing you have made in front of you. Place strong but transparent paper (such as typing paper) over each part that needs a separate pattern piece. (See Fig. 2–11.) Draw each component separately as a solid template pattern. Cut it out without adding the seam allowance. The pattern pieces can be drawn directly on their respective fabrics. Then the ¼-inch seam allowance is measured all the way around and the piece is cut out. Turn the edges back and baste but do not press; set aside.

Prepare the background by finding the horizon line—where the sky meets the ground. Cut out the ground color and the sky color and sew them together. If the line is relatively straight, then use a running stitch. If it is rather jagged, then applique the ground to the sky color. Now arrange the pieces of the applique on top of the background so they all fit together. Some pieces, such as a large tree or a long stream, will be carried out of the picture to the raw edges of the seam allowance. For the most part, fit the main applique pieces within the margin given in the basic drawing. This helps to give a little breathing space between the applique and the intersecting bordering bands. After all pieces have been appliqued, then embroidery can be added for a textural effect.

Windows can be made to look recessed by a technique called reverse applique. After the building is drawn onto the fabric, the windows are drawn; then a ¼-inch seam allowance is drawn in and the remainder of the inside is cut out. The seam allowance is slashed diagonally into the corners, basted back, and placed over another color background fabric slightly larger than the opening. This color represents the glass. The opening of the window is appliqued to the background. Embroidery around the windows can be added at this point, using a three-ply cotton yarn and a split stitch to give a heavy look. Then the house itself should be appliqued to the background.

# Ulster County Bicentennial Quilt

In 1975 a group of 42 women met at Ulster County Community College with Quilt Coordinator, Ruth Culver. A quilt was planned to include forty-two 12-inch blocks to be appliqued and embroidered. Each person was responsible for researching and writing the history of her individual block. After the quilt top was finished, it took seven weeks to quilt. The participants ranged from 20 to 79 years old and were strangers to one another at the beginning of the project; however, lasting friendships have grown through pride in their work which is shown on the front cover. The quilt is dedicated to the people of Ulster County in the hope that by examining their past, they will find inspiration for the future. It has been given to the Ulster County Community College where it is on permanent exhibition. It has the names of the original 242 settlers of Ulster County embroidered in the outer border.

# Delaware and Hudson Canal Sesquicentennial Quilt

In 1978, the sesquicentennial year of the Canal's opening, the Delaware and Hudson Canal Historical Society commissioned the Atwood Community Club to make a pictorial quilt which would tell the Canal story. Mr. Lewis Brown, artist and curator of the Society Museum, did the drawings from which the quilters worked; Alice Valentine was the quilt coordinator. The blocks are interspersed with plain squares with the names of canal towns embroidered on them. This is a checkerboard effect and the arrangement makes the pictorial blocks stand out beautifully. This quilt is on exhibition at the Delaware and Hudson Canal Historical Society Museum, High Falls, New York. A booklet in the form of a coloring book is available.

# The Onondaga County Bicentennial Quilt

Twenty-five women between the ages of 19 and 79 responded to an article written about Mary Helen Foster's proposed county wide quilt project. Topics were selected from a list prepared by Carol Wright of the Onondaga Historical Association. The octagonal shape of the quilt designs represents the many octagonal buildings in the area and depicts the growth and development of the county. The small diamonds represent the plants and wildlife native to the county. This type of banding of a quilt is called a lattice and the backing and banding made of dark brown calico print. It took 2,000 hours for the sewing

Fig. 6 – 4 Delaware and Hudson Canal Sesquicentennial Quilt. (The canal stretched from the Hudson River in New York to Honesdale, Pa.) Left to right, top to bottom: Digging the D & H Canal; Maurice and William Wurts and the D & H Canal; Maurice Wurts finding coal in Pennsylvania; canal boat mules; the Seaside Supply Store; Sturbridge Lion; canal boat entering lock; the D & H Canal aqueduct; the Hawk's Nest; coal boat in 1860; New York & Rosendale Lime & Cement Company; the Gravity Railroad; an early canal boat waiting to go through a lock; canal packets (passenger boats); winter on the canal. Photograph by David Fletcher.

Fig. 6–5 Onondaga County, New York, Bicentennial Quilt. Left to right, top to bottom: Saltmaking; Skaneateles Lake; Syracuse china; the Franklin car; Ephraim Webster; steam locomotive; the Erie Canal; the Williams house in Manlius—1813; the Cardiff Giant; New York State Fair; Syracuse—Typewriter City—1903; the Pompey store— 1828; Onondaga County Seal; Octagon House; St. Paul's Cathedral; settlers cabin in Elbridge; the Plank Road; Delphi Falls United Church; French Fort; the Jerry Rescue; Geddes Pottery; 1812 Seneca Turnpike Cemetery; the Canal Museum—Weighlock Building; Lafayette visits Onondaga Hill Court House—1825; candlemaking; Crouse College, Syracuse University; 1814 School House; Lafayette apple orchards; Onondaga County Court House; the military tract map. Photograph courtesy of Mary Helen Foster, quilt coordinator.

and quilting to be finished. It was presented on May 16, 1976, at the Civic Center, Syracuse, New York.

The names of blocks are listed under the photo of the quilt. There are post cards and a booklet available by writing to Ms. Ginny Rhoades, Cultural Resources Council, Civic Center, 411 Montgomery St., Syracuse, New York 13202.

## The Post Mills, Vermont, Quilt

This was conceived as a fund raiser and was ultimately raffled off to someone who moved to Hawaii. What is so interesting about this is the intense activity represented in this quilt. It was not conceived as a historical picture repository. It shows the life and times of the 1970s. There is an invitation to be part of the joy of the Vermont life—ice-fishing, sleigh riding, backpacking, fishing, sailing, flying, camping, biking, horseback riding. Even hanging one's laundry looks pleasant in Vermont. The freshness of spirit is so inviting. Credit goes to Kay Schlichting and her needlecraft friends. Kay came to me one day and asked how to go about such a project as her group had only limited knowledge of group quilting, and over a pot of tea she received the same information that is here in this chapter. There are thirty design blocks set in a gold border.

## Freedom Rider Quilt

This quilt (shown in the color section) depicts Paul Revere's ride in a silhouette figure on a rolling set of stripes. This use of the rolling stripes helps to add movement to the motions set by the horse's flying feet. The upper portion is in dark blue with the single star. The single star might represent the one light that told Revere that the enemy was coming by land. It has a white border bound in red. There are many different quilting textures carried out on the various parts of the overall design. The horse and rider have a diamond pattern (see Fig. 3–8a); the quilting behind the silhouette is of the pipe line type, following the movement of the stripes (Fig. 3–8d); the star has concentric lines outlining the inside; and the borders echo the same quilted star (Fig. 3–3) with pipe line quilting joining the stars together. In the large blue field at the top is a very intricate pattern of large and small stars. Embroidered on the blue field are the words taken from the Liberty Bell, "Proclaiming liberty throughout the land to all the inhabitants thereof. . ." and the dates 1776–1976. The overall measurement is 53 by 72 inches. At the time of this writing, it has received four national quilt prizes.

## George Washington at Valley Forge

This quilt (shown in the color insert) was inspired by the portrait of George Washington by J. C. Leyendecker which appeared on the *Saturday Evening Post* magazine in 1975. The figure is created in a hand-sewn direct applique and reverse applique. The main section is 45 by 60 inches with a pipe line quilting in the background. The border patterns are historically linked to George Washing-

Fig. 6-6 Assortment of blocks for pictorial quilts. (a) Shows the handling of a rural panoramic view. (b) Represents the importance of the train in early America. (c) Symbolic seals make interesting artwork and usually have a lot of embroidery. (d) Buildings, like this planked barn, come in all sizes, shapes, and perspectives. (e) The log cabin school house.

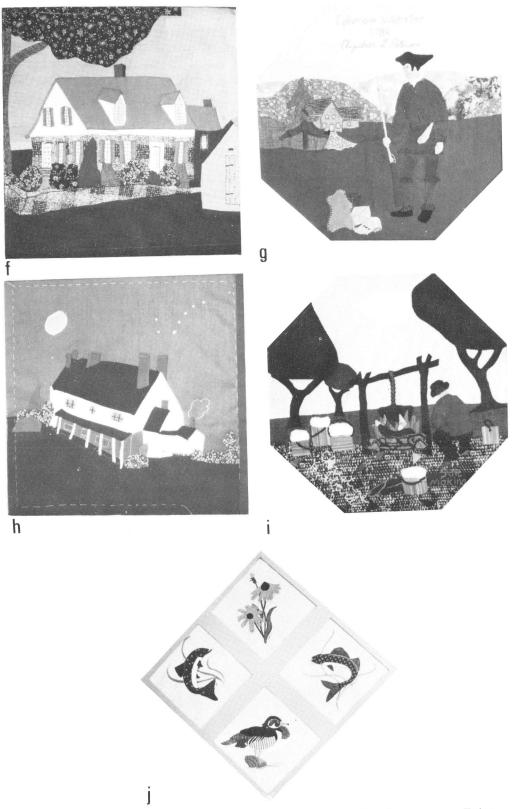

Assortment of pictorial blocks. (f) The stone house. (g) The frontiersman Ephriam Webster, 1786. (h) The underground railroad (note the Big Dipper in the sky and the candles burning in the windows to signal all is well). (i) Saltmaking, an early local industry. (j) Small vignettes commemorating the flowers and wildlife of Onondaga county.

Fig. 6−7 Post Mills, Vermont, Quilt. Photograph courtesy of Kay Schlichting, quilt coordinator.

ton's lifetime. The four sunflowers in the corners appeared on a quilt that he used during one of his stays in Valley Forge. The other patchwork pattern comes from a quilt known as Washington's Own or The President's Quilt. The traditional colors for this pattern were red and tan set together with white. There were 840 pieces to be sewn in the border. It took 90 days to complete to be entered in the Lawrence, Kansas, Bicentennial Quilt Show; it took first place. The quilt has won six more prizes up to the time of this writing. Its overall size is 81 by 96 inches.

# More Pictorial Quilts

For two other pictorial quilts, see the School Days and Bicentennial Friendship Quilts in Figs. 5–2 and 5–3.

These were made as a response to the Stearn's and Foster's "Mountain Mist" Quilt Contest. School Days has thirty 12-inch squares set in apple red bordering bands and was made in 1977. The Bicentennial Friendship Quilt was made in 1974. There are thirty design squares, depicting important historical events in the original thirteen states, set in red and white striped background and bordering bands.

Thanks to Mary Helen Foster and Victor Frager's enthusiasm, individual pictures were taken of the blocks before they were assembled finally into their respective quilts. I have chosen ten to show you different handling of the various categories. Some of the blocks are from the Onondaga County Quilt and are octagonal; the rest are from the Pascack Valley Historical Society Quilt.

# CHAPTER 7

# Block-by-Block Quilts

Up to now the concentration has been on assembling an entire quilt or very large sections of a given quilt which are then united. Due to the need for smaller project work that will ultimately be finished as a large project, I have developed the rather unique method of block quilting. (See American Stars Forever in Fig. 5 – 33.) It works as follows. First, the number of design blocks needed for the entire quilt are made. Each design block is placed in a staggered position over a piece of batting and a backing cut slightly larger. The three layer block is then basted in a sunburst pattern. The quilting can be done on a small frame, with no frame, or on the machine. After all the design squares have been quilted, they are then joined together. The backings are sewn together so that the seams appear on the right side of the quilt. The seams are then covered with a bordering band, thus creating one large quilt. Follow the instructions given and choose from the suggestions of assorted techniques described. The distinct advantage of this method is that the entire project remains comparatively small in physical size until final assembly. This method does away with the large floor frame.

There are three main steps to understand in this assembly: (1) producing the design block and the bands in proper proportions; (2) how the quilting is accomplished; and (3) how the bands are finally used to assemble this quilt with a smoothly finished backing.

One of the original problems to be solved was that of the seams that joined the quilted blocks together. The initial response to this problem in most needlecrafters' minds would be the old tried and true welt seam or the mock French seam used earlier in Chapter 5, Figs. 5 – 7 to 5 – 14, as a joining seam. Having one or two of these seams on the back of a quilt doesn't present a problem, but having them vertical and horizontally intersecting each other does make for a rather weak backing. It is the back of the quilt that gets most of the wear with the body shifting against it. To eliminate this, it is better to design a smooth back. To do this, it meant that bands had to be placed on the top of the quilt, forming an integrated part of the overall design. The bands could be plain or pieced. (See Fig. 7 – 1.)

156

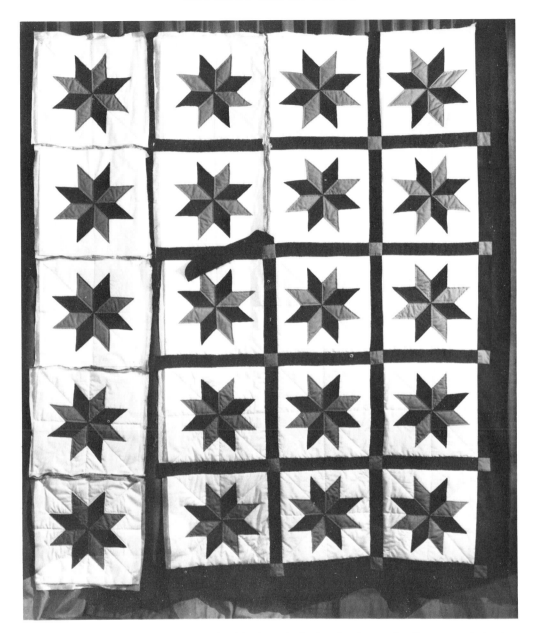

Fig. 7 – 1 Putting together a block-by-block quilt. Left side shows the first step of pinning and sewing full-length strips together. The seams are on the right side of the face and will be covered by bordering bands. Center shows a strip that has been banded and attached to two finished units. Right side and bottom shows 5-inch-wide one-piece border band being applied.

The most important part of this quilt is the planning, as the mechanics are relatively easy to understand. Not every quilt design will lend itself to being interpreted with intersecting bands on the face, but it is comforting to know that about 97 percent of the patterns popular today can be adopted beautifully to this assembly technique.

This method lends itself well to group work. Each participant prepares and quilts a design block; they then come together for a few hours work of assembling. This method is great for small quilt clubs or social groups that want to do a rather large money-making project.

For clarity's sake, it is best to consider applique and patchwork tops separately as the technique changes slightly with each medium.

# Applique

Select a design that will fit on the bed properly with enough room around the applique for quilting.

Draw out the design block, say 18 by 18 inches, on graph paper and trace in suggested quilting lines. Make patterns for each of the individual elements.

Select the size of the band that would best compliment the design block. Generally the 2 to 3-inch band is a good size. Divide the band *width* in half and add this measurement to the design block for seam allowances. In this example, we would select a band with a finished size of 2 inches. Therefore, we would add one inch all the way around to the background fabric, enlarging the background to 20 by 20 inches.

Using the graph paper as a guide, cut out the needed number of background pieces and appliques and stitch by hand or machine, using suggestions for applique given in Chapter 2.

Cut a sufficient number of framing borders (see Figs. 2−3 and 2−4), adding ¼-inch seam allowance all the way around on all bands. The quilt will be assembled in strips—first with the short horizontal bands; and then the resulting long strips will be joined with vertical bands, measuring the length of the quilt. In our example, a 2-inch wide finished band would be cut 2½ inches wide to allow for the seam allowance. The short bands that would be placed horizontally will be cut 20 inches long (see Fig. 7−1).

Cut the backing of the quilt into blocks ½ inch larger on all four sides than the face. In our example, this would be 21 by 21 inches, allowing for the extra ½ inch to be used in the seam allowance when the individual quilted blocks are joined together in the final assembly.

Place each completed applique design over a piece of batting that is cut the same size as the completed design square (see Fig. 7−2b). Center these two over the wrong side of backing material. There will be a ½ inch of the wrong side of backing fabric extending around the perimeter of the design square and batting (see Fig. 7−2c). In a sunburst pattern, baste the three layers together. Now this applique piece is ready for quilting. (See the suggestions for mini block quilting.)

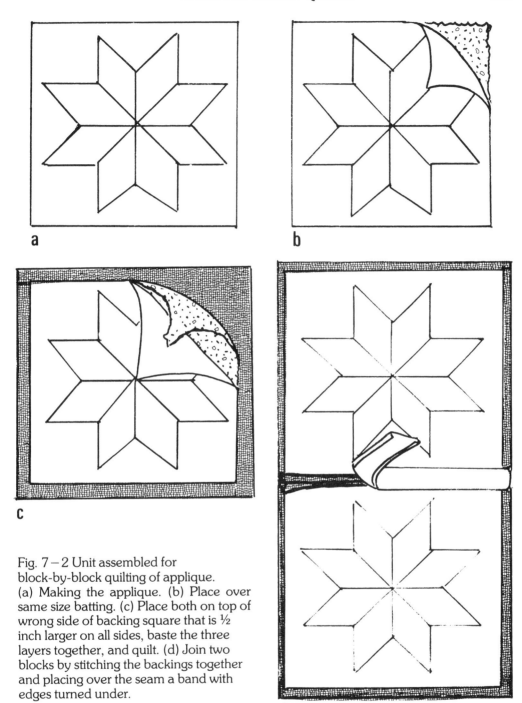

Fig. 7 – 2 Unit assembled for
block-by-block quilting of applique.
(a) Making the applique. (b) Place over
same size batting. (c) Place both on top of
wrong side of backing square that is ½
inch larger on all sides, baste the three
layers together, and quilt. (d) Join two
blocks by stitching the backings together
and placing over the seam a band with
edges turned under.

# Patchwork

Select a design block and border band that will complement the design. All sorts of intricate patchwork bands can be pieced together. Many times the actual design of the block is relatively simple, but the bands are so intricate that they carry the quilt to magnificence. Put the entire quilt design onto graph paper to make sure you have the sizes in proper proportion.

Draw out one design block on graph and make individual design patterns for both the block and the bands. Figure 7–3 shows our sample block in a "wrench" design. The finished size of the block is 14 by 14 inches.

Proceed to make the patchwork design squares and piece the bands if necessary. Piece together the short horizontal ones, then the long vertical ones and press the seams to the wrong side on the long edges.

The laying together of the face, batting, and backing to ready it for quilting is accomplished in a staggered manner. The backing is cut large enough to accommodate half the band and ½ inch additional for seam allowance on each side. In our example, the band is 4 inches wide finished; therefore, half the band will be 2 inches plus ½-inch seam allowance gives a backing cut 19 inches square (see Fig. 7–3b). Place the backing material on the work surface wrong side up. Cut the batting 18 by 18 inches and center on backing. Batting does not include seam allowance as we do not want to have batting in our seams. Center the completed design block on top of the batting face up (Fig. 7–3b). Baste the three layers together on the work surface. Try not to lift until the basting is complete. Now the patchwork is ready to be quilted. (See suggestions for Mini block quilting.) The bands will be used later to put the quilted block together and will cover the exposed batting and the ½-inch seam allowance of the patchwork.

# Quilt Stitching

The most satisfying method of quilting is on a frame. It must be kept in mind that we have accomplished the first two of the basic elements of a quilted object—*design* and *color*. Now the enriching last element is to be added—*texture*. By placing the three layers to be quilted into a frame to strengthen and hold the layers taut, the depressions of the quilting lines create the texture—a design element that should be used to its fullest to enhance the quilt.

## The Hoop Frame

This simple embroidery hoop can be purchased at a low cost in any needlecraft department, craft stores, department stores, or mail-order catalogs. The round or oval frame should accommodate the main portions of the area to be quilted. A smaller size can be used such as a 10-inch hoop on a 14 by 14-inch piece of patchwork. After the center is completed, move the frame to an unquilted area and quilt until it is finished. I find it most satisfying to use a hoop that will accommodate the central motif of the design and leave very little to be quilted into the corners without a frame. Try to get a hoop that has a screw closure, rather than the spring closure type. The spring closure forces the upper

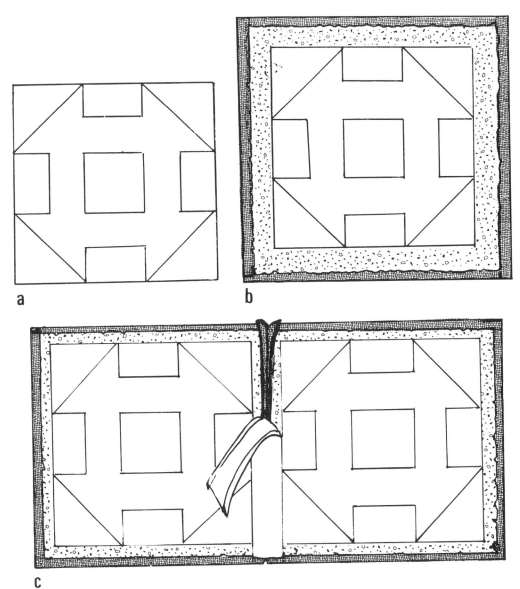

Fig. 7−3 Unit assembly for block-by-block quilting of patchwork. (a) Make a patchwork block. (b) Set it over batting that is cut ½ inch smaller than backing, baste three layers together, and quilt. (c) Join two blocks by stitching the backings together so seam appears on front, and center a band over the extra batting, covering the raw edge of the patchwork block. Baste and then quilt stitch the bands down.

hoop over the lower and a lot of pulling takes place to get the three layers even. Where the screw closure is used, the basted layers are placed over the lower hoop and the screw on the top hoop is opened to its maximum and placed gently over the fabrics. Tighten the screw slowly while adjusting the tensions of the layers. Do not leave the work to be quilted in the hoop when not working on it. The hoop creates too much tension and is abrasive to appliques that may be caught under the edge of the two hoops. The screw type may be loosened and set to the side carefully without complete removal of the work. Always work from the center out when quilting (see Fig. 7−4).

## The Four-Board Mini-Frame

This small piece of quilting may be placed in a mini facsimile of the larger full floor frame. (See Fig. 7−4 top.) This can be purchased from quilt and needlecraft shops around the country or mail-order suppliers. It can be made

Fig. 7−4 Mini quilt frames (top and right) and large embroidery hoop (bottom left).

very simply at home with easy to handle tools and ¼ by 1½-inch lumber. This frame is made up of four slats that are cut 22 inches long. The slats will be laid one on top of the other and at each end center and drill three holes one inch apart. A folded piece of fabric is stapled to the edges below the holes with the raw edges against the wood; anywhere from ½ to a full inch will be serviceable. The slats are assembled with corner holes overlapping. The two horizontals are placed on the work surface and the verticals are placed on top of the slats. A set of small screw and bolts are placed into the corners to hold them fast.

The basted design block is stretched into the frame by first placing four pins at north, south, east, and west points. Then by gently pinning all around and into the corners, keeping fabric tight. The pins may be left in for the duration of the quilting, provided the pins are rust-proof, or the block can be basted onto the fabric around the frame (Fig. 7−4 right). Only in this mini-frame can we utilize the flexibility of straight pins to hold the work into the frame.

## Lap Quilting

A third method would be to dispense with the frame altogether and quilt in the lap. This produces quilting that is a little puffy because it lacks the tautness of the frame and the quilting loses some of its dimension. This author feels that her stitches are much longer when quilting without a frame; but if this method turns you on to quilting, it's for you, and have no reservations about it. Crafts should be as much fun as possible; no need to be a Patty Perfection.

## Machine Quilting

This fourth method is to quilt the basted unit on the machine. Review suggestions in Chapter 3 on machine quilting. It would be advisable to use a small stitch, perhaps 12 stitches to the inch. Remember always to start from the center when possible. The tendency with machine quilting is to quilt on the diagonal to fill in the background on an applique. Do not stop at the edge of the upper layers of face and batting, but continue the stitching to the raw edge of the backing.

# Assembling the Blocks

When all the design blocks have been quilted, they should be pressed. For an appliqued block, press on the right side with a cool iron. For a patchwork block, press with the design side of the face down. This will prevent the exposed batting from melting under an iron that may be too hot.

The quilted and pressed blocks are now arranged as they will look in the finished quilt on a large work surface (usually the floor). The blocks will be sewn in strips from top to bottom by placing the right sides of the backing together and seaming at the ½-inch seam line on the wrong side of the backing fabric. Do not catch the batting in this seam, only the backing. Keep repeating this until all the top to bottom strips are sewn. Finger press seams open. As each strip is sewn, replace it on the work surface, checking the alignment of the horizontal seams across the quilt. (See Fig. 7−1.)

On *applique* work, the edge of the face will be laying under the newly made opened seams. On *patchwork,* the raw edge of the design square of the patchwork will be some distance away, allowing a great deal of batting to show intentionally.

Turn the ¼-inch seam allowance to the back on the long sides of the short horizontal bands. Position the short bands over the center of the seams that are open and pin in place. Baste the sides of the band in place over the face of the quilt stitching through the face, batting, and backing (see Fig. 7−2d). Lay aside each long strip until all the horizontal bands are basted to the front. These will be again placed on the work surface to make sure that all the horizontal bands line up. Adjustments can be made at this time.

To stitch the bands permanently, you may then quilt stitch them in place by hand, either in your lap or in an embroidery frame. If you would prefer not to have a row of quilt stitching along the edges, then handstitch the bands with a hidden slipstitch and place the banded area into a hoop frame and apply intricate design quilting. Keep in mind that any band that is wider than 2 inches will have to have quilting on the edges or along the inside to hold it in place. This also strengthens the quilt. Plain bands can have novelty motifs at the intersections (see Figs. 3−6 and 3−7 for suggestions on band quilting).

If the quilting of the blocks has been done on the machine, the band should be applied with a straight or novelty stitch which also can be used for the quilting. It is a help to know that the diamond type of quilting is both fast and works very well with minimum distortions for machine quilting.

The same process of band application is then repeated for the long vertical bands of the quilt (see Fig. 7−1 center).

The distinct advantage of this method is seen immediately when the quilt is turned over. The back is smooth and appears to be made of large blocks, but most important, it is sturdy and attractive. For people with limited workspace or in need of a lap project, this method is ideal. There is another popular scrap technique for putting a blanket item together as you cut and sew; it is called Pre-Quilted Log Cabin and is found under Scrap Quilts in Chapter 8.

# American Stars Forever

American Stars Forever, shown in Fig. 5−33, was made by author for James Frager. The overall size is 74 by 92 inches and the pattern is given in Chapter 9.

*Materials*

   1 yard red for star and corners
   2½ yards navy for star and bands
   6 yards white for background
   6 yards backing (small overall pattern)
   72″ × 90″ batting

*Cutting*

20 white 18'' squares
80 navy star points
80 red star points
20 pieces batting 18'' squares
20 pieces backing 20'' squares
16 navy bands 2½'' × 20''
3 navy bands 2½'' × 94''
5'' wide navy bands for outer binding
2 bands 6'' × 72'' for top and bottom
2 bands 6'' × 94'' for sides

# Borders for Block-by-Block Quilts

The use of borders on quilts serves two purposes. One is to enlarge the quilt and the second is to add an outer boundary to the quilt. As a picture frame enhances the picture, the border enhances the quilt. In previous chapters, the border has been an integral part of the totally assembled face. Now the quiltmaker is faced with an entirely different problem since the borders have to be added after the main section is made and quilted. There are two approaches to this border—either a one-piece border or a multipieced border. The width of the border can be the same width as the bands or wider. When making a quilt with bands, it is best to keep the border the same shade as the bands in the quilt since this gives it uniformity.

## One-Piece Border

Select the width of the border that best suits your quilt. Double the width and add ½ inch to each side and length. Begin by applying the border to the face of the quilt, right sides together. Then sew through all the layers, attaching the border permanently to the quilt. Turn the quilt right side down on the work surface. Place batting, cut the width of the desired border, near the newly sewn raw edge. Fold the remaining border material to the back folding the ½ inch raw edge to the inside and slipstitching in place against the backing. Attach the top and bottom borders first and add the two side borders last. Then turn the ends of borders to inside and slipstitch.

If the borders are 2½ inches or larger, apply quilt stitching to hold the batting from shifting. Put the border into an oval frame if available and quilt in a complimentary pattern. It might be good to point out that if you buy 45-inch fabric for the border equal to the length of the quilt and divide it lengthwise four times, you will have no waste. Each panel will then be 11 inches wide by the length of the quilt. When this is folded in half and applied, it will yield a 5-inch finished border. If you want to add a wide border, purchase a double length of fabric and cut in half lengthwise. Each panel will be 22 inches wide, but 10 inches finished when folded and attached to the quilt.

## Multipiece Border

This offers an intricate look to the border, but it has a simple application. The width of the multi-strip border may vary as well as the number of bands used. For example, let us say we have a red, white, and blue quilt and we want to add a 6-inch border. First cut two 2½-inch strips of each color for each side of the quilt to be bordered (a total of 24 strips). Then begin work on top and bottom bands only. First, place one red band in position on the top of the quilt right sides together and baste in place. On the back of the quilt, baste another red band with the right side of the band against the right side of the backing of the quilt (Fig. 7—5a). Sew permanently, catching the two bands and the quilt layers in one row of stitches and press both bands away from the quilt. Fill with batting and baste the edges together (Fig. 7—5b). Repeat for other sides. Apply the second, white set of bands onto the red bands as the red bands were applied to the quilt. Apply the blue bands to the white bands after pressing and filling. Turn the two outer raw edges to the inside and finish with a hidden slipstitch or a row of quilt stitches. This last band may be finished with binding as described in Chapter 3.

Knowledge of this border method is important in several other situations. If you have made a quilt but find that you would have liked it bigger, put on a border this way. Baby quilts can be made to grow with a youngster by adding borders. This method can be used to replace a border on an old quilt where the border is worn or nonexistent.

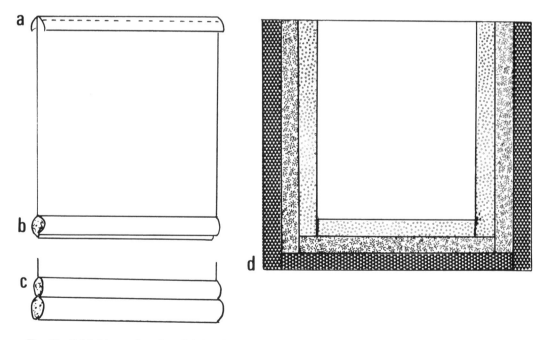

Fig. 7—5 Multi-strip border. (a) Apply two strips to the edge of the quilt. (b) Turn forward, fill with batting, and baste closed. (c) Repeat with two more strips. (d) Three finished strip borders on three sides of a quilt.

# CHAPTER

# *Scrap Techniques and Crazy Quilting*

One thing that is common to all home sewers is the large amount of unused yardage in odd shapes. One and two hundred years ago when almost all garments were made at home, this excess material was used up in quilting. Quilting was often done with little more thought than to use up the scraps, cutting them into common shapes such as pyramids and squares.

For many, this may be an opportunity to turn one's creativity onto a hodgepodge of scraps and to magically turn them into a work of art. Two traditional techniques still used today are "strip work" and "crazy quilting." One is the use of strips of fabric and the other uses odd shaped pieces of fabric sewn together with decorative stitches.

## Strip Techniques

The three most popular designs are Rail Fence, Roman Stripe and the intricate looking, but simple to make, Log Cabin. In this technique, long strips of the same size are made from the scraps and are separated into color groups of lights and darks.

### Rail Fence

Flip back to the directions for this quilt in Chapter 5 and to the color insert. It can be made as shown with careful color coordination of each patch. To the scrap artist, it can be worked in four color tones—dark, medium, light, and no color or white. An alternate to the method described in Chapter 5 is to cut long strips across 45-inch width fabric, or whatever width you have, and assemble long lengths in color groups such as assorted browns, oranges, yellows, and whites. Cut the strips all the same width. For example, cut strips 2 inches wide by maximum length and sew on the machine with 10 stitches to the inch or by hand using ¼-inch seams, and press. When you are finished, you will have a multicolor strip 6½ inches wide, including both outer seam allowances. Cut the strip horizontally 6½ inches across (Fig. 8–1a) and follow the pattern given in Fig. 5–20. This method uses up a lot of scrap yardage quickly.

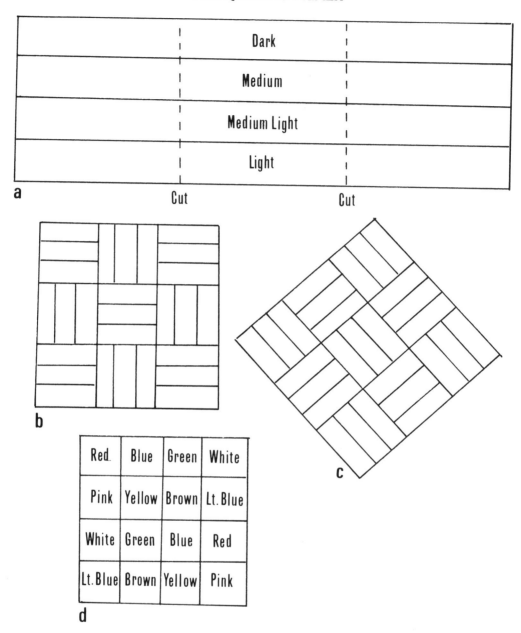

Fig. 8–1 (a) Stripping colors together for Rail Fence. (b) Setting triple strips together for Roman Stripe. They can be set into the quilt horizontally and vertically or (c) on the diamond. (d) Setting assorted colors together for Hit or Miss.

## Roman Stripe

This version is made the same way as above, but it uses three strips and its most effective coloration is to use a very light strip in the middle with assorted colors on either side. The best size for this pattern is 3 to 4-inch square blocks. For a finished 3-inch square, cut the strips 1½ inches wide, including the ¼-inch seam allowance. When the three strips are assembled in long lengths, then cut

Fig. 8–2 Background: Diamond Pyramid quilt, made by Barbara Hillerman. Left: Diagonal stripe pillow. Center: Roman Stripe quilt, in which the pattern is set on the diagonal, made by Vivian Talbot. Right: Mixed Wrench quilt, made by Mary Gormley. Foreground: Pyramids quilt, owned by Doris Wickman.

across at 3½-inch intervals. Sew the small squares, alternating the small blocks horizontally and vertically until you have formed a block of say four across and four down. After a number of these blocks are made, then put them together to form a quilt top (see Figs. 8—1b and 8—1c).

Hit or Miss is a perfect name to apply to a scrap quilt and many beginners are encouraged to work on a series of assorted squares to perfect their basic skills. Having gained some knowledge of strip techniques, the quilt called Hit or Miss proceeds at a fast pace. Instead of cutting and marking each small square, cut long strips all the same width from existing fabric. Stitch three to five strips together down the length. Repeat the process but alternate the color sequence (Fig. 8—1d). Press seams open or toward the dark color and cut horizontally, forming four even sized squares. Arrange them into larger squares of four by four, turning the colors upside down and assorting the strips as you go. You have to have at least three long strips of differing color combinations before starting to set them back to squares. Do not fuss too much about what color sits next to what color. Remember this is called Hit or Miss. If you have a large amount of scraps, then you may color them into coordinate color groupings such as earth tones, pastels, or monotones of one shade.

## Log Cabin

This is a true American design which originated in this country about 1850. Although it looks intricate, it is one of the easiest patterns to make up after the initial logs or strips are cut. The pattern must be understood to be effective and it is best worked in two color values—lights and darks. It is best to discard the medium colors.

When I first examined this pattern in depth, I could not understand why some quilts were such gems of color perfection and others were such a hodgepodge. The answer lay in the quilters basic intention. The well-colored quilts had a quiltmaker who understood the meaning of the pattern and the effect of the light and dark colors and the assorted-colored quilts had a quiltmaker who wanted merely to use up her small scraps.

This pattern takes its name from the intersecting logs of the original log cabins brought to the new world from the Scandinavian countries. This type of cabin spread quickly in the new colonies due to the abundance of wood in this country. As the sun rose and set on the cabins, traveling the sky in its east to west direction, part of the cabin was left in shadow. This is why the patch is colored in lights and darks—divided on the diagonal. The small square in the middle represents the chimney and is most often found in a warm color tone.

An assortment of dark colors such as navy, kelly green, burnt orange, brown, wine, and black and light colors such as pale yellow, pink, tan, sky blue, green or orange are cut in strips. The colors used may be all in the same color family with a wide range of lights and darks. Traditionally, the quilt is made of small calico prints. The smaller the logs, the smaller the prints must be to be effective. Another important fact is that there should be two to three times as many prints and/or solids as the number of logs on one side, counting out from the center. For example, the largest pattern given here has four logs from the center; there should be 8 to 12 different prints or solid colors for each side. The outside logs should have a good assortment of patterns (Fig. 8−3, top left.)

The pattern can be adapted to a modern look by using shades of two strong colors for the logs, thus accenting the geometric effect (Fig. 8−3, top right). Most often, it is made of solid colors such as black and white with a red chimney and/or red and navy with a gold chimney.

Among quilt collectors, a real prize is a log cabin quilt made of ribbons. Since ribbon was known to be plentiful in the making of clothes of the Victorian Day, the leftovers were used in quilts. (See color insert and Fig. 8−3, bottom.)

*Cutting a Log Cabin Quilt Top*   Understanding the strip techniques of making Log Cabins will save hours of measuring, marking, and cutting individual light and dark strips. For our example, we are going to use a standard size measurement. Wash and press all fabric to be used. Select at least eight different light and eight different dark prints. Cut strips of fabric across the width of the fabric 2½ inches wide, including seam allowance. If using scraps, these strips should be left as long as possible and rolled into whatever length you have, but

Fig. 8−3 Log Cabin pattern in assorted sizes. The two pillows are made of cotton blend fabric, and the quilt is made of ribbons.

must be on the straight of the grain. Roll each strip of fabric and place in light or dark groups.

To start a patch, cut one bright colored chimney for center, 3 by 3 inches, and call this square 1 (Fig. 8–4b). Select a light strip of fabric (piece 2) and place it against square 1, right sides together. Make a ¼-inch seam along one edge. Sew from raw edge to raw edge. Cut strip 2 the same size as square 1. Finger press the seam allowance away from the chimney. Turn the patch so that strip 2 is to the right of square 1 and place another dark strip 3 across the top of the 1–2 piece, right sides together (Fig. 8–4c). Make a ¼-inch seam and open; finger press seam allowance away from the chimney. Cut piece 3 so that it is even with square 1. Turn the patchwork so that piece 3 is to the right of 1. Select a dark

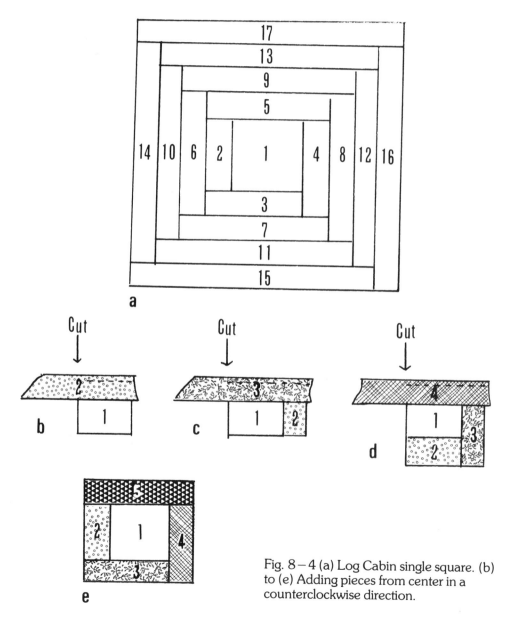

Fig. 8–4 (a) Log Cabin single square. (b) to (e) Adding pieces from center in a counterclockwise direction.

strip 4 and stitch across the $1-3$ raw edge. By now you realize that you are working in a circular fashion. Cut strip 4 evenly with the $1-2$ length and add another dark strip 5, measuring as above. Repeat the darks and lights.

Add three strips on each side of the center chimney and the block will measure 15½ by 15½ inches, raw edge to raw edge, with a total of thirteen pieces. Or add another set of light and dark logs to make a total of seventeen pieces or a finished block of 19½ by 19½ inches.

As you work, two things must be remembered: press all seams away from the center and use numerous prints on the outer edge. Try to have enough variety of prints so that when the patterns come together in the final quilt they will continue to look interesting. Try a few samples—remember it will take a little longer for the first ones, both in the sewing and the selecting of colors. This truly is a very fast method of working and that fact is borne out by the number of surviving antique quilts and the number of new quilts made today.

Make a sample as suggested and you will soon see how easily this pattern can be varied. The square can be any size and logs can be ½ to 2 inches wide. The smaller the log size and the more of them in a quilt, the greater its intrinsic value.

After you make a few samples that please you, it is easy to plan your quilt. Measure the bed and decide how many patches you will need across and down the bed. Yardage is difficult to figure out on an exact basis, but what most of us do is to select 8 to 12 dark and 8 to 12 light prints and buy about ⅓ to ½ yard of each. If you need more, just go back to the shops and buy some additional, different ones. A good rule of thumb would be that double bed quilts take about 6 to 8 yards. As you work, remember this is a good way to use up all the small scraps that have been around for years.

The most popular arrangement of this pattern is called Barn Raising. It forms concentric diamonds of light and dark. Start with the 4 corners of light or dark to the center and build the concentric lines of color from there (see Fig. $8-5$). The second most popular overall design is to arrange the lights and darks to form diagonals across the entire quilt; that is called Straight Furrow. This is the only popular pattern I know of that has both a pattern name and a variety of names for the ways in which the design squares are placed. (Study Fig. $8-3$ and color insert for designs.)

This pattern may be quilted around the inside of each log or every other log or it may be tied. (See suggestions under Crazy Quilts at the end of this chapter.) It is generally finished with a bias binding although sometimes the back is used as a border.

*Pre-Quilted Log Cabin*    This is a very old method in which each block is quilted at the same time it is being assembled. Cut the backing square for each block ½ inch larger than the finished square of the top. Cut a piece of batting the same size as the finished design square. Fold the backing square into four to find the center and place a pin coming through from the right side to the wrong side at that center. Place the backing on the work surface right side down. Center the batting on top of the wrong side of the backing, allowing the upright pin to come through the batting at the center. Baste two diagonal lines of basting stitches

Fig. 8 – 5 Log Cabin used in a Barn Raising design; must have an even number of blocks to be effective.

across the batting and backing to hold them firm (Fig. 8 – 5a to c). Take the square of fabric to be used for the center chimney and fold it twice to find its center. Place the center of the chimney square over the upright pin with the wrong side down against the batting. All three pieces are now lined up to the center. Turn the pin back into the fabric to hold the square in place temporarily. Baste around the edge of the square, making sure it is centered over the backing. You are stitching through all three layers.

Now proceed as above for additional strips, quilting through the strip, batting, and backing. When a row of stitches is finished, make sure the last stitches are very secure by using an overcast or backstitch. Keep working until you come to the outside of the square. The quilting will not show on the face of the quilt but this is a rather strong and a relatively quick way to work. When all the pre-quilted blocks are ready to be assembled into a quilt, lay them out on the floor in either of the suggested overall designs—Barn Raising or Straight Furrow. Assemble the squares into strips the length of the quilt by placing the tops together and sewing along the seamlines for the tops. To facilitate easy handling, pin the backing out of the way. If you find that you prefer to do this on the machine, it is best to use a zipper foot as in Fig. 5 – 11. The batting will not be caught in the seam since it should be the exact size of finished block. Open the blocks and place them face down on the work surface. Proceed with suggestions for joining seam in Figs. 5 – 11 to 5 – 14 for a piece that will receive hard wear. For a piece that will receive limited wear, extend one piece of the backing over

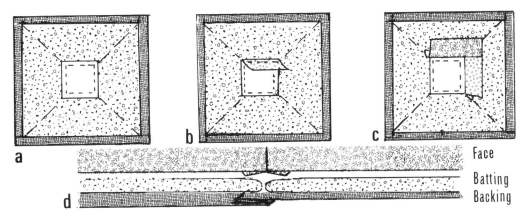

Fig. 8−6 Prequilted Log Cabin block. (a) Square sewn down. (b) Place the first strip over one side of the square. (c) Turn the square counterclockwise to add each additional piece. (d) Alternate seam finishing technique.

the freshly made seam and fold the edges of the remaining lining piece under ½ to ⅓ inch and place so it will overlay the other lining edge. Baste through all three layers and blindstitch the two linings together, but do not go through to the other side. Repeat this until you have strips the length of the quilt; then sew the strips together to finish the quilt. Bias bind the edges.

# Pyramid Scrap Quilts

Pyramid Patterns. The pyramid shape is a little more interesting to use in a scrap quilt than the square or the rectangle. Even in scrap quilts there is a great sense of appreciation for the triangular-shaped patterns. The simplest ones are the equilateral triangles as seen in Fig. 8−2, left bottom. Here a random selection of solid colors live in happy harmony. This quilt was made from silky type fabrics and tied to a backing of taffeta. To do this make rows of triangles as shown in Fig. 2−7a. This places one triangle upward and the next downward. Then sew the rows together.

## Diamond Pyramid Quilt

The Diamond Pyramid Quilt on the wall in Fig. 8−2 is a super easy beginners quilt, using solids, checks, and small prints. The assortment was made in blue and brown colors. The pattern elements are three different sized triangles and one square. The pleasing effect in this pattern is the alternate use of blocks of a predominating color. The square begins with a medium or light color, a small triangle is dark, and a medium triangle is light with the largest triangle being dark and solid. The finished block is 17 by 17 inches and there are three blocks across and five down the quilt, with a border of 10 inches on the sides and 7 inches on top and bottom. A diamond patterned quilting design enhances the borders. The overall size of the quilt is 71 by 99 inches and was made as a beginner quilt by Barbara Hillerman.

Since this was a scrap quilt, its face yardage cannot be estimated accurately. The best way to do this is assemble several of the small yardages sleeping in your remnant box. Start with the biggest triangle in the corners and pick two dominant colors for the corners. Then work the remaining colors from the scraps at hand. Yardage for the backing would be 6 yards, batting would be 71 by 99 inches. Two inches of the backing is used as a binding. This quilt would look just as well with narrow binding. I can see it in wool remnants tied to a smooth cotton backing with its edges turned to the back with binding. To make patterns for a 17-inch finished design square, add a seam allowance to each of the following:

$6'' \times 6''$ center square;
$4\frac{1}{4}'' \times 4\frac{1}{4}'' \times 6''$ small triangle;
$6'' \times 6'' \times 8\frac{1}{2}''$ medium triangle;
$8\frac{1}{2}'' \times 8\frac{1}{2}'' \times 12''$ large triangle.

# Mixed Wrench Scrap Quilt

*Mixed Wrench* is a scrap quilt that uses a traditional pattern in a variety of colored scraps. The wrench comes in many shapes, generally an even nine-patch motif but some people prefer it with an elongated cross through the center. Often the center itself is cut into another nine patch. (See Fig. 8−2 and color insert.) The word mixed before the pattern names usually indicates that it is a scrap pattern, like pot luck supper would mean.

The quilt in Fig. 8−2 was made in bright colors of lavender, purple, and pink with a little green as an accent color. The strong lavender print used on the outer most triangles and the center square creates unity in this quilt. The other triangles and two side strips are of differing prints. A scrap quilt of this type looks best in color families such as earth tones, pastels, or flag colors. This quilt has a

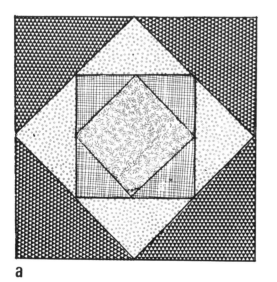
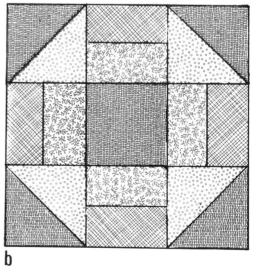

a                                                          b

Fig. 8−7 (a) Diamond Pyramid (b) Mixed Wrench.

15-inch block and the face was made from scraps; the strong lavender color accounted for about 2 yards. There are 5 blocks across and 6 down the quilt. The backing, a complimentary paisley print in pastels, was used as a 2-inch binding. Use 6 yards for the backing if made as suggested with 79 by 94 inches of batting. Overall completed size of quilt is 79 by 94 inches. This pattern uses one 5-inch square for center, one 5-inch square divided on the diagonal for corners (using two colors), and a 5-inch square divided in half lengthwise (using two different prints).

# Crazy Quilting

Surprisingly the needlecraft form referred to as Crazy Quilting is never really quilted with a batting and backing. The quilt is made with a very flat type filler such as a sheet or thin blanket. The Crazy Quilt reached its peak of popularity in the Victorian Period. It was mostly used as a show piece in the parlor or thrown over a table or piano. Although you can find them in wools and cottons, rayon and its predecessor silk dominated the face decoration. The arrangement of the pieces were as individual as their colors, some people preferring soft, rounded shapes and others stiff, angular shapes. The selected pieces were sewn to a very thin piece of backing material. Generally they were made in blocks of a consistent size which were then sewn together to form the entire quilt top. Sometimes, you will find one where the pieces were all applied to a large solid background. Since they were decorative pieces, they also served as a memory book for the family. The quiltmaker gathered her pieces of fabric from favorite pieces of clothing that had special sentimental value. Remnants of party, wedding or baby dresses, special ribbons, labels, and old ties all held their special place. The texture was enhanced with moire silks, lustrous satins, novelty brocades, and plushy velvets, all laying side by side.

How well these basic elements of shapes, color, and texture are arranged depend on the crafter's eye. The ultimate crowning glory is the embroidery over seams. The intricacy and the originality of the needlework that covered the seam lines was in itself another display of the needlecrafter's skills. The embroidery was also a place to use up remnant thread left over from other projects. Today on the cotton blend quilts, three-strand cotton embroidery floss is used. The most common stitch is the feather stitch, with herringbone running a close second. One thing they both have in common is that they span the seam line evenly. Sometimes pieces would be embroidered with small designs before they were attached; I've seen designs painted on velvet. It was common to embroider names and initials onto the fabrics for memories sake.

## Starting a Crazy Quilt

Most of us do not have access to a lot of silky material, but can work in cotton and cotton blends successfully (Fig. 8−8). It is advisable to start with a small project such as a pillow, set of place mats, a handbag, a table cloth or throw, a centerpiece for table, a Christmas tree base cover, or Christmas

Fig. 8—8 Close-up of two pieces of crazy quilting: a pillow cover and a large quilt (see also Fig. 5—33).

stocking. To make a piece of clothing, you must have a shaped and fitted base such as a muslin vest or skirt.

Assemble what fabric you have on hand and purchase small yardages to compliment your selection. This is the time to ask friends for small scraps of fabric from their work baskets. You will be surprised what you will turn up.

Select a base fabric that is easy to sew on and has been pre-shrunk. It is best to work on pre-cut background squares. Begin by placing one small piece of fabric in the upper left hand corner, if you are right handed (if left handed, start from the upper right corner). This way you will be working toward the most educated hand. Baste down the outside corner edges, but leave the inner edges open (Fig. 8–9a).

Turn under the inner edges and baste only the edges, do not baste to the backing fabric. Insert a second patch under the first and baste down where it touches the previous patch, leaving its edge free. Select a third piece and slip under the remaining open edges of first or second pieces (Fig. 8–9b), continuing to work in this manner until all the surface is covered (Fig. 8–9c and d). Sometimes an opening in the work will appear where you cannot find a suitable piece to fit. Then applique a shaped piece on top all the way around. It is also good to use some appliques to dress up the work as long as the shapes are kept simple, such as stars, hearts, crescent moons, clovers, spades, clubs, diamonds, and even fans.

Before doing any stitching, you may wish to arrange all the pieces on a given background. Do so by pinning all pieces in place until you are satisfied. Then go back to top left corner and begin to turn under edges as you proceed with basting. Remember, no raw edges should show.

When all the patches are basted into place, use a hidden slipstitch or a running stitch to attach them firmly to the background. Then apply embroidery as an embellishment. This embroidery work can also be done on the machine. It's best to use the brightest color thread in machine work so it will be seen as well as the three-strand hand embroidery thread.

## Beginner's Crazy Quilt

The quilt shown in Fig. 5–33 and 8–8 has been simplified and updated by using a combination of blues of differing values. The work has been made into a decorator piece for a specific room and uses a contrasting color thread in the feather stitch. Throughout the years, the crazy quilt was used as a way of getting rid of a multitude of scraps of fabric and yarn, and it still has great appeal to today's homemaker.

The base square of fabric is 18½ inches. Each square was started with approximately a 5-inch piece of blue at one corner. That keyed the patches to the matching blue border. There are four squares across and five squares down the length or twenty squares altogether with a 5-inch solid border and a print backing. The approximate overall size is 82 by 100 inches.

### Materials
5 yards backing
king-size sheet, blanket, or flannel for batting, seamed together to
measure same as backing

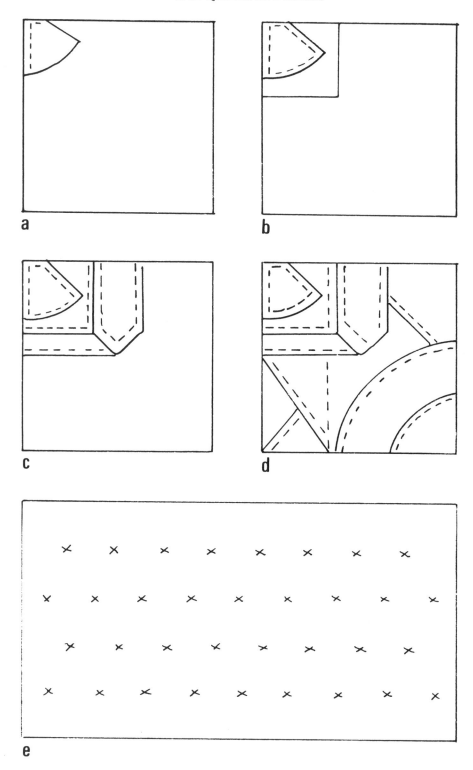

Fig. 8–9 Making Crazy Quilt patch. (a) to (d) Start by putting the first pieces in the upper left corner. (e) Classic pattern for tying a quilt.

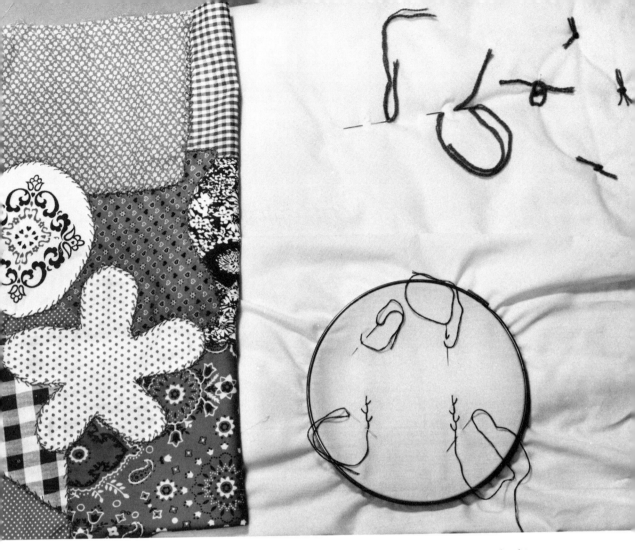

Fig. 8—10 Left: close-up of piece of Crazy Quilt. Top right: Steps in tying a quilted item (left to right). Bottom right: Steps in feather stitching (clockwise from upper left).

½ yard each of 12 to 15 different prints and solids for face
6 yards of thin cotton fabric for base of each block
20 skeins of cotton embroidery floss

After the blocks have been sewn together and border added, baste together as you would for a quilt to go into a frame. However, for the batting use a woven filler such as a pre-washed sheet, thin blanket, flannel or soft thermal summer blanket. Then proceed to tie each square with embroidery floss, crewel wool, or two-ply synthetic knitting yarn. It may be tied on the front or back and finished with a bow or a simple knot. Place one stitch through all layers of the quilt leaving a 1-inch end on the surface (Fig. 8—10). A second stitch is made over the first and the end is cut to 1 inch to match the first one. Then make a square-knot and allow the ends to hang loose, or trim to a pleasing length, or even tie them in a bow. This method is most secure if tied 4 to 6 inches apart along each row. A second row is spaced alternately between the ties of the first row. The tie placement can be in coordination with pattern of quilt (see Fig. 8—9e).

181

# CHAPTER

# *Patterns*

## How to Use Patterns

The patterns given here have been sized to the most popular ones used today. There are no small or odd-sized hand-me-down patterns—no quilts sized for yesterday's citizens who slept in 5-foot-square beds. The text lists, where possible, the number of light, dark, medium, or background pieces to be used. Here patterns are given exactly for most of the quilts pictured in the book. If it is a patchwork pattern, then each element can be found same size. If it is an applique pattern, almost all the elements are given here for the suggested size background. If the pattern is given alone or appears in a Sampler quilt, each pattern will give the number of pieces to cut per design block and size of background. There are variations on the star patterns given in conjunction with the basic 8-Point Star pattern that are difficult but all-time favorites.

*To all pattern elements, the ¼-inch seam allowance must be added.*

### Patchwork Patterns

One of the reasons patchwork is so well loved in America is that it is so easy to understand due to basic geometric shapes. All basic patchwork patterns are made from dividing a large square—usually into nine or more parts. Using a ruler and paper any combination is possible. The patchwork art is mostly based on various combinations of squares, rectangles, and triangles. Having this multiple set of basic geometric shapes, the crafter is not bound to just patterns that may appear in a text. It is easy to make a favorite pattern in a mini-size for a crib quilt worked in pastels or to enlarge the same pattern for your favorite football player and work with team colors. To provide a great many pattern elements in a small amount of space, there are a series of concentric sized basic squares, triangles, and rectangles.

If a pattern calls for cutting four 5-inch squares, simply look for the 5-inch square under basic squares. If it calls for a triangle, it will state, for example, a 5-inch square cut on the diagonal. If it calls for a quarter of a square, it will always mention the basic size of the square from which it is derived, saying 5-inch square cut in quarters. Find the basic square and sub-divide that twice on the diagonal to find the correct size triangle. If a patchwork pattern has odd shaped pieces, then the pieces are drawn for you here.

Color combinations in vogue today are suggested throughout the text. Be mindful that in some cases background colors are suggested. This often helps to define a design that has a rather definite motif such as a star. Use the line drawings in Chapter 2 as a guide for color tones; check to see if these designs appear in the photographs and then follow the suggested colors to get started.

## Applique Patterns

The applique patterns given in the first part of this chapter will coincide with the patterns as they appear in the book. Included here also are most of the patterns from the Friendship Sampler. There are much loved applique patterns such as the School House, Sunbonnet Sue, Farm Boy, and five different stars.

To save space we have not included enlarged circles as they are easily obtainable by using the compass or, as my mother taught me, the dinner plate. There are two ways to make the circles such as the Fig. 2 – 13c wreath; one is by cutting out an entire ring and placing it on the background with the edges turned back and flower over it, or by cutting out a piece of bias fabric sewing on the line, right sides together, with running stitches as one would do with a binding. This would cause the bias to stretch and curve along the widest arc of the circle's circumference. Then flipping the binding downward and slipstitching. This is the method used on the wreaths that appears in the Friendship Sampler.

There are assorted four, six, and eight petaled flowers given to accommo-date floral designs in Chapter 2 (Fig. 2 – 13). This will help you to design your own feelings on these garden specials. If you use dark color flowers and leaves, then you will have to use a spacious neutral background. If you are going to use light colors in the florals, then bring the floral pieces and the blocks closer together to help the eye delineate the designs. If the size of the flower motif is not exactly what you feel you need to do justice to your color sense, enlarge or reduce by adding quarter inches, using your ruler to measure ¼ inch in every direction.

Many patterns appear with a fold mark. It is best if you make a full-sized pattern from which to work, rather than place half a pattern on a fold of fabric, as in dressmaking. In this craft it is necessary to mark the cutting and sewing lines completely on each piece for a quilt.

As the sampler quilts were sent from around the country, the makers listed the patterns used with the pattern names they knew them by. In the case of patchwork, most patterns could be worked out by using Figs. 9 – 1 and 9 – 2. For applique, check for patterns in the index, but don't be afraid to work free-hand, combining pattern elements in Chapter 9.

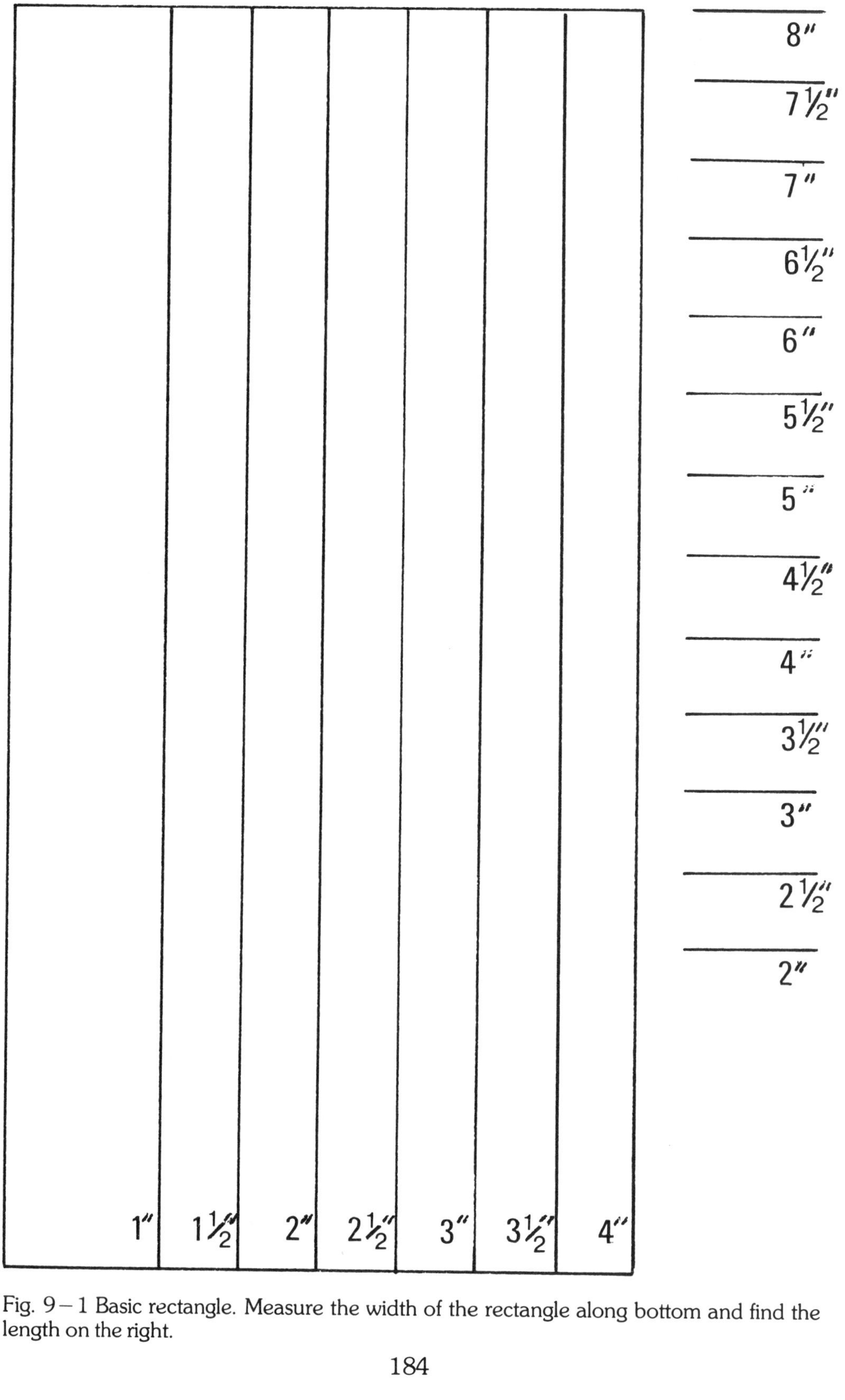

| 8" |
| 7½" |
| 7" |
| 6½" |
| 6" |
| 5½" |
| 5" |
| 4½" |
| 4" |
| 3½" |
| 3" |
| 2½" |
| 2" |

1"  1½"  2"  2½"  3"  3½"  4"

Fig. 9−1 Basic rectangle. Measure the width of the rectangle along bottom and find the length on the right.

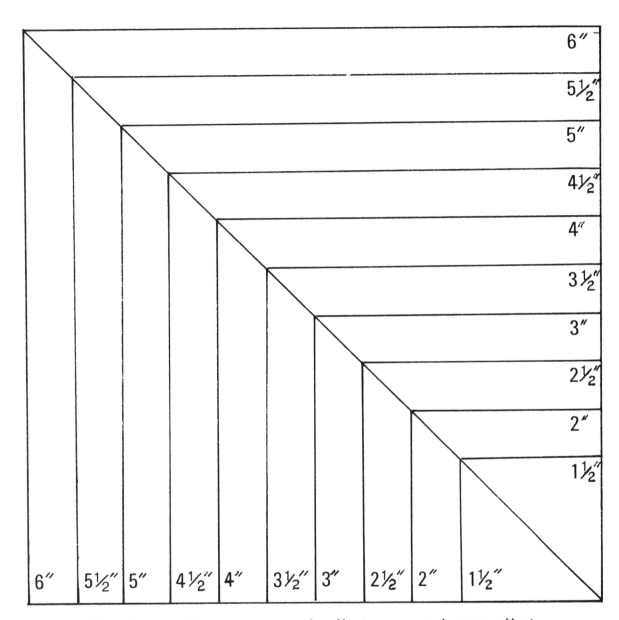

Fig. 9 – 2 Basic Square. All basic squares, triangles of basic squares, and quarters of basic squares can be worked from this shape. Trace the needed pattern element, add ¼-inch seam allowance, and transfer to a cardboard or plastic template.

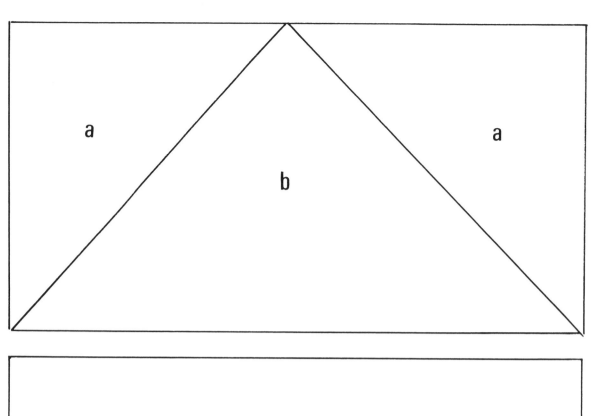

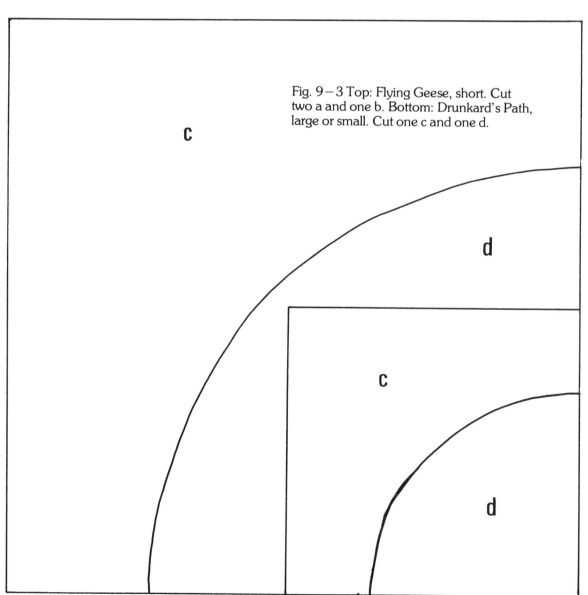

Fig. 9 – 3 Top: Flying Geese, short. Cut two a and one b. Bottom: Drunkard's Path, large or small. Cut one c and one d.

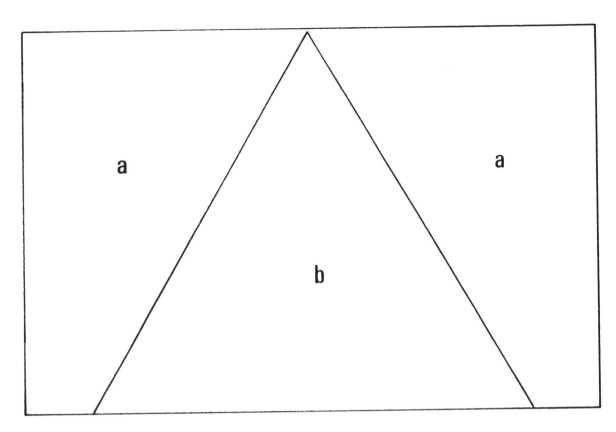

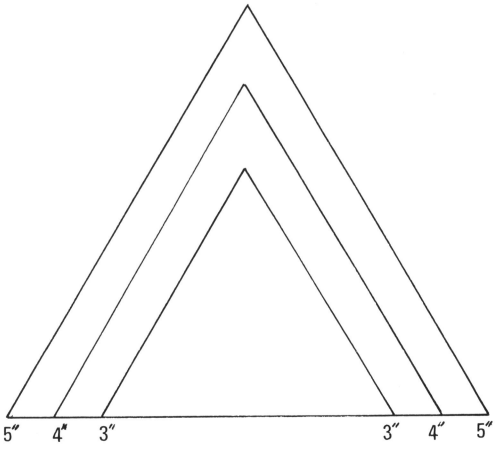

Fig. 9–4 Top: Flying Geese, tall. Cut two a and one b. Bottom: Equilateral triangles, 3 inches, 4 inches, and 5 inches.

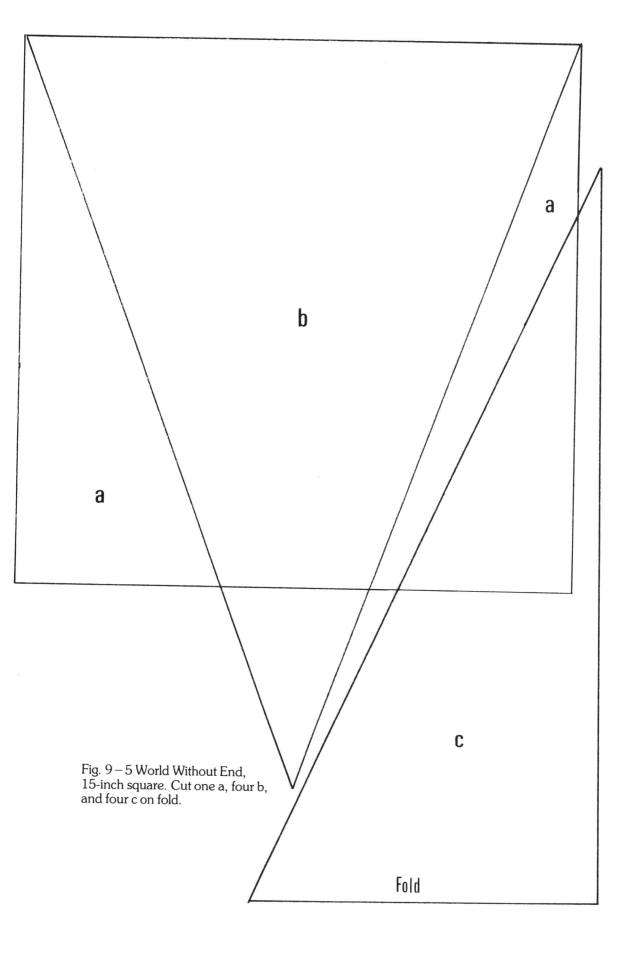

a

b

a

c

Fig. 9−5 World Without End,
15-inch square. Cut one a, four b,
and four c on fold.

Fold

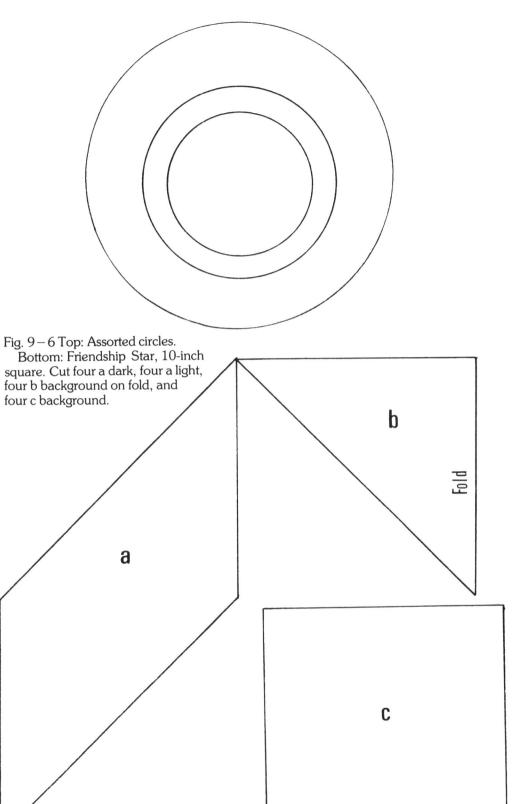

Fig. 9 – 6 Top: Assorted circles.
   Bottom: Friendship Star, 10-inch square. Cut four a dark, four a light, four b background on fold, and four c background.

b

Fold

a

c

189

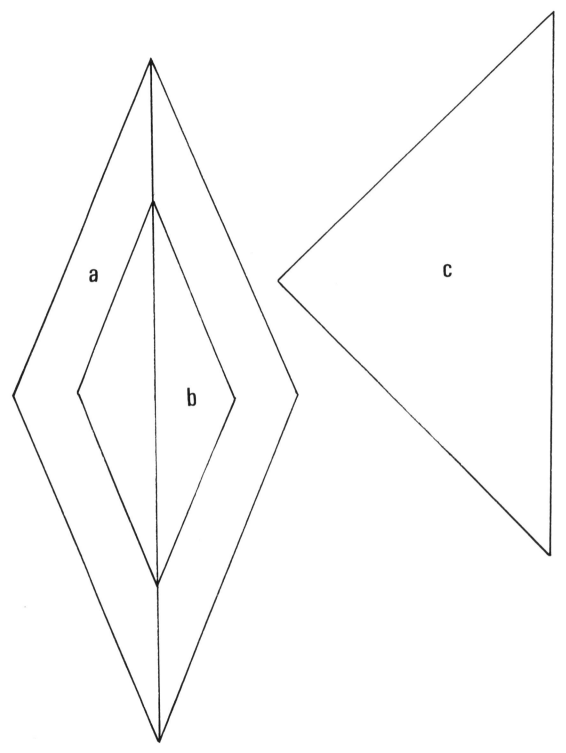

Fig. 9 – 7 Eight-Point Star. Use diamond a for 14-inch star and diamond b for 8-inch star. For background, cut four c. To make LeMoyne Star, cut the diamonds down the center.

190

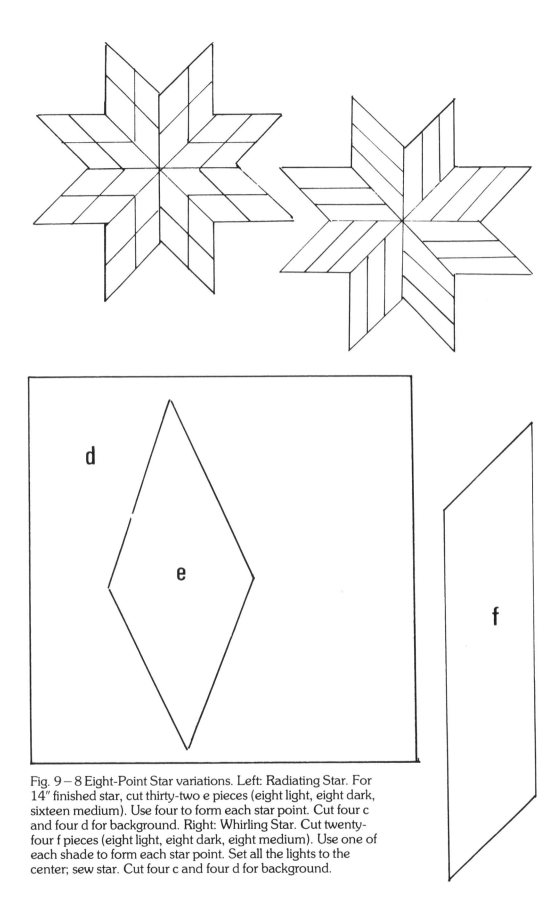

Fig. 9 – 8 Eight-Point Star variations. Left: Radiating Star. For
14″ finished star, cut thirty-two e pieces (eight light, eight dark,
sixteen medium). Use four to form each star point. Cut four c
and four d for background. Right: Whirling Star. Cut twenty-
four f pieces (eight light, eight dark, eight medium). Use one of
each shade to form each star point. Set all the lights to the
center; sew star. Cut four c and four d for background.

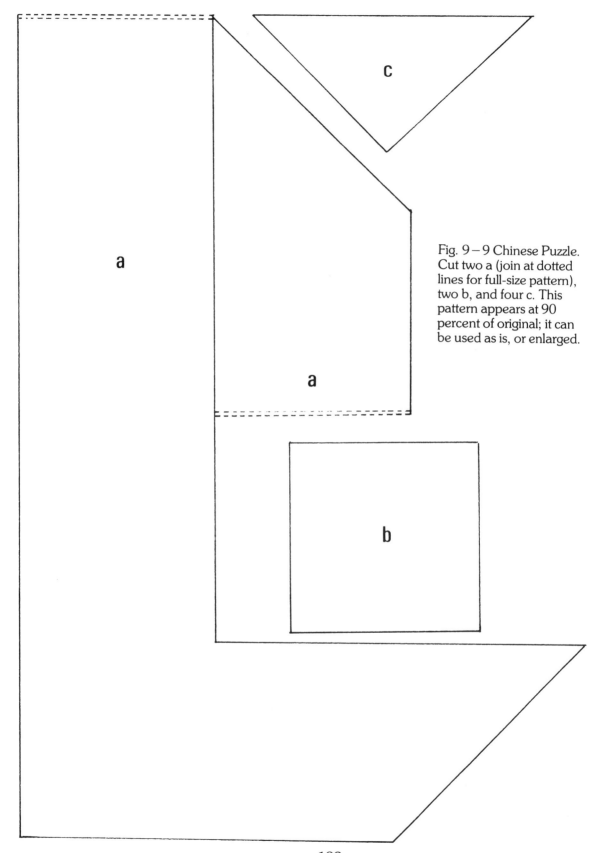

a

c

Fig. 9 – 9 Chinese Puzzle.
Cut two a (join at dotted
lines for full-size pattern),
two b, and four c. This
pattern appears at 90
percent of original; it can
be used as is, or enlarged.

a

b

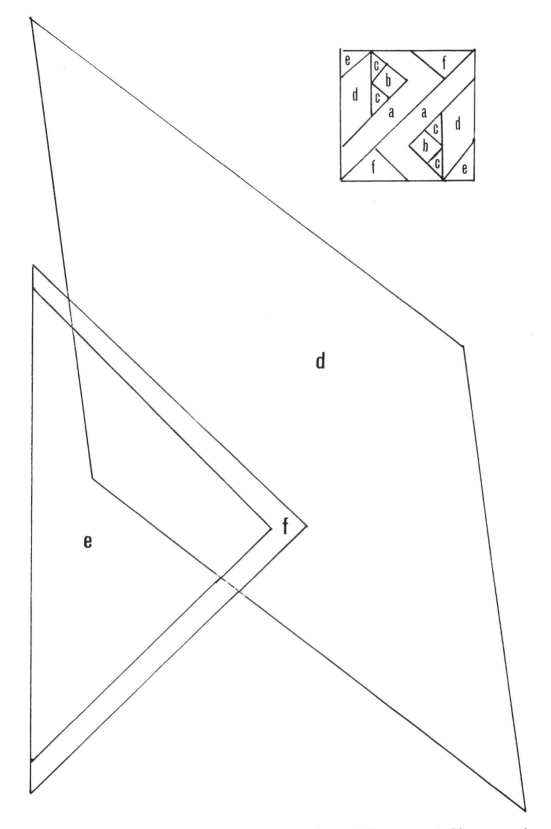

Fig. 9–10 Chinese Puzzle. Cut two d, two e, and two f. This pattern is 90 percent of original size.

193

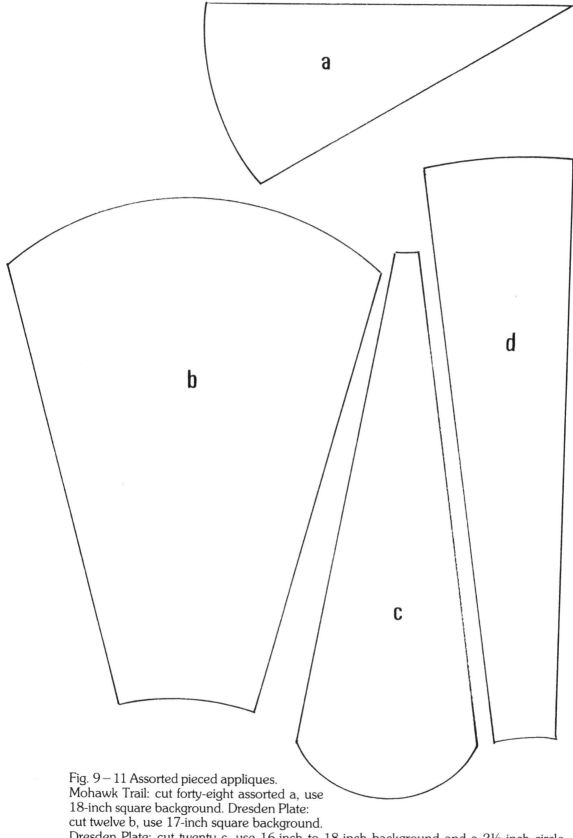

Fig. 9 – 11 Assorted pieced appliques.
Mohawk Trail: cut forty-eight assorted a, use
18-inch square background. Dresden Plate:
cut twelve b, use 17-inch square background.
Dresden Plate: cut twenty c, use 16-inch to 18-inch background and a 2½-inch circle
for center. Lace Trimmed Fan: cut thirteen assorted d and use 18-inch square background,
or cut twelve d and use 16-inch background. To make Grandmother's Fan, use five
assorted c, applique to 8-inch square, using ¼ of a 3-inch circle for the center.

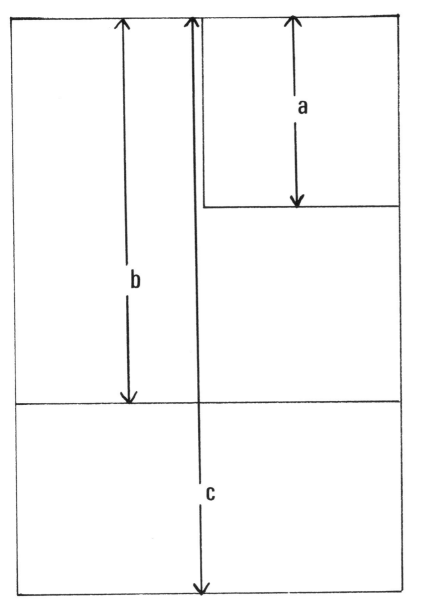

Fig. 9 – 12 Honey Bee. Cut nine a (five dark, four bright solid), four b (dark background), four c (dark background), and twelve d (four dark print, eight bright solid).

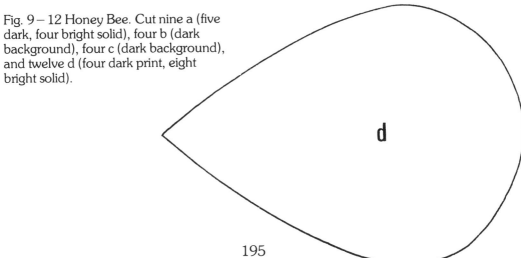

195

Fig. 9 – 13 Four-petal flowers.

Fig. 9 – 14 Six-petal flowers. Floral Wreath: cut four a or b, a 1-inch center circle if using a or a 2-inch circle if using b, and eight c. If using a, reduce c by ¼ inch; if using b, use c as is. Place the a flowers on a 14-inch background and the b flowers on an 18-inch background. Adjust the circle behind to your taste using any round object.

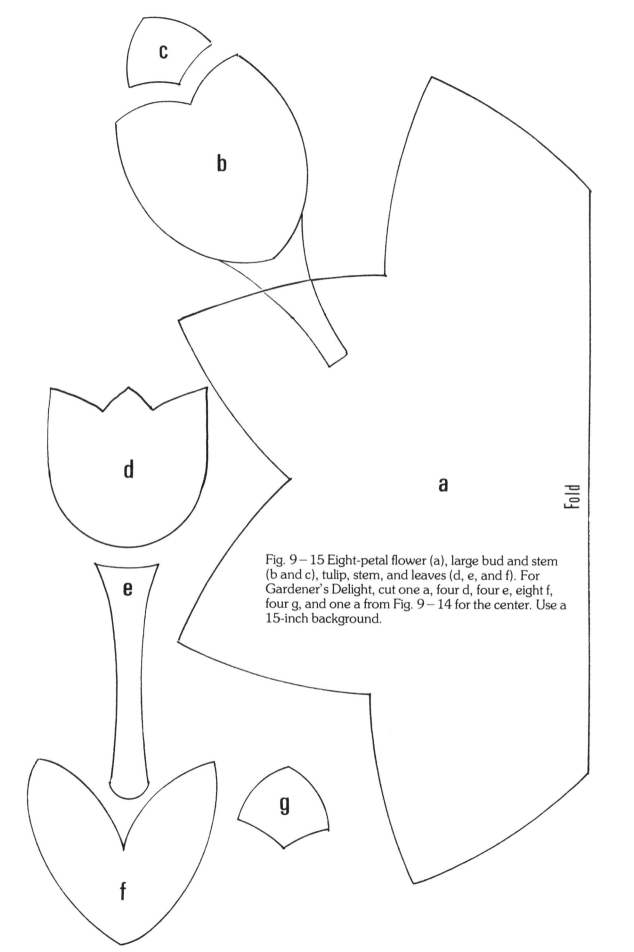

c

b

a

Fold

d

e

g

f

Fig. 9−15 Eight-petal flower (a), large bud and stem (b and c), tulip, stem, and leaves (d, e, and f). For Gardener's Delight, cut one a, four d, four e, eight f, four g, and one a from Fig. 9−14 for the center. Use a 15-inch background.

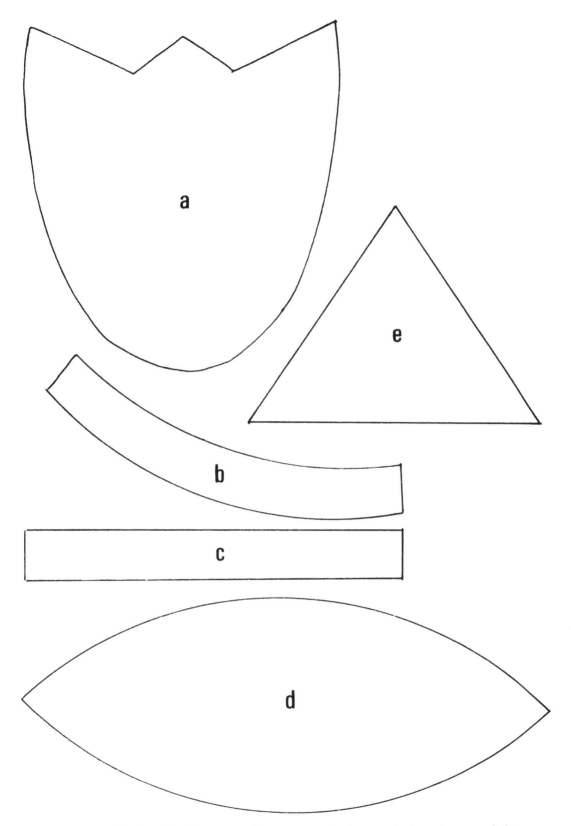

Fig. 9–16 Tulip Basket. Cut three a, two b, two c, two d, eleven e dark, and seven e light for patchwork basket. Add handle of your choice and place on 17-inch background.

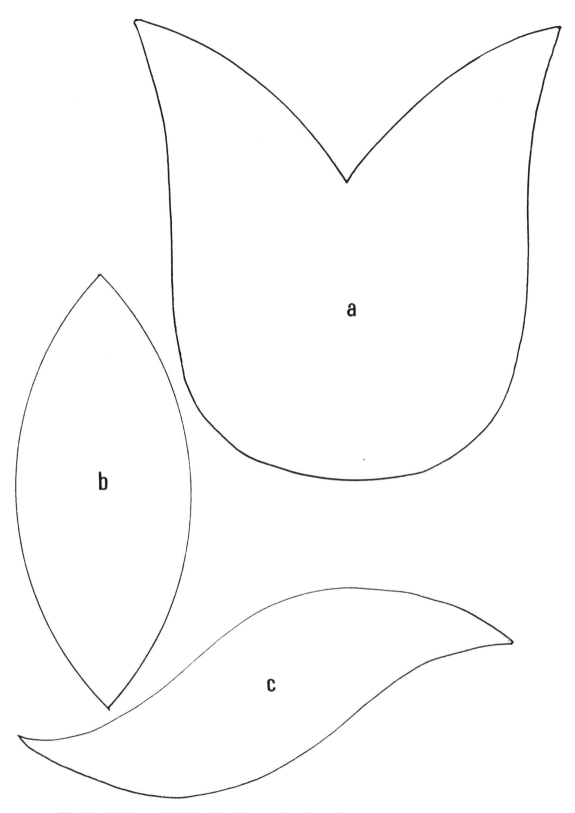

Fig. 9–17 Crossed Tulip. Cut four a, four b, and four c; place on 14-inch to 16-inch background.

200

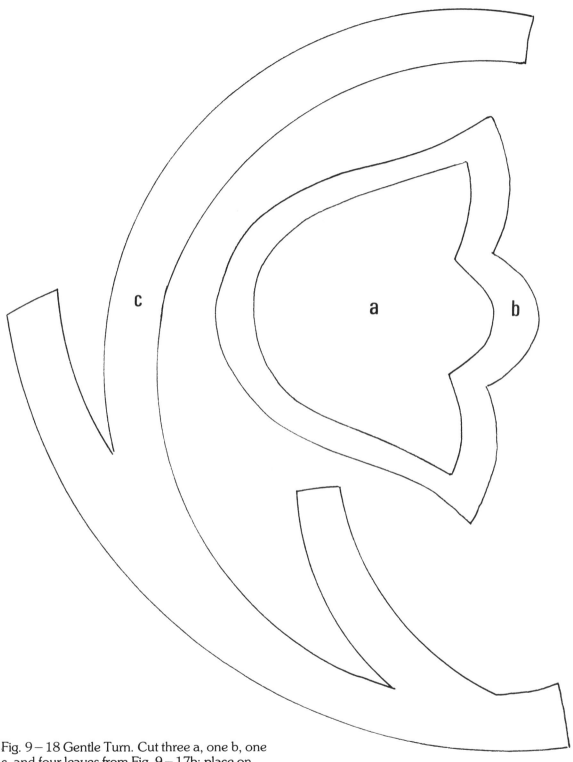

c

a

b

Fig. 9–18 Gentle Turn. Cut three a, one b, one c, and four leaves from Fig. 9–17b; place on 16-inch background.

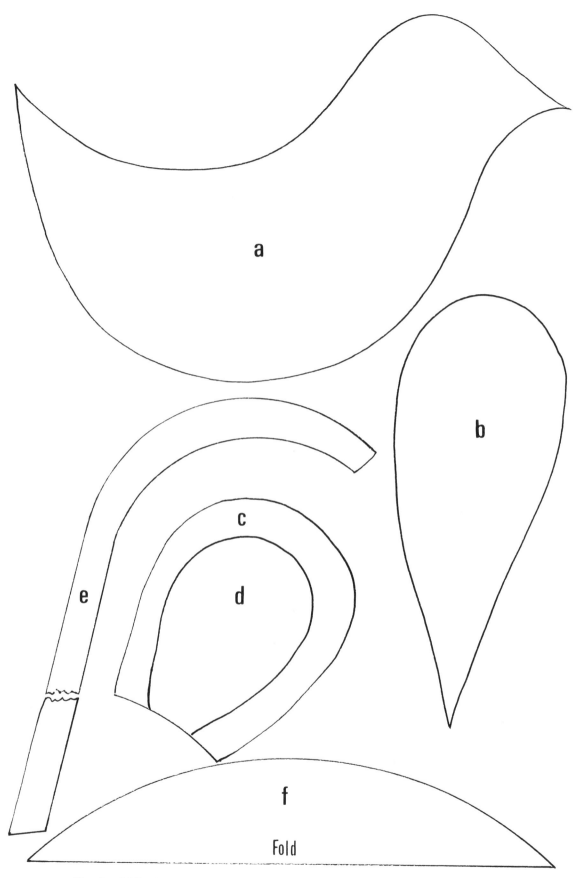

Fig. 9 – 19 Bird in the Bush. Cut one a, one b, five c, ten d, one e (9 inches long), and two f; place on 15-inch background.

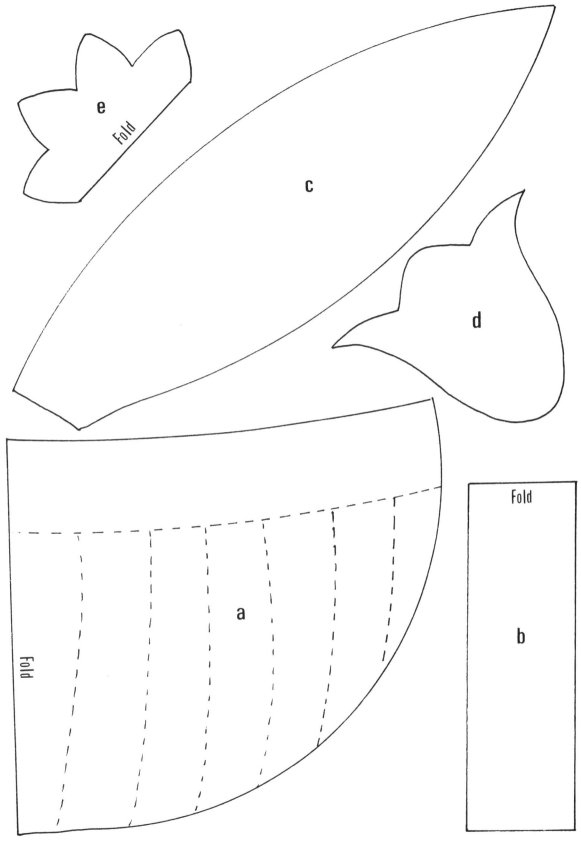

Fig. 9–20 Tulip Basket can have any set of flowers that appeals to you, such as flower d or e given here or the small flower from Fig. 9–14. Cut one a, one b, ten c, and five to seven d. Put on a 15-inch background and quilt or embroider a slat texture on the basket.

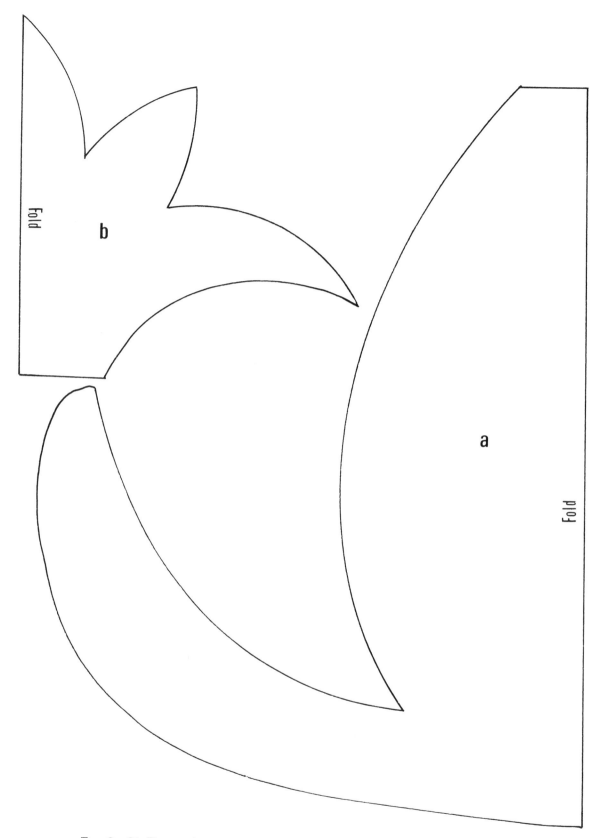

Fig. 9–21 Pineapple, approximately 14 inches when finished, can be placed on the diagonal on a 12-inch background or upright on a 15-inch background. Cut one a and one b. The large crescent piece at bottom may be a third color or the same color as b. This also looks good as a silhouette in one color.

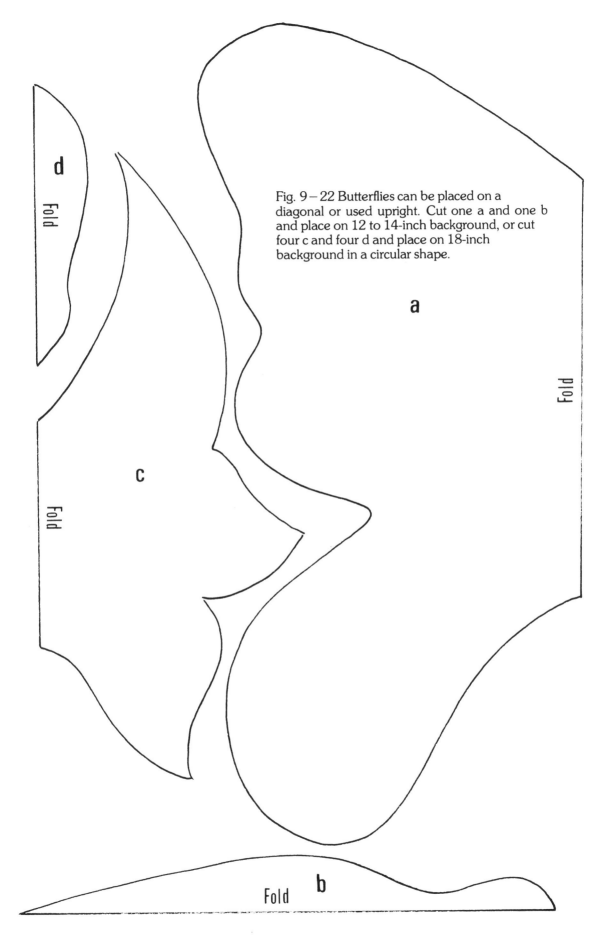

d

Fold

Fig. 9 – 22 Butterflies can be placed on a diagonal or used upright. Cut one a and one b and place on 12 to 14-inch background, or cut four c and four d and place on 18-inch background in a circular shape.

a

Fold

c

Fold

Fold    b

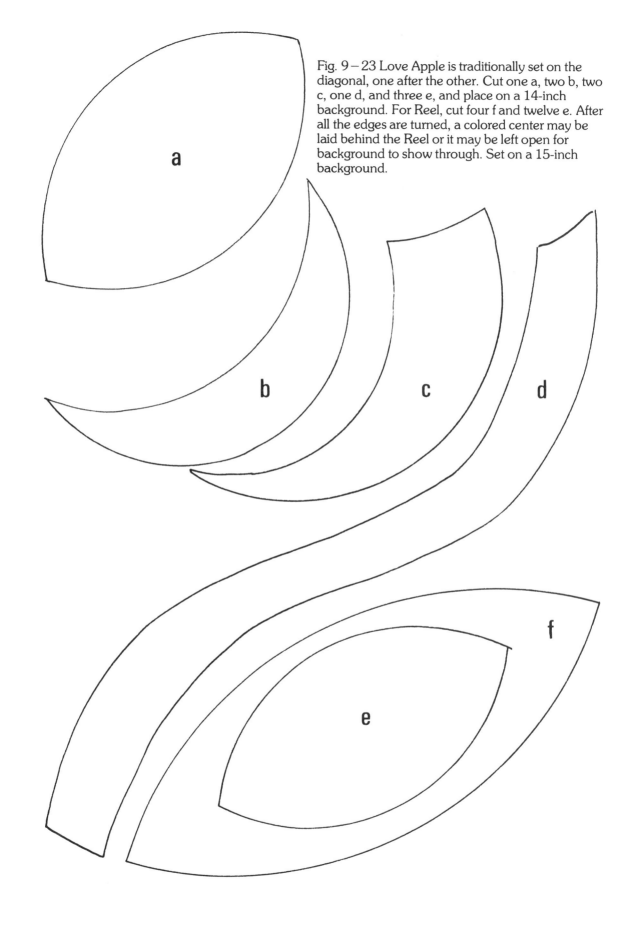

Fig. 9 – 23 Love Apple is traditionally set on the diagonal, one after the other. Cut one a, two b, two c, one d, and three e, and place on a 14-inch background. For Reel, cut four f and twelve e. After all the edges are turned, a colored center may be laid behind the Reel or it may be left open for background to show through. Set on a 15-inch background.

a

b

c

d

e

f

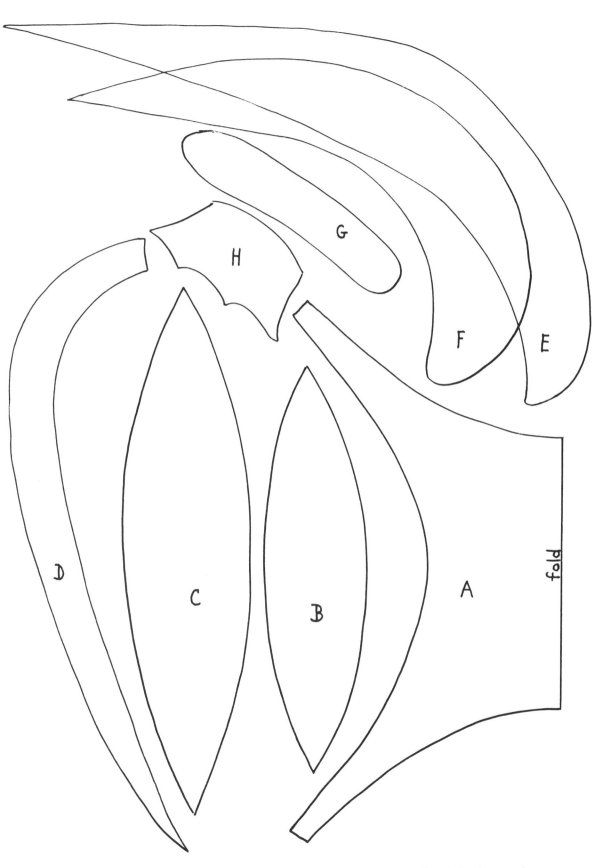

Fig. 9−24 Turkey Tracks: cut one a, eight b, and four c; place on 16-inch background.
Wind Blown Daffodil: use four 8-inch squares for background or one 16-inch square
background; cut four e, four f, four g, and eight h.

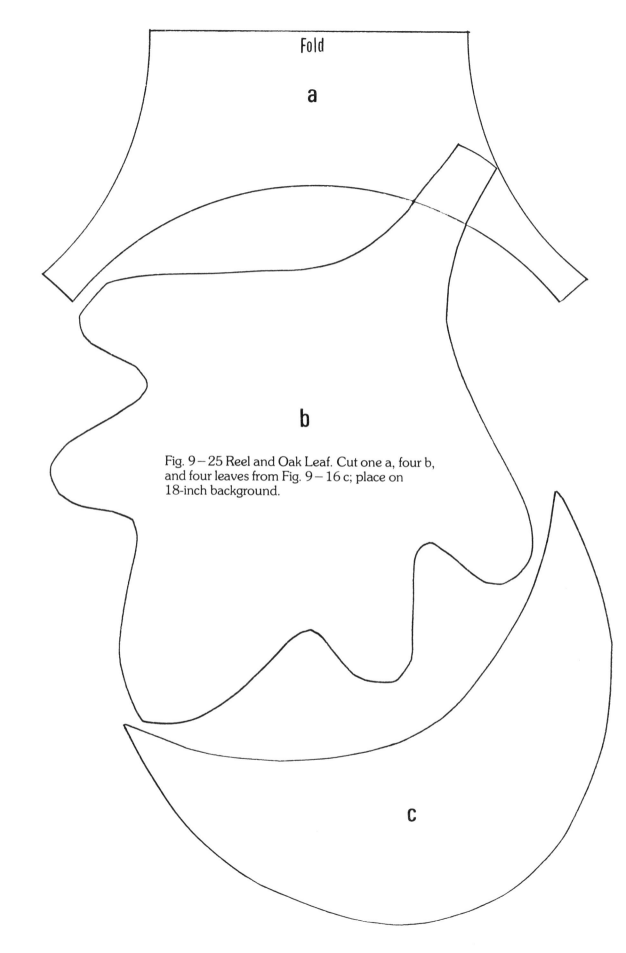

Fold

a

b

Fig. 9–25 Reel and Oak Leaf. Cut one a, four b, and four leaves from Fig. 9–16 c; place on 18-inch background.

c

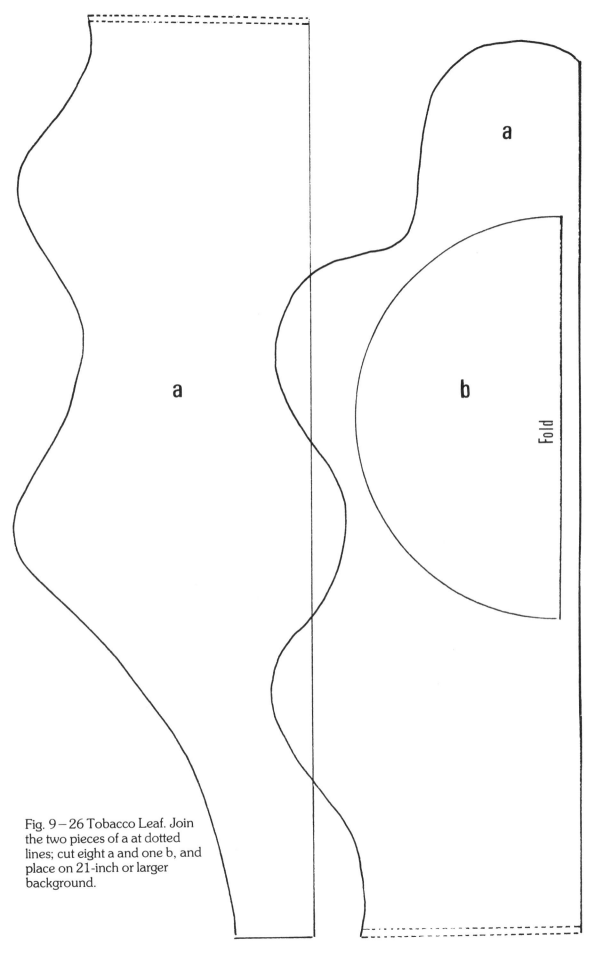

Fig. 9–26 Tobacco Leaf. Join
the two pieces of a at dotted
lines; cut eight a and one b, and
place on 21-inch or larger
background.

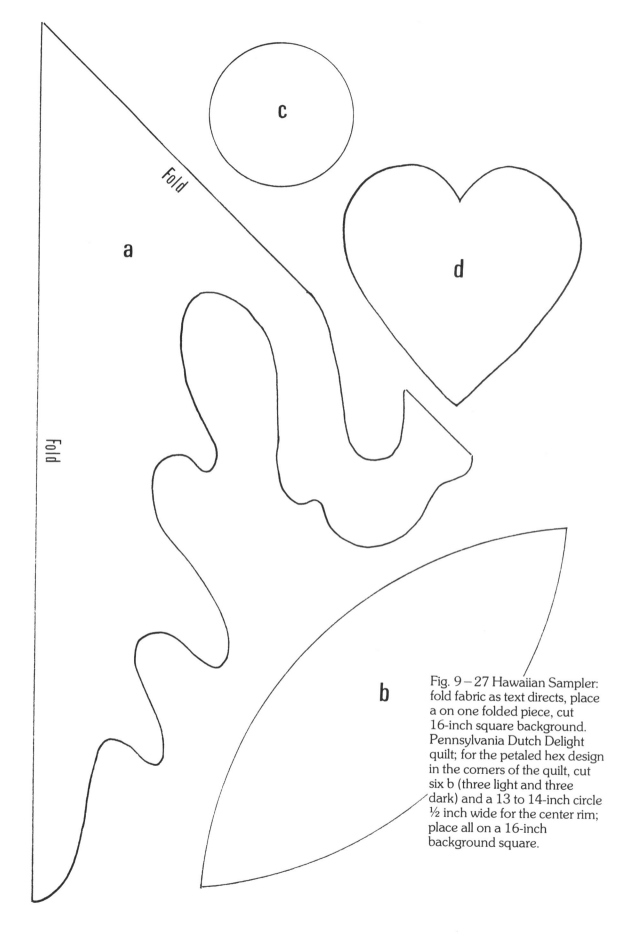

Fold

Fold

a

c

d

b

Fig. 9 – 27 Hawaiian Sampler:
fold fabric as text directs, place
a on one folded piece, cut
16-inch square background.
Pennsylvania Dutch Delight
quilt; for the petaled hex design
in the corners of the quilt, cut
six b (three light and three
dark) and a 13 to 14-inch circle
½ inch wide for the center rim;
place all on a 16-inch
background square.

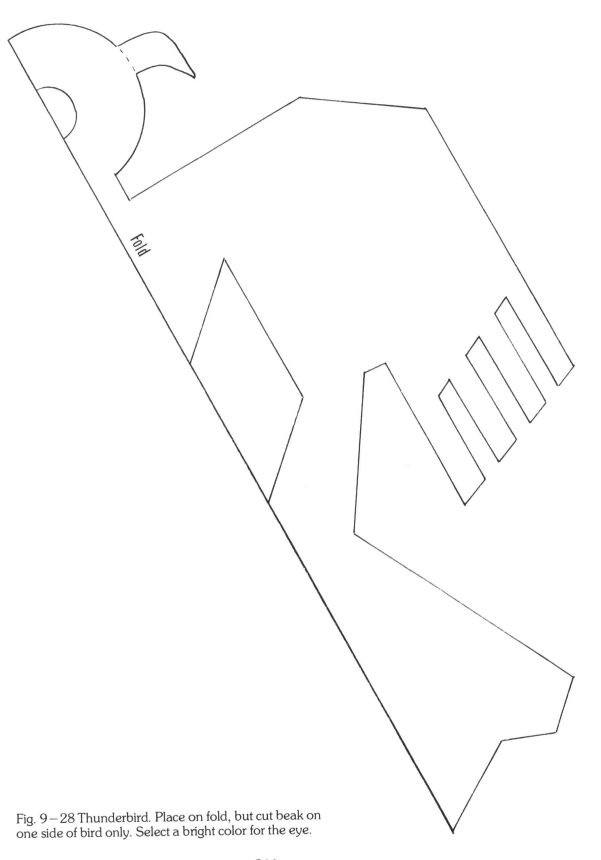

Fold

Fig. 9 – 28 Thunderbird. Place on fold, but cut beak on one side of bird only. Select a bright color for the eye.

211

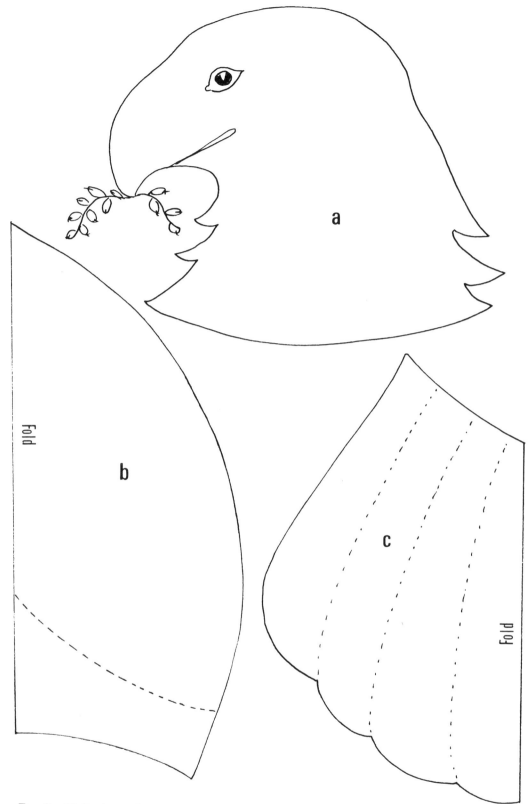

Fold

a

b

c

Fold

Fig. 9–29 Eagle applique measures 14 by 23 inches. Place it upright on 16 by 25-inch background or place on the diagonal on a 20-inch square. Cut one a, one b, one c, and two d (Fig. 9–30). Embroidery can finish off any details such as eye, mouth, or claws. Use quilt stitches on tail and wings to give texture.

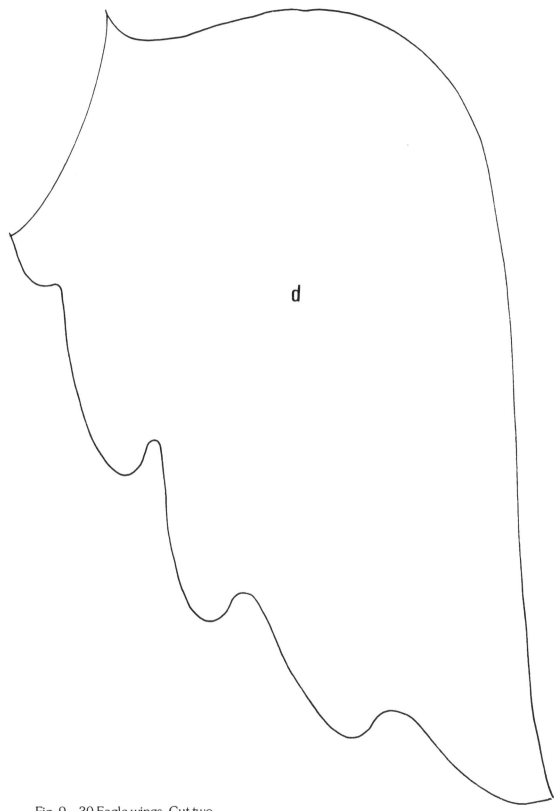

d

Fig. 9 – 30 Eagle wings. Cut two.

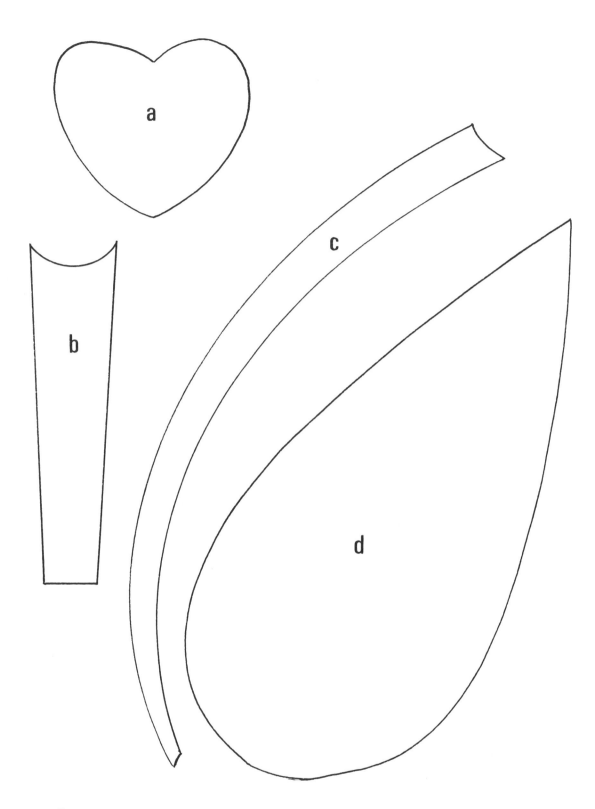

Fig. 9–31 Border of Wind Blown Tulips. For one side border 70 inches long by at least 10 inches wide, cut eight a, four b, four c, and nine d. Multiply according to number of borders planned and length of the border. This border can be used on any quilt.

214

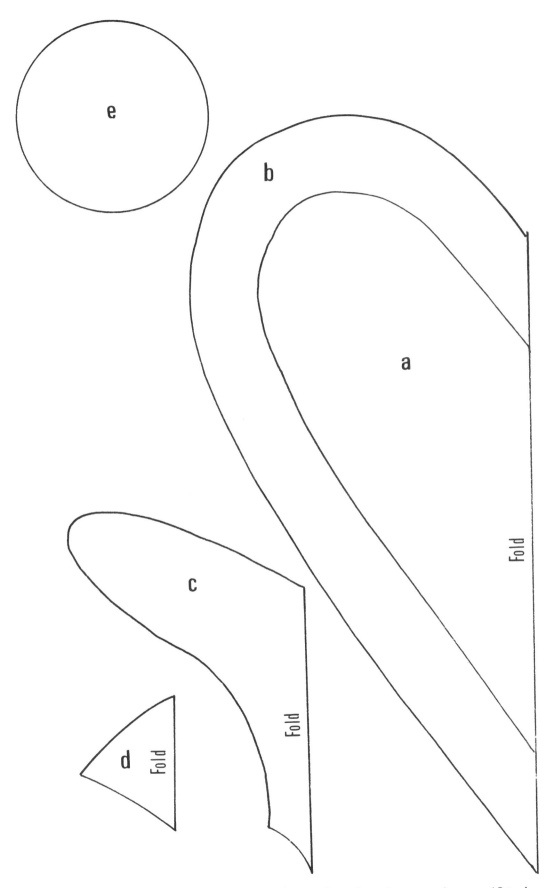

Fig. 9–32 Ohio Rose. Cut four a, four b, four c, four d, and one e; place on 19-inch background.

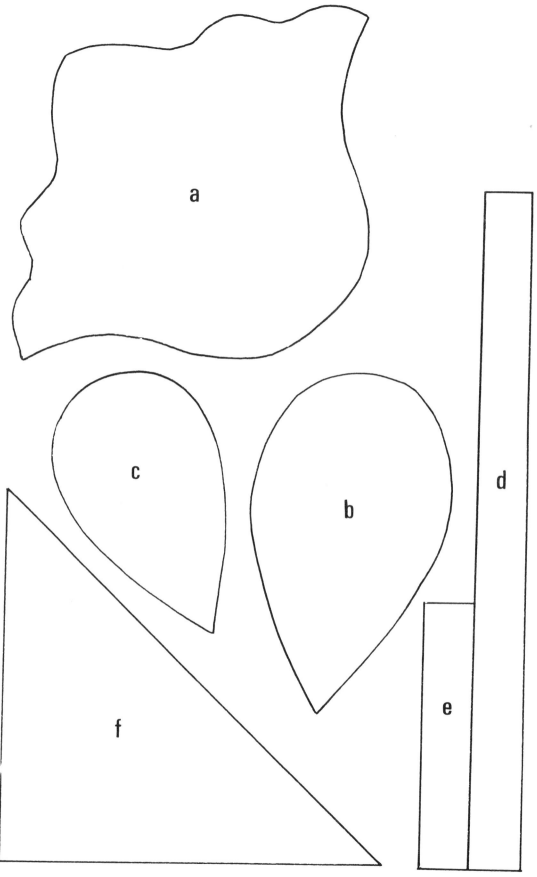

Fig. 9–33 Country Blossom. Cut three a, two b, two c, one d, two e, and one f; place on 11-inch or larger background.

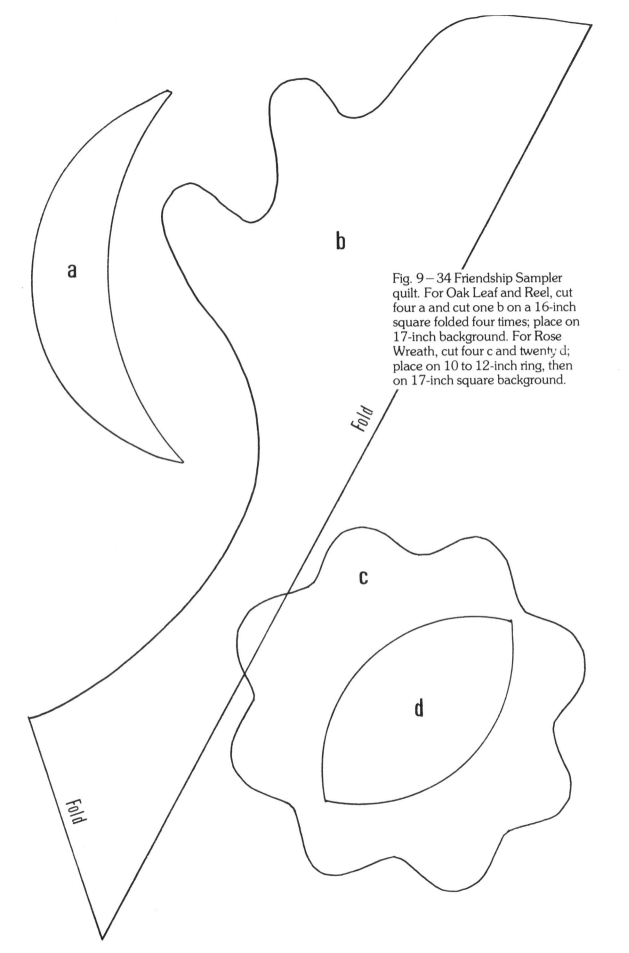

a

b

Fig. 9 – 34 Friendship Sampler quilt. For Oak Leaf and Reel, cut four a and cut one b on a 16-inch square folded four times; place on 17-inch background. For Rose Wreath, cut four c and twenty d; place on 10 to 12-inch ring, then on 17-inch square background.

Fold

c

d

Fold

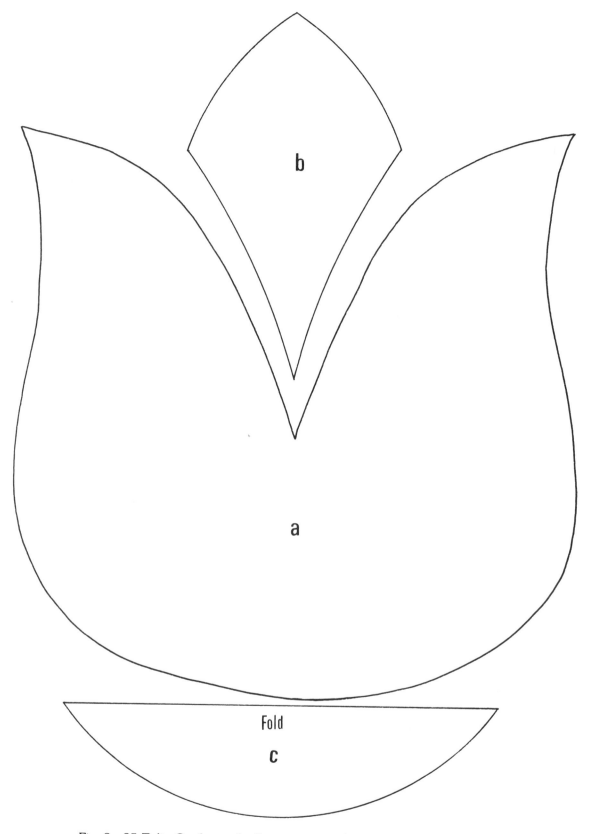

b

a

Fold

c

Fig. 9–35 Tulip Garden quilt. Cut one a, one b, two c, and one stem 1¼ by 7 inches. Place on 15 by 18-inch background.

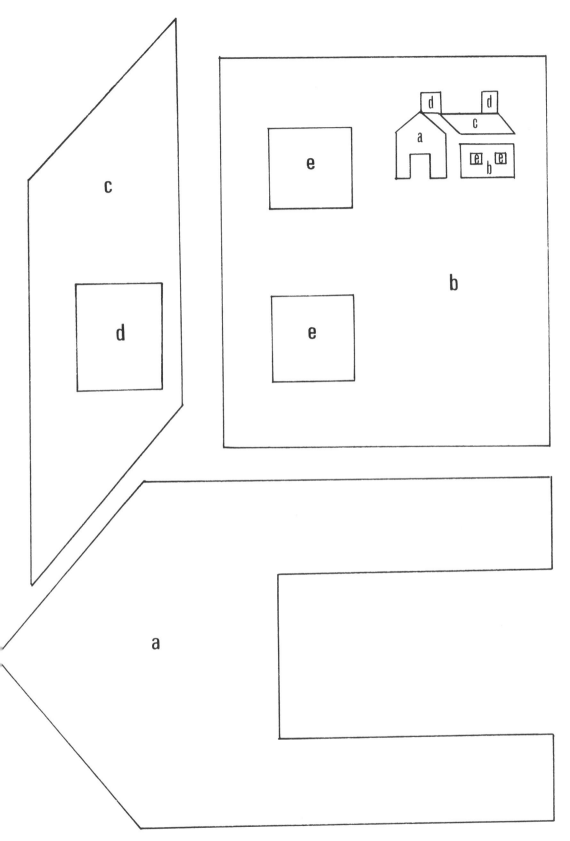

Fig. 9–36 School House. Cut one a, one b, one c, two d, and two e (of background to applique on b; or else cut windows out of b to show background). Pieces are set apart from each other, as shown in picture inset, with same background showing between pieces.

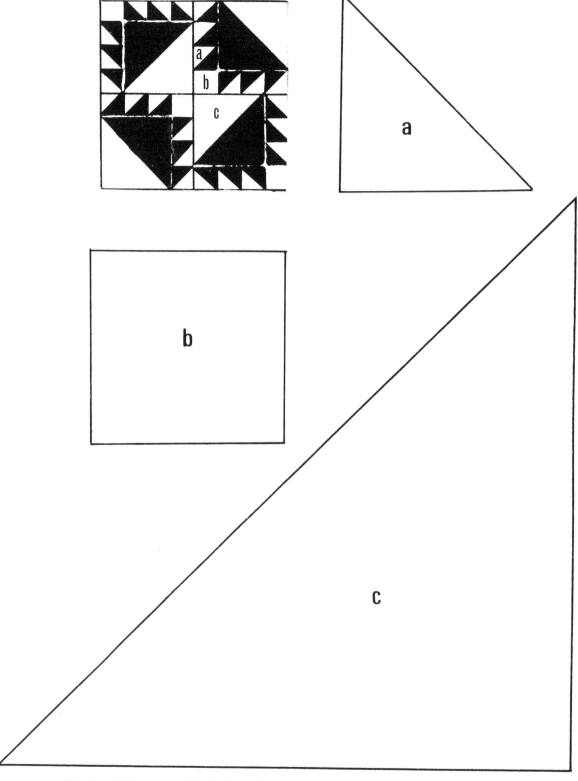

Fig. 9–37 Barrister's Block, from Hudson Highlands Quilt. Shown on small inset is only one fourth of Barrister's Block. Finished block is 32 inches square. For complete block, cut a (ninety-six dark print and ninety-six background), sixteen b background, and thirty-two c (sixteen background and sixteen print).

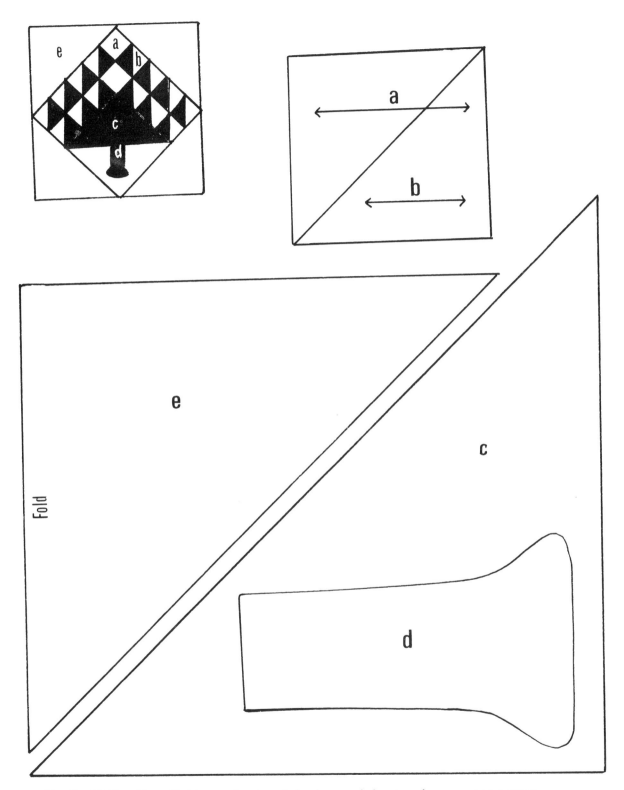

Fig. 9–38 Pine Tree. Cut two a, fourteen b background, fourteen b green, one c green, one c background, one d (center and applique to c background), four e background. Finished size is 14 inches square.

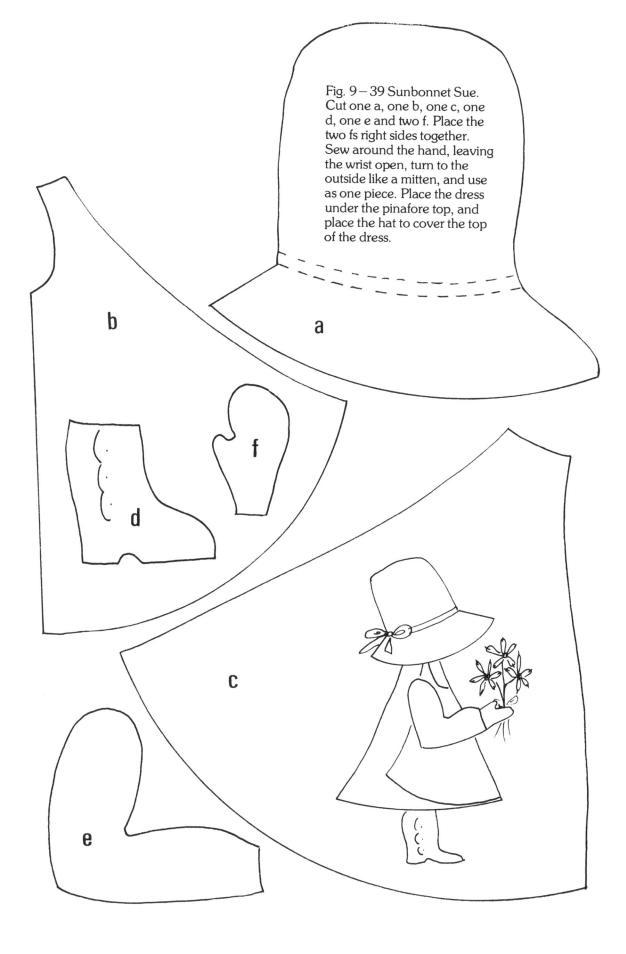

Fig. 9−39 Sunbonnet Sue. Cut one a, one b, one c, one d, one e and two f. Place the two fs right sides together. Sew around the hand, leaving the wrist open, turn to the outside like a mitten, and use as one piece. Place the dress under the pinafore top, and place the hat to cover the top of the dress.

a

b

f

d

c

e

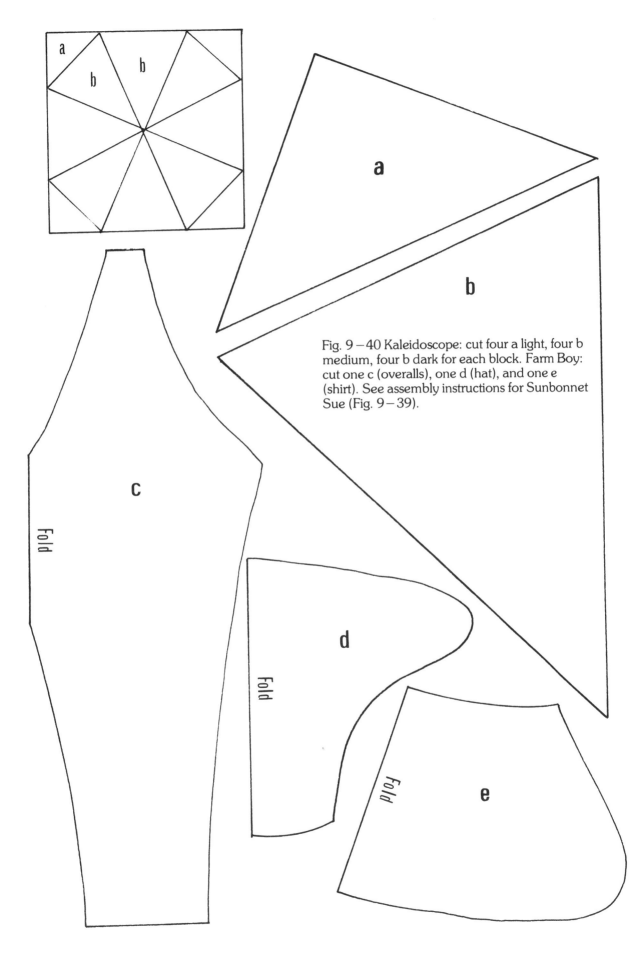

a

b

b

a

b

Fig. 9−40 Kaleidoscope: cut four a light, four b medium, four b dark for each block. Farm Boy: cut one c (overalls), one d (hat), and one e (shirt). See assembly instructions for Sunbonnet Sue (Fig. 9−39).

c

Fold

d

Fold

Fold

e

# Index

Page numbers in **bold type** indicate
information found in illustrations.